T0301594

Making Inclusion Work

Making Inclusion Work

Experiences from Academia around the World

Edited by

Saija Katila

Professor of Innovation Management, University of Eastern Finland, Finland

Susan Meriläinen

Professor of Management, University of Lapland, Finland

Janne Tienari

Professor of Management and Organization, Aalto University School of Economics, Finland

Edward Elgar
Cheltenham, UK • Northampton, MA, USA

Published by
Edward Elgar Publishing Limited
The Lypiatts
15 Lansdown Road
Cheltenham
Glos GL50 2JA
UK

Edward Elgar Publishing, Inc.
William Pratt House
9 Dewey Court
Northampton
Massachusetts 01060
USA

A catalogue record for this book is available from the British Library

Library of Congress Control Number: 2009941138

Mixed Sources
Product group from well-managed
forests and other controlled sources
www.fsc.org Cert no. SA-COC-1565
© 1996 Forest Stewardship Council

ISBN 978 1 84844 084 5

Typeset by Cambrian Typesetters, Camberley, Surrey
Printed and bound by MPG Books Group, UK

Contents

Contributors

Myrtle P. Bell, PhD, is Professor of Management at the University of Texas at Arlington, USA. She has degrees from the University of Notre Dame, Louisiana State University, and UT-Arlington. Her research focuses on diversity and social issues at work, including diversity education, obesity, disability, age, appearance and religion as aspects of diversity, and employment discrimination against immigrants. Myrtle's research appears in numerous academic journals, including *Journal of Applied Psychology, Academy of Management Journal, Equal Opportunities International, Journal of Applied Behavioral Science, Journal of Managerial Psychology, Journal of Vocational Behavior, Violence against Women* and *Journal of Interpersonal Violence* in multiple-edited volumes. Her book, *Diversity in Organizations* (Thomson, 2007), is the first comprehensive, research-based book of its kind for teaching diversity. Myrtle is an Associate Editor of *The Academy of Management Learning & Education* journal, the Professional Insights Editor of *Equality, Diversity and Inclusion: An International Journal*, and past Chair of the Gender and Diversity in Organizations division of the Academy of Management.

Regine Bendl, PhD, is Associate Professor at the Department of Management (Working Group on Gender and Diversity in Organizations) in Vienna University of Economics and Business Administration, Austria. Her fields of research and teaching include gender and diversity management, gender subtext in organization theory, critical management studies, and feminist theory. She has published in *British Journal of Management, Journal of Management and Organization, Zeitschrift für Betriebswirtschaft, Gender Work and Organization, Gender in Management: An Interdisciplinary Journal* and *Finnish Journal of Business Economics*. She was awarded with the following prizes: Prize of the Chamber of Labour (1997), Prize Dr Maria Schaumayer Stiftung (1997), Käthe Leichter Prize for Special Achievements in Women's and Gender Studies (2005), Best Paper Award EURAM 2007 (Track 'Gender Equality and Diversity in Management'), EMERALD Highly Recommended Paper Award (2009).

Sandra Billard, PhD, is a Lecturer in Management at the School of Business, University of Ballarat, Australia. She uses action research to encourage processes of creativity and learning within organizations. She teaches action learning and action research methods to graduate business students. Sandra has used participatory action research to investigate gender relations and participation in industrial democracy in an Australian public sector agency, and to inquire into teaching practices that can be effective with business students.

David M. Boje is endowed Bank of America Professor in the Management Department at New Mexico State University, and past holder of the Anderson professorship. His main research is the interplay of storytelling methods and ethics. His current books include *Storytelling Organizations* (Sage, 2008), *Critical Theory Ethics for Business and Public Administration* (Information Age Press, 2008) and the *Handbook of Managerial Psychology* (with co-editors; Sage, 2008). Boje's books also include *Managing in the Postmodern World* (with Dennehy) and *Narrative Methods for Organization and Communication Research*. He has published over 120 journal articles, including ones for *Administrative Science Quarterly*, *Management Science*, *Management Communication Quarterly*, *Organization Studies*, *Leadership Quarterly* and other journals. He is President of the Standing Conference for Management & Organization Inquiry (http://scmoi.org), editor of *Tamara Journal* (http://tamarajournal.com) and associate editor for *Qualitative Research in Organization & Management* (QROM) and *Journal of Organization Change Management*. He serves on 14 other editorial boards.

Mary Ann Danowitz, EdD, is a Visiting Professor at the Vienna University of Economics and Business Administration at the Institute of Gender and Diversity in Organizations. She has held faculty positions at the University of Denver, Ohio State University and the College of William and Mary, and several university administrative appointments in the United States. Mary Ann has been a Fulbright Scholar in Austria and Indonesia and a visiting scholar in Australia and Malaysia. Her research and publications focus on leadership and governance, the academic profession, careers and human resources, and gender and racial equality. Her most recent book is an edited contribution: *Women, Universities, and Change: Gender Equality in the European Union and the United States* (Palgrave Macmillan, 2007).

Ulla Eriksson-Zetterquist, PhD, is Associate Professor at Gothenburg Research Institute, School of Business, Economics and Law, University of Gothenburg. Her research interests concern organizing, especially gender, technology, intersectionality and risk. She has enlarged on these themes in such books as *Organisering och intersektionalitet* (*Organizing and Intersectionality*) (2007) co-authored with Alexander Styhre and *Institutionell* *teori – idéer, moden, förändring* (*Institutional Theory – Ideas, Fashion, Change*) (2009). Since 2004 she has been an Associate Editor for the journal *Gender, Work and Organization* for which she was also guest editor for a special issue on 'Gender and new technology' (2007: 14.4).

Silvia Gherardi is a full Professor of sociology of work and organization at the University of Trento, Italy, where she is responsible for the Research Unit on Communication, Organizational Learning and Aesthetics (RUCOLA, www.unitn.it/rucola). In 2005 she was named Doctor Honoris Causa by Roskilde University (DK), and in 2007 was appointed as Egos Honorary Member. Her research activities focus on workplace learning and knowing. Her theoretical background is in qualitative sociology, organizational symbolism and feminist studies.

Jean Helms Mills, PhD, is a Professor of Management at the Sobey School of Business, Saint Mary's University in Halifax, Canada. She is the author of *Making Sense of Organizational Change* (Routledge, 2003) and has co-authored and edited six additional books. Jean is an Associate Editor for *Gender, Work and Organization* and past Associate Editor of *Culture and Organization*, as well as serving on the editorial boards of *Management and Organizational History*, *The Journal of Workplace Rights*, *Equal Opportunities International* and *The Journal of Change Management*. She has presented and published her work on gender, change and culture nationally and internationally.

Ella Henry is a Senior Lecturer in the Faculty of Maori Development at AUT University, where she coordinates the Maori Media major for undergraduates and teaches Maori business and research methods to postgraduate students. Her most recent publication is a chapter for an international edited collection entitled *Kaupapa Maori Entrepreneurship* (Edward Elgar, forthcoming).

Elina Henttonen is a Researcher and Doctoral Student at the Department of Marketing and Management of Aalto University School of Economics, Finland. Her research interests include gender, organization and management, women entrepreneurs and gendered professions. She has published several journal articles and book chapters. She teaches qualitative methods.

Saija Katila, PhD, is Professor of Innovation Management at the Department of Business and Management, University of Eastern Finland, Finland. Her research deals with the relational practices of management, gender, ethnicity, diversity and family in different organizational contexts. She teaches diversity and innovation management as well as leadership with a critical twist. She has published in international journals such as *Gender, Work and Organization* and her work is forthcoming in *Canadian Journal of Administrative Sciences* and *International Journal of Gender and Entrepreneurship*. She has also authored several book chapters. She is an Associate Editor of *Gender, Work and Organization* and editorial board member of *Equal Opportunities International*.

Kirsi LaPointe is a Researcher and Doctoral Student at the Department of Marketing and Management of Aalto University School of Economics, Finland. Prior to joining academia, she worked in HR consulting and corporate education. Her research interests include identity, narrative, changing careers and gendered professions.

Susan Meriläinen, PhD, is Professor of Management at the University of Lapland, Finland. Her research interests centre on the doing of gender in knowledge work, including academia, and on gender and information technology. She has published in international journals such as *Organization* and *Gender, Work and Organization* and co-authored several book chapters.

Beverly Dawn Metcalfe, PhD, is a Research Fellow in HRM and Development in the Institute for Development Policy and Management, Faculty of Humanities, University of Manchester, UK. She is also a Research Associate at the Centre for Equality and Diversity in Manchester Business School, UK. She has published widely in the area of women's learning and leadership development in the international economy, feminist theory, international management and globalization and international HRD.

Albert J. Mills, PhD, is Director of the PhD (Management) programme at the Sobey School of Business, Saint Mary's University, Halifax, Nova Scotia, Canada. He is the author, co-author and co-editor of 14 books, including *Gendering Organizational Analysis* (1991), *Managing the Organizational Melting Pot* (1997) and *Sex, Strategy and the Stratosphere: The Gendering of Airline Cultures* (2006). He has just completed the *Sage Encyclopedia of Case Study Research* (2009).

Judith K. Pringle, PhD, is Professor of Organisation Studies, and co-ordinator of the Gender and Diveristy Research Group at the Auckland University of Technology. Her research focuses on issues of gender, diversity, the experiences of women in organizations and reframing careers. She is co-editor of *Handbook of Workplace Diversity* (2006), Gender and Diversity editor for *Columbia Journal of American Studies* (CJAS) and has published numerous journal articles.

Angelika Schmidt, PhD, is Assistant Professor at the Institute of Change Management and Management Development at the Vienna University of Economics and Business Administration (WU). Her fields of research and teaching are: Employment – Workforce – Commitment, Work–Life Boundaries, Career Management, Gender Management and Organizational Discourse. She has published in *Journal of Managerial Psychology, Zeitschrift für Personalforschung* and *Gender Work and Organization*.

Hans Siebers, PhD, is Associate Professor at Tilburg University, the Netherlands. He leads the Master programme on Organisation of Cultural Diversity and the research group Diversity at Work. His research focuses on ethnic identity and ethnic inequality in organizations and in the labour market. He has worked at several Dutch universities and abroad and has been trained as an anthropologist. His dissertation investigated identity constructions of the Q'eqchi'es of Guatemala between global and indigenous influences. Recent publications include Siebers, H. (2009) '(Post)bureaucratic organizational practices and the production of racioethnic inequality at work', *Journal of Management and Organization*, **15**(1): 62–81; Siebers, H. (2009) 'Struggles for recognition: the politics of racioethnic identity among Dutch national tax administrators', *Scandinavian Journal of Management*, **25** (1): 73–84; and Siebers, H. (in press) 'The impact of migrants – hostile discourse in media and politics on racioethnic closure in career development in The Netherlands', *International Sociology*.

Janne Tienari, PhD, is Professor of Management and Organization at Aalto University School of Economics, Finland, and Editor of the *Scandinavian Journal of Management*. His research interests include cross-cultural studies of gender and organizing. He has published in, for example, *Academy of Management Review, Organization, Organization Studies, Journal of Management Studies, Gender, Work and Organization, British Journal of Management* and *Human Relations*.

Frank A. Tuitt, EdD, is an Assistant Professor and Director of the higher education programme in the Morgridge College of Education at the University of Denver. His research explores a range of topics related to access and equity in higher education, teaching and learning in racially diverse college classrooms and diversity and organizational transformation. Frank received his BA from Connecticut College in 1987 and currently serves his alma mater as a member of its Board of Trustees. Dr Tuitt is a member of The Association for the Study of Higher Education (ASHE), American Educational Research Association (AERA), and the Professional and Organizational Development in Higher Education Network (POD). He also serves as a consultant to universities, colleges and education-related organizations on diversity training throughout the United States.

Rachel Wolfgramm, PhD, holds an academic position at the University of Auckland, New Zealand. Her teaching includes sustainability in business and society, organization behaviour and management. Her research areas include spirituality at work, sustainable business, creative ecologies, leadership, indigenous entrepreneurship and cultural innovation. She has published research locally and internationally.

Patrizia Zanoni, PhD, is currently Associate Professor at the Faculty of Business Economics of Hasselt University, Belgium, where she directs SEIN, the research institute on identity, diversity and inequality. She previously worked at the Catholic University of Leuven and Tilburg University. Her research critically deconstructs diversity, attempting to embed its meaning within specific productive contexts. Her dissertation 'Beyond demography: Essays on diversity in organizations' received the 2007 CMS PhD Award of the Academy of Management, and her paper 'Diversity in the lean automobile factory: Re-doing class along socio-demographic identities' was awarded the 2009 CMS Best Paper Award. Her work has been published in *Organization Studies*, *Human Relations* and *Journal of Management Studies*. Patrizia is currently working on the translation of the institution of diversity into organizations, the notion of inclusion, and the theorization of the relation between difference, control and resistance in organizations. She teaches diversity and economic sociology.

Preface

This book originates from a panel discussion that Professors Marta Calás and Silvia Gherardi asked us to organize in their Diversity Management track at the 2006 International Federation of Scholarly Associations of Management (IFSAM) conference in Berlin, Germany. We came up with an idea for a participatory panel discussion, which we named 'Action! What We Can Do to Make the Academic World a More Inclusive Place'. The panel was enthusiastically received. It became clear that the track participants felt a need to talk about their own experiences in working for inclusion in teaching and research. Based on this experience, an idea was conceived to edit a book where academics around the world would share their stories about bringing in new voices, themes and methods in teaching and research. We were curious to learn how people working in different local contexts account for their relative success – and what insights they can offer others. We are grateful to Professor Mustafa Özbilgin for advising us to contact Edward Elgar Publishing to find a publisher that would understand the value of such an undertaking. We would like to extend our thanks to Francine O'Sullivan at Edward Elgar for proving that Mustafa was right. Francine has supported us from the very beginning. We also want to thank the Foundation of Economic Education (Liikesivistysrahasto) in Finland for their generous funding, which made this book possible.

Saija Katila, Susan Meriläinen and Janne Tienari

1. Introduction: making inclusion work in academia

Janne Tienari, Susan Meriläinen and Saija Katila

This book is *for* inclusion and multiplicity in academia. To this end, it is *against* standardization. As academics in Western countries, we are being organized to conform to rigid standards of teaching and research. This book shows how we can meaningfully challenge such standardization through inclusive practices in our everyday work. We – the authors in this edited volume – present inclusive ideas and ways of interacting that have worked in different university contexts around the world. We share our personal experiences on working for inclusion, account for the relative success of our efforts and provide insights that may prove helpful for others, too.

We care passionately about inclusion in academic work. For us, inclusion means bringing in new voices, themes and methods in teaching and research. Most often, inclusion refers in this book to incorporating considerations of gender and ethnicity in the ways in which curricula, courses and research projects are developed and run. By questioning established power relations, privileged knowledge and locally held truths regarding good and proper academic standards and practice, we have each in our own way sought to challenge the status quo. We have sought to make alternative understandings and practices visible.

We are aware of current criticism of 'positive scholarship' (Fineman, 2006). We distance ourselves from this notion. As feminist organization and management scholars we have learned not to be naive. We are aware of unequal power relations and structures of domination that our work is embedded in. These relations and structures are woven into the fabric of our academic lives, even if we sometimes refer to particular experiences as positive. Also, our stories relate to relative success in changing everyday academic practices, not to great breakthroughs or unselfish service to community. In this way, we also distance ourselves from the notion of 'engaged scholarship', which has in recent years become a popular concept to describe meaningful academic work. Engaged scholarship can refer to admirable efforts to incorporate key stakeholders' perspectives in the study of complex social problems

(Van de Ven, 2007). However, especially in the US, it has been appropriated as a label by the university institution – and it has thus become marketized. Ours is a more bottom-up approach, with a focus on everyday practices in local units embedded in particular institutional and cultural contexts.

We have crafted this book with three main audiences in mind. First, we aim to bring hope to those teachers and researchers who feel disheartened in the contemporary globalizing academia that sets the stage for organizing teaching and research. We want to show that it is possible to challenge standardization and survive. Second, PhD students may find the book helpful in their search for meaningful ways to navigate an academic world that often seems awkward and incomprehensible – at least judging from our own experiences and those of others with whom we have discussed the issue. Third, we are bold enough to hope that more mainstream scholars and decision-makers will also get hold of this book and find some food for thought in it.

Our message is that we *can* make a difference, although working for inclusion today takes place in a global system that does not appear to be receptive to such efforts. There are strong forces for convergence in academia according to an Anglo-American model, which is obsessed with audits and assessments based on standardized criteria (Engwall, 2007). Beyond these supposedly global processes, however, local contexts continue to differ. Local standardizers differ with respect to both outlook and room for manoeuvring. Crucially, then, enhancing inclusive practices and carving out a space for action demands understanding of local power structures, actors and established practices. For this reason, the authors of this book turn to their own experiences to highlight the emotional and political struggles in bringing about change. At the same time, we argue that there is something to be learned in each chapter that can be tailored to fit local conditions elsewhere.

IN THE SYSTEM

Most contributors to this book are organization and management scholars. Many of us work in business schools, where it is clear that the nature of academic work is changing. There is increasing control over what we do as academics, when and how we do it, and to whom we are responsible. The hegemonic global academic system standardizes work through three intertwining elements: teaching, research and funding. Yet, as Myrtle P. Bell (2009) puts it, we must constantly seek to do work that matters.

First, what and how we teach is increasingly determined by the logic of the market and business enterprise. The paradox is obvious. There are increasing pressures to provide academic education that is both innovative enough to satisfy the needs of business, yet cost-effective enough to satisfy policymakers in their quest for lean government. On the one hand, rhetoric that celebrates excellence and innovativeness affects the content and form of our work. Universities are in a quest for global quality certificates, and different kinds of rankings and indexes play a huge role in the provision and assessment of education (Hedmo et al., 2005; Wedlin, 2007). Deans, department heads and administrators eagerly follow university rankings provided by global business media and the like.

On the other hand, paradoxically, volume continues to be king for most of us. In practice, universities continue to be governed by principles of cost-effectiveness. We are required to produce (sic) an adequate number of MSc, MBA and PhD degrees for our student-customers every year, and we are monitored on the basis of the volume of our output. While the excellence rhetoric urges us to compare ourselves to, and compete with, the likes of Harvard and MIT, our resources remain trifling by comparison. At the same time, the power of the business community and student-customers limits our possibilities to make curriculum changes that are considered by deans and department heads as risky. It is difficult to offer courses not considered part of the so-called core of the field. In these conditions, it is hard to be different and to offer, for example, teaching that draws on critical feminist or race theory. The very notion of being critical tends to make students, colleagues and administrators feel uncomfortable or even threatened. This is the case specifically if there is no time and space to explain to them what critical theorizing is about and what it can offer.

Second, practices of research are changing worldwide. Rankings and indexes are, if possible, even more influential in assessing research than they are in teaching. With the touch of a button,[1] the output of each and every individual scholar is available online to deans and department heads. Journal articles are (over)valued as our academic performance indicators. We are encouraged by our host universitites to report our research findings in article format, and to plan our publication strategies so that we target our work in journals that are thought to have the highest impact as measured by popular rankings and citation indexes.[2] As individuals, we are encouraged to climb the rankings and indexes; to strive for world class performance as if objective and individual standards were possible.

The politics of distribution affects our work – and the gatekeepers in the system are typically mainstream scholars who have little tolerance for what they consider unorthodox research (Westwood and Clegg, 2003). The high-impact 'top' journals idolized in the system tend to favour particular kinds of research and reporting (Adler and Harzing, 2009). They cherish positivist and functionalist research that is technically elegant. In doing so, they scorn original and avant garde contributions, especially critical ones. They seldom provide opportunities for alternative or critical theorizing that would foster more inclusion (Özbilgin, 2009). Critical theorists often need to make do with alternative channels for making their work known.

To be sure, many scholars are critical or even hostile towards rankings that for them represent unnecessary control and interference with academic freedom. Journal rankings and the publishing practices these rankings support have been criticized for being circular, self-fulfilling and marked by gamesmanship (Macdonald and Kam, 2007). Also, as all the 'top' journals in fields such as business and management are published in the Anglo-American cultural sphere and in the English language, we non-native English speakers from peripheral countries face an extra burden in the contemporary global academic system (Thomas et al., 2009; Tietze and Dick, 2009).

Third, the doing of research is increasingly tied to successful efforts to obtain external funding for research projects that are focused, on the one hand, and that address issues that are considered directly relevant for business practice, on the other. Needless to say, obtaining external funding often depends on the support of mainstream scholars and on adherence to topics deemed timely by those who finance the undertaking, that is state apparatuses (directly and through intermediary organizations), private foundations and business as well as supranational institutions such as the European Union. Those who fund research not only dictate the relevant topics, but often also the number and type of (international) partners in the research, thus also influencing the creation of collaborative networks among academics.

In sum, the contemporary hegemonic global academic system appears to be unwelcoming to those who question standardization and the mainstream. Why do we call the system *hegemonic*, then? Well, it is not a given that an article published in a high-prestige journal contributes more to knowledge than work appearing in less prestigious journals (Starbuck, 2005). Yet, we are led to believe that this is the case, and provided with incentives to act accordingly. The system seduces us to do what everyone else seems to be doing, not by direct force but by consent (Meriläinen et al., 2008; Nkomo, 2009). At the same time, the wide range of examples in this book demonstrates that to work for inclusion in contemporary academia is not impossible. On the contrary, it is not only possible, it can be meaningful – and it can lead to what we would consider positive experiences and outcomes.

DOUBLE STRATEGIES

Clearly, it would be safer to comply with the contemporary system and do mainstream teaching and research, rather than to follow one's passion. Many of us who are not lucky enough to have an established position are forced to carry out *double strategies* in order to be taken seriously. We have chosen a path of engagement with the mainstream (Grey, 2008). In this vein, we call double strategies those practices that scholars like us engage in to cope with the pressures for standardization in academic work, without compromising (too many of) our principles and ideals. Below, we reflect upon such double strategies from the position and viewpoint of scholars outside the Anglo-American core, in our case Finland.

One example of a double strategy is to attempt to publish actively in sufficiently highly ranked international journals that are open to non-mainstream research, and in this way carve out a local position for being critical or different, with a proven track record in global academia. With experience in publishing internationally (in English), it is often a little less difficult back home to find room for tackling alternative research topics and to introduce these topics in teaching. Conforming to the hegemonic academic system can thus be used as an advantage in the local context. Rankings and indexes can be used strategically as long as there are journals that are open to the non-mainstream *and* enjoy a relatively good standing in the international community.

The catch is that in order to get stuff published, one must usually sacrifice some of one's principles. For example, we have found it difficult to convince our colleagues in other countries that reporting on data from Finland is interesting *per se*. Sometimes we are forced to downplay the Finnish context in our research reports when we try to make our theoretical point. A viable double strategy, then, is to engage in cross-cultural comparative studies. This not only proves our international outlook back home, but it gives us an opportunity to both highlight the Finnish context (which is important for us Finns) and to put it into scruniry *vis-à-vis* other cultural contexts. Comparative studies across national boundaries can also be great fun, given that the collaborators are prepared to reflect upon the joint experience. This is particularly pertinent when the cross-cultural comparison involves scholars from the Anglo-American core, who – unlike us – are not encouraged by the system to reflect on the specificities of their own cultural context (Meriläinen et al., 2008; Thomas et al., 2009).

Yet another possible strategy is to build on sophisticated, alternative and critical theories in teaching, and to carve out a position locally on this basis. There is a distinct possibility that a divide between teaching universities and research universities is currently being manufactured, and that this affects what it means to be an academic in each setting. For academics working in teaching universities in peripheral countries such as Finland, being theoretically sophisticated may prove important in two ways. First, on the individual level, it helps in constructing a comfortable academic identity. Second, theoretically oriented people may be appreciated in teaching universities because they keep up academic standards. This, in turn, is based on the fact that keeping up standards is important for legitimizing the university within the national system of higher education.

In this book, we share positive experiences of intervening in teaching and research. We reflect on inclusive practices that seem to have worked in the Netherlands, Austria, Sweden, Finland and the United Kingdom, the United States and Canada as well as Australia and New Zealand. The contributors to this book – with very different backgrounds, acting in very different academic milieus – have each tried out some of the double strategies outlined above, carving out solutions that work for them. The geographical scope in this book is far from exhaustive, but we hope that the contributions offered will serve as a catalyst for scholars in other contexts to bring their stories forward.

WRITING ABOUT POSITIVE EXPERIENCES

There is a strong element of autobiography and autoethnography throughout the book. We look at academic work through personal accounts, which are reflexive and contextual (Ellis and Bocher, 2000, 2006). We write about ourselves in relation to others, and connect the personal with the social and the cultural (Katila and Meriläinen, 1999, 2002). The concept of situated knowledge captures this well (Haraway, 1991; Calás and Smircich, 2006). We view knowledge as contextualized. It is linked to time and place; to particular situations and actors. The authors in this book are viewed as situated knowers who reflect upon their own everyday experiences, practices and understandings. A sense of confession is inherent in the stories – it cannot, and should not, be avoided (Lemons, 2008).

However, we are conscious of the fact that what stands as autoethnography remains unclear and contested, and that the form of autoethnography advocated in this book may have its limitations (Anderson, 1999; Buzard, 2003; Charmaz, 2006). Throughout the book, the authors' claims to autoethnographic authority are not attempts to close meaning and advocate singular interpretations of social reality. The stories reflect on how the authors have each acquired knowledge of the particular local contexts – that is, universities and their particular traditions and practices – they describe and make sense of, and how, on this basis, they assume a form of authority to speak about these contexts.

Our goal is also to be critical in an approachable way (Grey, 2008). Approachable means that as editors of this book, we have tried to persuade the authors to be personal and practical and to avoid theorization in their texts. However, as you can see in the various chapters, academics manage to be personal and reflexive, but it seems to be difficult for them to avoid the temptation of framing their experiences *vis-à-vis* particular theories. This is only natural and, reconsidering the issue, we came to the conclusion that it adds to the appeal of the book. This is *how academics are...* and how they choose to frame their experiences theoretically is interesting in its own right. Also, it enables readers to follow the reasoning on the basis of which the authors assume autoethnographic authority. In a similar vein, this introduction is merely one possible interpretation of the variety of experiences and under-standings offered in the chapters. Other interpretations may be equally plausi-ble.

Furthermore, as feminist organization and management scholars we know that by being personal *and* positive we are easy prey to fellow critical schol-ars who like to remind us about the futile nature of our efforts in the big picture, in supporting the hegemony rather than challenging it. This is under-standable because working for inclusion is a notoriously difficult task (Danowitz Sagaria, 2007). There are plenty of texts documenting disappoint-ments, and for good reason. In a recent book, a team of Swedish feminist scholars led by Professor Anna Wahl shared their experiences and insights in struggling to make their voices heard in public arenas (Wahl et al., 2008). Sweden is popularly considered an egalitarian society where gender issues are a serious concern. However, Wahl and her colleagues have first-hand experi-ences of another Sweden. They tell stories of being ignored, ridiculed and attacked with aggressive rhetoric when they have worked to promote feminist scholarship and ideas.

Our point of departure in the present book is that to work for inclusion, 'we must begin with understanding our subjective orientations and commitments as well as our motivations and desires' (Nkomo, 2009, p. 109). On this basis, the journey to inclusion is often step-wise. First, we need to be able to describe and account for current practices in different academic milieus. Second, we need to be prepared to ask questions about the status quo; the taken-for-granted practices it sustains and the knowledge it privileges. Third, and only then, we are ready to offer constructive alternatives and provide suggestions for change. In other words, we must be prepared to move from constitutive questions (*what? how?*) via critical and evaluative questions (*how good is it?*) to constructive questions (*how could it be otherwise?*). We need to be prepared to move from practical questions to more political and moral ones (Räsänen et al., 2005; Korpiaho et al., 2007).

The authors of the chapters of this book have in their own local contexts and in their own distinctive ways gone through these steps (though not always in the same order). We feel that the time is right for sharing experiences of alternatives and alternative understandings. Of course, the three-step journey outlined is no guarantee for positive outcomes. Anna Wahl and her colleagues have followed the steps, but nevertheless experienced a mixed response to their efforts.

We are also aware that our efforts for inclusion are affected by gendered and racialized power relations that are difficult to challenge, let alone change (Mohanty, 2004; Acker, 2006). We know that we are privileged. Unlike many people around the world, we do not have to worry about how to get food on our tables every day – or to fear being imprisoned or worse if we speak our minds and work for inclusion. We also realize that what we mean by inclusion in our Western local settings may not make sense in other contexts. In fact, we do not even claim that we have managed to change or seriously challenge power relations in our own societies as a whole. What we have done, however, is introduce change in everyday local practices that we are involved in.

MAKING INCLUSION WORK

Without conscious efforts to the contrary, the content and form of our curricula, the courses we offer our students and the research we carry out will address a decreasing number of topics deemed legitimate by a maintream elite. A decreasing number of 'truths' about social life will be privileged. Without intervening in mundane everyday practices the voices heard and appreciated will become ever fewer. Throughout the book, we offer examples of interventions that have challenged standardization. The book is structured in three parts.

Developing Curricula

The first part of the book includes contributions by Patrizia Zanoni and Hans Siebers (The Netherlands), Mary Ann Danowitz and Frank Tuitt (USA), and Regine Bendl and Angelika Schmidt (Austria). The three chapters present examples of how curricula are developed and institutional arrangements are challenged to foster inclusiveness in different university settings.

In Chapter 2, Patrizia Zanoni and Hans Siebers share with us their experiences and insights in tackling ethnic and cultural inequality in The Netherlands. Patrizia and Hans work in Tilburg University, a relatively new university in a small city in the southern part of the country. They take us through a journey that resulted in the successful introduction of a new Masters' Programme in the Organization of Cultural Diversity. Reflecting on their joint efforts with a number of colleagues, Patrizia and Hans call themselves tempered radicals who seized the moment to make a difference (Meyerson and Scully, 1995). Dutch society is currently marked by ethnic tensions, and there is a dire need for competences related to diversity. The double strategy of Patrizia, Hans and their colleagues was to draw on this need and to work towards building a more inclusive society.

In Chapter 3, Mary Ann Danowitz and Frank Tuitt introduce us to the University of Denver in western USA. Mary Ann and Frank offer us an opportunity to follow in their footsteps the building of an inclusive curriculum for doctoral studies. Similarly to Patrizia and Hans, the focus in Mary Ann and Frank's chapter is on ethnicity and culture. They designed and implemented a PhD programme that builds on inclusive knowledge and pedagogies. To do so successfully, Mary Ann and Frank needed to adopt a strategic approach, starting from the description of positions and search committee membership to the precise ways course offerings and pedagogies were changed. Changes that appeared minor and technical eventually became substantial and structural.

In Chapter 4, Regine Bendl and Angelika Schmidt take us to Vienna in Austria. Regine and Angelika work at the Vienna University of Economics and Business. They provide us with a historical account of the joint efforts of a large number of female scholars to institutionalize gender studies and the inclusion of women in a traditionally male-dominated university. Through their personal reflections, Regine and Angelika offer insights on what it means to be an active feminist scholar at an Austrian university. Their story brings forward the ambiguity of 'success' and how it is linked to particular viewpoints and interpretations.

Reworking Pedagogy

The second part of the book includes contributions by Myrtle P. Bell (USA), Sandra Billard (Australia), Ulla Eriksson-Zetterquist (Sweden), and David M. Boje (USA). The four chapters focus on efforts by scholars to set examples and to rework pedagogy.

In Chapter 5, Myrtle P. Bell shares with us her personal account of teaching diversity issues in a university in a conservative southern state in the US. Myrtle reflects on her own solutions that have worked at the University of Texas in Arlington. She discusses challenging erroneous views and misunderstandings that students in the US have about minorities, and about different people in general. Using herself as an example, Myrtle offers us hands-on advice on how to tackle diversity in the classroom. By coupling her own experiences and those of the students with research evidence and statistical data, Myrtle has managed to make students rethink their deeply held stereotypical perceptions of different groups of people.

In Chapter 6, Sandra Billard moves our focus down under to the state of Victoria in Australia. Sandra works at the University of Ballarat, a small town near Melbourne. She shows how respecting difference and inclusion can be taught to business school students in courses that are not explicitly created to tackle these issues. Sandra reflects on her experiences in teaching a year-long action learning and research programme, and explores the practical interventions, strategies and methods that can be used to facilitate effective 'doing' of difference in such a setting.

In Chapter 7, Ulla Eriksson-Zetterquist provides an account of promoting gender equality at the School of Business, Economics and Law at Gothenburg University on the western coast of Sweden. As a novice PhD student some ten years ago, Ulla became involved in a project that shaped her identity as a feminist academic. Together with a colleague, she managed a state-funded project that aimed at increasing academics' knowledge of the role of gender in teaching. Ulla reflects on how despite several obstacles along the way the project successfully raised awareness of gender issues throughout the School, and provided an important learning experience for her personally. Ulla's chapter highlights the importance of taking different university sub-cultures – or academic tribes (Ylijoki, 1998) – into account when working for inclusion.

In Chapter 8, David M. Boje takes a different perspective on inclusion. David works in New Mexico State University, on the Rio Grande river in Las Cruces, USA. David is a critical postmodernist scholar who over the past ten years has been active in using the internet as a means of sharing his insights on society and on different ways to make it more inclusive. David discusses the pros and cons of developing websites as a free-to-public pedagogy, moving beyond linear and sequential approches into networked interconnectivity.

Shifting Strategies and Identities

The third part of the book includes contributions by Judith K. Pringle, Rachel Wolfgramm and Ella Henry (New Zealand), Jean Helms Mills and Albert Mills (Canada), Beverly Dawn Metcalfe (UK), and Elina Henttonen and Kirsi LaPointe (Finland). The four chapters focus on shifting research strategies and academic identities.

In Chapter 9, Judith K. Pringle, Rachel Wolfgramm and Ella Henry provide us with an account of what it means to do research in a cross-ethnic team in contemporary New Zealand, which is marked by historical relations between Mäoris (the indigeneous people) and Pakeha (settlers of European origin). Judith and Ella are affiliated with Auckland University of Technology, while Rachel works at the University of Auckland. The three scholars with different ethnic backgrounds share their joint experiences in research projects, and reflect on how they have managed to find a shared epistemological terrain, and create equitable research relationships across historically fractured ethnic lines while studying indigenous communities.

In Chapter 10, Jean Helms Mills and Albert Mills reflect on their lives as researchers and teachers. Jean and Albert work in St Mary's University in Halifax, Nova Scotia, on the eastern coast of Canada. They explore the influence of what they call sensemaking communities on events that they have been part of and on theoretical work that they have been engaged in. Jean and Albert's chapter offers a self-consciously retrospective sense of the development of ideas and strategies over time, offering critical sensemaking as a valuable heuristic for examining gender discrimination in particular.

In Chapter 11, Beverly Dawn Metcalfe shares with us her journey as an academic in several universities in the United Kingdom. Acknowledging that a feminist pedagogy is increasingly difficult within the neo-liberal, market-oriented UK academia (Morley, 1999), Beverly tells us a story of how she has developed different modes of teaching and research identities dependent on local context. She describes how different spaces have provided her with different opportunities and obstacles as a feminist scholar. Beverly offers positive reflections of her feminist pedagogic practice while teaching a range of undergraduate and postgraduate equality and diversity courses in UK universities.

In Chapter 12, Elina Henttonen and Kirsi LaPointe take us up north to the Helsinki School of Economics in Finland. Elina and Kirsi relate their experiences and emotional turmoil in becoming academics at the Department of Organizations and Management in HSE. This is an academic community that we – the editors of this book – know only too well. Saija and Susan both did their PhDs there, before moving to other universities in Finland. Janne has just moved back to the HSE after eight years at another university. Elina and Kirsi's account reflects on Saija and Susan's work to foster gender equality in the Department in the 1990s and early 2000s. Elina and Kirsi provide a story of how they have benefited from their predecessors' work, on the one hand, and how it is a constant struggle to keep gender awareness on the departmental agenda, on the other.

Conclusions

Finally, in Chapter 13, Silvia Gherardi from the University of Trento in northern Italy comments on the key points in the various chapters of the book, and offers her insights on inclusion in academia. Silvia's work first got us interested in gender studies in the early 1990s (Gheradi, 1995). We found Silvia's insightful ideas – for example, in developing the notion of doing gender (West and Zimmerman, 1987) – helpful in moulding our respective identities as academics. Later, we discovered her work on practice-based theorizing on learning and knowing in organizations (Gherardi, 2000). In this book, Silvia comments on notions such as being critical and positive, provides a practice-theoretical reading of the other chapters, and offers a theorization of inclusion on this basis. Silvia maintains that 'this is a book which discusses academic practice without directly naming it', and goes on to offer the missing piece in the puzzle.

CONTEXT MATTERS

In brief, the thread running through the chapters in this book is that local context matters in working for inclusion (cf. Klein and Harrison, 2007). Despite the forces for convergence, national academic systems and cultures remain distinct. Within the Anglo-American core itself, there is a lot of variety to be cherished (Korpiaho et al., 2007). The space for working for inclusion varies (Meriläinen et al., 2009). Different spaces must be enacted differently.

Considerations of context lead us back to the notion of situated knowledge. We seek to account for why particular practices seem to have worked in particular contexts (Haraway, 1991). In general, the answer is simple: the scholars in this book have managed to make inclusion work because they have been sensitive to local traditions, power relationships, social practices and situations. What works in one place does not necessarily work elsewhere, and what does not seem to work in a specific setting may well work elsewhere. Similarly, what works at one point in time may not work in another, and vice versa (Bell and Berry, 2007).

The chapters in this book differ in their specific messages. However, there are also notable similarities across the chapters. It is safe to say that in making inclusion work, academics need to be able to rely on one or, usually, several of the following. First, a little help from your friends is always a good idea. Making inclusion work is generally more productive and definitely more fun if you embark upon the journey together with others. Second, it is not a cliché that support from the top is often crucial if you want to do something new or different. Many of the authors in this book are candid about the fact that they have benefited from the open mind of one or several people in positions of authority in their universities.

Third, carpe diem. Timing is crucial. Seizing the right moment to act is paramount. This relates to the three steps presented above. Sometimes it suffices to describe and account for current practices in different academic milieus. Sometimes scholars need to be prepared to go beyond this and ask questions about the status quo; the taken-for-granted practices it sustains and the knowledges it privileges. Sometimes windows of opportunity are open to offer constructive alternatives and work for change. Fourth, and finally, courage and patience are necessary. Doing things differently takes a lot of guts, because someone is bound to judge you – or even to stab you in the back (metaphorically speaking). Criticism may come both from the mainstream elite and from fellow critical thinkers. Challenges can, however, be overcome in time. Used wisely, a bit of passion and reflection goes a long way.

NOTES

1. For example, http://www.harzing.com/pop.htm.
2. For example, *ISI Web of Knowledge*, owned by the global publishing house *Thomson Reuters*, has managed to become one of the current global standards.

REFERENCES

Acker, J. (2006), *Class Questions. Feminist Answers*, USA: Rowman & Littlefield Publishers.

Adler, N.J. and A.-W. Harzing (2009), 'When Knowledge Wins: Transcending the Sense and Nonsense of Academic Rankings', *Academy of Management Learning & Education*, **8** (1), 72–95.

Anderson, L. (1999), 'The Open Road to Ethnography's Future', *Journal of Contemporary Ethnography*, **28** (5), 451–9.

Bell, M.P. (2009), 'Introduction: Special Section, Doing Work That Matters', *Academy of Management Learning & Education*, **8** (1), 96–8.

Bell, M.P. and D.P. Berry (2007), 'Viewing Diversity Through Different Lenses: Avoiding a Few Blind Spots', *Academy of Management Perspectives*, **21** (4), 21–5.

Buzard, J. (2003), 'On Auto-Ethnographic Authority', *The Yale Journal of Criticism*, **16** (1), 61–91.

Calás, M.B. and L. Smircich (2006), 'From the "Woman's Point of View" Ten Years Later: Towards a Feminist Organization Studies', in S.R. Clegg, C. Hardy and W.R. Nord (eds), *The Sage Handbook of Organization Studies*, London: Sage, pp. 284–346.

Charmaz, C. (2006), 'The Power of Names', *The Journal of Contemporary Ethnography*, **35** (4), 396–9.

Danowitz Sagaria, M.A. (2007), 'Reframing Gender Equality Initiatives as University Adaptation', in M.A. Danowitz Sagaria (ed.), *Women, Universities, and Change – Gender Equality in the European Union and the United States*, New York: Palgrave Macmillan, pp. 1–6.

Ellis, C. and A.P. Bocher (2000), 'Autoethnography, Personal Narrative, Reflexivity – Researcher as Subject', in N.K. Denzin and Y.S. Lincoln (eds), *Handbook of Qualitative Research*, London: Sage, pp. 733–68.

Ellis, C. and A.P. Bocher (2006), 'Analyzing Analytic Autoethnography', *Journal of Contemporary Ethnography*, **35** (4), 429–49.

Engwall, L. (2007), 'The Anatomy of Management Education', *Scandinavian Journal of Management*, **23** (1), 4–35.

Fineman, S. (2006), 'On Being Positive: Concerns and Counterpoints', *Academy of Management Review*, **31** (2), 270–91.

Gherardi, S. (1995), *Gender, Symbolism and Organizational Cultures*, London: Sage.

Gherardi, S. (2000), 'Practice-Based Theorizing on Learning and Knowing in Organizations', *Organization*, **7** (2), 211–23.

Grey, C. (2008), *A Very Short, Fairly Interesting and Reasonably Cheap Book About Studying Organizations*, London: Sage.

Haraway, D. (1991), *Simians, Cyborgs and Women – The Invention of Nature*, New York: Routledge.

Hedmo, T., K. Sahlin-Andersson and L. Wedlin (2005), 'Fields of Imitation: The

Global Expansion of Management Education', in B. Czarniawska and G. Sevón (eds), *Global Ideas: How Ideas, Objects and Practices Travel in the Global Economy*, Lund, Sweden: Liber & Copenhagen Business School Press, pp. 190–212.

Katila, S. and S. Meriläinen (1999), 'A Serious Researcher or Just Another Nice Girl? Doing Gender in a Male-dominated Scientific Community', *Gender, Work and Organization*, **6** (3), 163–73.

Katila, S. and S. Meriläinen (2002), 'Metamorphosis: From "Nice Girls" to "Nice Bitches": Resisting Patriarchal Articulations of Professional Identity', *Gender, Work and Organization*, **9** (3), 336–54.

Klein, K.J. and D.A. Harrison (2007), 'On the Diversity of Diversity: Tidy Logic, Messier Realities', *Academy of Management Perspectives*, **21** (4), 26–33.

Korpiaho, K., H. Päiviö and K. Räsänen (2007), 'Anglo-American Forms of Management Education: A Practice-Theoretical Perspective', *Scandinavian Journal of Management*, **23** (1), 36–65.

Lemons, G.L. (2008), *Black Male Outsider – A Memoir. Teaching as a Pro-Feminist Man*, Albany, NY: State University of New York Press.

Macdonald, S. and J. Kam (2007), 'Ring a Ring O'Roses: Quality Journals and Gamesmanship in Management Studies', *Journal of Management Studies*, **44** (4), 640–55.

Meriläinen, S., J. Tienari, R. Thomas and A. Davies (2008), 'Hegemonic Academic Practices: Experiences of Publishing From the Periphery', *Organization*, **15** (4), 629–42.

Meriläinen, S., K. Räsänen and S. Katila (2009), 'Autonomous Renewal of Gendered Practices: Interventions and their Pre-conditions in an Academic Workplace', in Sunne Andersen and Dorother Ludke Koreuber (eds), *Gender and Diversity: Albtraum oder Traumpaar? Interdisziplinärer Dialog zur 'Modernisierung' von Geschelechter-und Gleichstellungspolitik*, VS Verlang fur Sozialwissenshaften, Wiesbaden, Germany, pp. 209–30.

Meyerson, D.E. and M.A. Scully (1995), 'Tempered Radicalism and the Politics of Ambivalence and Change', *Organization Science*, **6** (5), 585–600.

Mohanty, C.T. (2004), *Feminism Without Borders – Decolonizing Theory, Practicing Solidarity*, Durham & London: Duke University Press.

Morley, L. (1999), *Organising Feminisms – The Micropolitics of the Academy*, London: Macmillan.

Nkomo, S.M. (2009), 'The Seductive Power of Academic Journal Rankings: Challenges of Searching for the Otherwise', *Academy of Management Learning & Education*, **8** (1), 106–12.

Özbilgin, M.F. (2009), 'From Journal Rankings to Making Sense of the World', *Academy of Management Learning & Education*, **8** (1), 113–21.

Räsänen, K., K. Korpiaho, A. Herbert, H. Mäntylä and H. Päiviö (2005), 'Emerging Academic Practice: Tempered Passions in the Renewal of Academic Work', in S. Gherardi and D. Nicolini (eds), *The Passion for Learning and Knowing* (Vol I), Trento, Italy: University of Trento e-books, pp. 242–75.

Starbuck, W.H. (2005), 'How Much Better Are the Most-Prestigious Journals? The Statistics of Academic Publication', *Organization Science*, **16** (2), 180–200.

Thomas, R., J. Tienari, A. Davies and S. Meriläinen (2009), 'Let's Talk about "Us": A Reflexive Account of a Cross-Cultural Research Collaboration', *Journal of Management Inquiry*, **18** (4).

Tietze, S. and P. Dick (2009), 'Hegemonic Practices and Knowledge Production in the

Management Academy: An English Language Perspective', *Scandinavian Journal of Management* **25** (1), 119–23.

Van de Ven, A.H. (2007), *Engaged Scholarship. A Guide for Organizational and Social Research*, Oxford: Oxford University Press.

Wahl, A., M. Eduards, C. Holgersson, P. Höök, S. Linghag and M. Rönnblom (2008), *Motstånd & fantasi. Historien om F* [Resistance & Fantasy. The Story of F], Stockholm, Sweden: Studentlitteratur.

Wedlin, L. (2007), 'The Role of Rankings in Codifying a Business School Template: Classifications, Diffusion and Mediated Isomorphism in Organizational Fields', *European Management Review*, **4** (1), 24–39.

West, C. and D.H. Zimmerman (1987), 'Doing Gender', *Gender & Society*, **1** (2), 125–51.

Westwood, R. and S. Clegg (2003), 'The Discourse of Organization Studies: Dissensus, Politics, and Paradigms', in R. Westwood and S. Clegg (eds), *Debating Organization. Point-Counterpoint in Organization Studies*, Oxford: Blackwell Publishing, pp. 1–42.

Ylijoki, O.-H. (1998), 'Akateemiset heimokulttuurit ja yliopistoyhteisön itseymmärrys' [Academic Tribe Cultures and the Self-Understanding of the University Community], *Tiedepolitiikka*, **3** (98), 7–11.

PART I

Influencing institutions and developing
curricula

2. Tempered radicals seizing the moment: creating a Master's programme on cultural diversity in a Dutch university

Patrizia Zanoni and Hans Siebers

INTRODUCTION

Ethnic and cultural diversity has featured high in the Dutch public arena in the last decade. The higher unemployment rates of ethnic minorities, lower school achievements and higher criminality rates of migrant youth, the problems of lower class and ethnically mixed neighbourhoods, murders and possible terrorist action inspired by religious conviction, the debates on criteria for awarding citizenship to immigrants, political asylum policies, and minimum requirements for granting social and unemployment benefits have been at the top of the political agenda and often in the media. As in other European countries, the multicultural character of Dutch society is today perceived as highly problematic. An ethnicist interpretation of societal problems is feeding a nationalistic ideology that threatens to exclude 1.7 million people with a non-Western foreign background residing in the Netherlands.[1]

The current social and political context is calling us, Patrizia Zanoni and Hans Siebers, to consciously reflect on our role as diversity scholars. As currency expendable not only in the academic but also in various public arenas, our scientific knowledge is today particularly politically loaded. To what extent and in which forms are we to engage in these debates? How can we, as academics, counter dominant ideas and foster inclusion of ethnic minorities in society?

In this piece we reflect on our engagement by discussing our experience of setting up a Master's programme in Organization of Cultural Diversity at Tilburg University, together with a multidisciplinary, culturally diverse team including anthropologists, linguists, psychologists, organization studies and religion scholars from the faculties of Social and Behavioural Sciences and the Humanities. We believe this programme can contribute to building a more inclusive society by forming professionals who raise embarrassing questions and confront orthodoxy and dogma rather than mere 'technicians' of diversity

(Said 1994; Ball 1995). The programme attempts to achieve this aim by targeting a culturally diverse student audience and a three-fold strategy including multidisciplinarity, interactive didactics and close collaborations with culturally diverse organizations.

While the programme is only at its beginning, there are some early indications of success. It has put cultural diversity on our university's educational agenda, providing the first cohort of students with a safe evironment to debate on diversity-related issues in a theory-informed way. In their research projects, they have not only been able to investigate various mechanisms through which ethnic minorities are excluded, but also to draw the attention of the host organizations to such mechanisms. In the longer run, success will depend on the capacity to maintain the synergy between a variety of actors within and outside the university who, recognizing the societal relevance of the programme, have been willing to invest in it.

Before discussing the philosophy of the programme, we outline the increasingly negative perception of migrants and ethnic minorities in the Netherlands since the 1980s. We then elaborate on the factors we see as key to the programme's success. We conclude with a reflection on how this experience has given us the chance to build meaningful professional practices and a rewarding professional identity as 'tempered radicals', individuals with a double allegiance to our profession and university on the one hand and to our ideals of democracy and inclusion on the other (see Meyerson and Scully 1995) at the interstices of Dutch academia (see Sweet 1998).

CHANGING VIEWS ON CULTURAL DIVERSITY IN DUTCH SOCIETY

In the Netherlands, the political debate on cultural diversity is intrinsically linked to immigration. It originated in the 1980s, when it became clear that 'guest workers' from Turkey and Morocco, who had immigrated since the 1960s, were to stay in the country and their families were to rejoin them. At the same time, new immigrants from the former Dutch colonies Surinam and The Antilles and, later, asylum seekers from various countries also arrived.

In the context of economic recession and mounting unemployment, the government passed policies intended to remove barriers to equal treatment before the law and foster equal participation in the labour market. For example, a law passed in 1994 obliged companies to report on the share of ethnic minorities among their employees and their diversity management initiatives to increase it. At the same time, the state approached immigrants as members of distinct ethnic communities, for instance by subsidizing education for minority children 'in their own language and culture' (Entzinger 2003).

The cultural relativism underlying this approach, according to which cultures can be only understood on their own terms (Siebers 2004), however de facto inhibited the possibility of expressing critique, which contributed to the erosion of good-will towards minorities.[2] A more negative stance on migrants was also triggered by the increasing number of asylum seekers, which reached a peak of 55 000 in 1994 (*Trouw* 23 March 1995). The debate on asylum gradually shifted from how to guarantee human rights to how to close the country for 'fortune-hunters' (Geuijen 2004). Naturalization and double citizenship were made more difficult and minority children's education in their mother-tongue virtually disappeared (Entzinger 2003).

At the turn of the century, a provocative article entitled *The Multicultural Tragedy* by Paul Scheffer, a journalist and university professor, crystallized the new terms of the debate on multicultural society (*NRC Handelsblad* 29 January 2000). The author claimed that problems with minorities were dramatic and called for a revival of 'Dutch national awareness'. Populist politician Pim Fortuyn – also a university professor – later capitalized on tensions in ethnically mixed neighbourhoods and on the lack of political debate under the government coalition of right-wing liberals and social democrats. He harvested large support among the Dutch public by characterizing Islam as a 'backward culture' and calling for the abolition of the article in the Dutch constitution banning discrimination (*de Volkskrant* 9 February 2002). After his assassination in 2002, other public figures took the lead in the anti-Islamic offensive. One of them has been Ayaan Hirsi Ali, a young, female politician of the Liberal Party with a Somali Muslim background. In 2004, together with filmmaker Theo van Gogh, she produced a documentary suggesting that the Koran authorizes violence against women. She subsequently received death threats and Van Gogh was actually murdered later that year by a radical Muslim. His assassination triggered a spiral of violence against Muslim schools and mosques and retaliation against churches. Other politicians have joined her anti-Islamic battle, harvesting again wide electoral success.

The escalation of violence after 2000 accelerated the substitution of cultural relativism with a nationalistic 'monoculturalism'. In 2004, the Prime Minister Jan Peter Balkenende launched a nationwide debate on Dutch 'norms and values'. The national identity has been increasingly constructed in opposition to ethnic minorities' norms and values, particularly of those inspired by Islam. The problems ethnic minorities face in education and on the labour market are today often seen as the effects of their 'clinging to their own culture', as stated by the former Minister of Integration. Accordingly, government interventions in favour of ethnic equality in the labour market have been abolished and migrants are obliged to attend and pay for a civic integration programme to 'learn' Dutch culture. Many have been expelled, often in violation of Dutch and international laws.[3]

The government that took office in 2007 has had a more tempered position on cultural diversity and minorities in society. Nonetheless, the position of ethnic minorities in the Netherlands remains highly problematic, as in many other European countries (see Stolcke 1995; Heath and Cheung 2007; Alghasi et al. 2009). Many countries struggle with issues related to cultural diversity, pluralism and migration. Liberal democracies have come under severe pressure, yet so far not many viable scenarios have been developed to escape from the extremes of social fragmentation, exclusion and fundamentalism (Siebers 2004). As diversity researchers, we feel we can contribute to making society more inclusive.

OUR CHANGING ROLE AS ACADEMICS

The societal developments sketched above have made our research and teaching more relevant to the 'outside world'. In the Netherlands, there are particularly strong connections between academia, the mass media and the political world. Political decisions are often legitimated drawing on scientific reports drafted by academic experts. Significantly, the major policies dealing with issues related to cultural diversity over the last decades were preceded by official reports by the Scientific Council for Government Policy in which prominent scholars are represented. Leading academics have developed the official categorization of 'autochthonous' versus 'allochthonous' populations and, within this latter category, between 'Western' and 'non-Western allochthonous' people. Reflected in all official statistics, these categories have been instrumental in developing the we-versus-them discourse delineated above. Also in the academic community, they are today widely used with little questioning.

For scholars, the risk of (unintentionally) creating or reproducing exclusive ideologies is very real. Yet our position also allows us to play an important role in the development of critiques countering hegemonic thought (Saul 1997; Aronowitz 2000). If intellectuals may be functional to legitimizing a given social order, they are also particularly well placed to call it into question, becoming agents of change (Boyce 2002). As educators, we can provide students with the critical tools to articulate their lived experience and to play an inclusive role in society. We have chosen to focus on our teaching because we believe that pedagogy is a core means of engagement of 'tempered radicals'. In the words of Henry Giroux:

> Pedagogy at its best is about neither training nor political indoctrination; instead, it is about a political and moral practice that provides the knowledge and skills to deepen and extend the possibilities of living in a substantive and inclusive democracy. Rather than assume the mantle of a false impartiality, pedagogy recognizes that education and teaching involve the crucial act of intervening in the world and the recognition that human life is conditioned not determined. (2006, p. 31)

THE MASTER'S IN ORGANIZATION OF CULTURAL DIVERSITY

A few years ago a group of academics from the faculties of Social and Behavioural Sciences and of the Humanities of Tilburg University, members of the Babylon Centre for Studies of the Multicultural Society, joined forces to develop a new Master's programme. We shared the desire to restore critical distance, as scholars, from the increasingly negative dominant discourse on multiculturalism, and agreed about the need for preparing students to play a critical and constructive role in society after graduating.

As a result of our efforts, a new Master's programme in Organization of Cultural Diversity was created, leading to a diploma of Master of Science in Organization Studies. Its objective is to provide students with the multidisciplinary knowledge and critical analytical skills to deal with issues related to cultural diversity in their future work as, for example, policy developers, advisors, managers, consultants and human resource officials in public, non-profit and for-profit organizations. The focus is on understanding and addressing the challenges and the opportunities that emerge when people with different languages, religions, ethnic identities and cultural backgrounds come together in the same companies, schools, hospitals, associations, public agencies and neighbourhoods. It is a one-year intensive Master's with an international orientation, fully run in English, and so far unique in its genre within the European context.

After a year and a half of preparation, in August 2007, the first cohort of 26 students started attending classes. Candidates holding a university Bachelor's degree or an equivalent diploma providing basic knowledge about organizations, cultural diversity and research methodologies were admitted. Students who entered the programme had a background in organization studies, culture studies, sociology, anthropology, business studies and philosophy. Seventeen were women, three were Dutch nationals with an ethnic minority background and two were white South-Africans.

THREE GUIDING PRINCIPLES OF THE MASTER'S PROGRAMME

Our commitment to a critical pedagogy that fosters inclusion is articulated along three basic principles of the Master's: a multidisciplinary character, an interactive didactic approach and close collaborations with organizations dealing with cultural diversity.

Multidisciplinarity: Including Ideas on Culture and Identity

The programme consists of modules exposing students to diversity-related concepts and theories from different scientific traditions. This is made possible in the first place by the collaboration between staff with diverse disciplinary backgrounds, in itself an act of openness and inclusion. It is further supported by the research seminars organized by Babylon, the Centre for Studies of the Multicultural Society, to which students are invited.

Let us take core concepts such as culture, identity and diversity. In the different modules of the programme, they are approached from different disciplinary and epistemological perspectives. Students can thus reflect on how culture can have different meanings. It can refer to a specific set of psychological traits that are acquired through socialization and are therefore more often found within a certain community, as in classical psychology. Or it can refer to a set of social habits, traditions, meanings and myths, which are passed from generation to generation, as in classical anthropology (Geertz 1973). In both cases culture is understood as rather integrated and relatively static. But it can also be conceptualized in more relational terms, as a social process of boundary construction, stressing how the definition of the self is achieved by differentiation from the other, as in Barth's work (1969). Or culture can also be conceptualized as a politically loaded collective discourse or a more subjective, narrative phenomenon (Gullestad 1996). It thus becomes something contested and contradictory rather than shared and systemic (Featherstone 1995). Similarly, the concept of identity can be approached from a more positivistic or social constructivist stance, stressing its psycho-biological basis or its narrative dimension, allowing more or less room for continuity and closure versus fluidity and openness (Flax 1990; Baumann 1999). Also conceptualizations of diversity vary from a group's socio-demographic heterogeneity to socially constructed differences (Litvin 1997; Zanoni and Janssens 2004).

We let students become familiar with these distinct, even opposed understandings of key concepts because they inform explanations of related social phenomena such as the acculturation of minorities and, possibly, socioeconomic inequality between ethnic groups. They are therefore necessary to deconstructing dominant discourses in the social and political arena. Take, for example, acculturation theory (Berry 2001, 2005), which portrays immigrants as positioned between two distinct cultures: the culture of the country of origin and the culture of the host country. Its static and monolithic understanding of cultures can easily be appropriated by political actors to argue that the cultures of origin are incompatible with the host culture, and that ethnic minorities need to abandon the former and adopt the latter. This is an often-heard argument in Dutch politics. Yet, other perspectives would contest the very existence of one homogeneous Dutch culture as well as monolithic cultures of origin. Recognizing diversity within cultures allows shifting attention to specific practices that are considered problematic, and reconsidering the possible reasons why they are so. By focusing on specific problems, the discussion can be circumscribed to more specific practices, rather than ethnic minority communities or 'cultures' as integrated wholes. While considering a broader variety of possible causes of these problems, such as socio-economic factors or intolerance by the host community, such an approach re-frames responsibilities for them and allows considering alternative solutions.

If theory facilitates disidentification with taken-for-granted reality (Ball 1995), multiple theories are likely to stimulate it even more by enabling its systematic deconstruction. Multidisciplinarity further helps them learn to deal with complexity, rather than ignore it for theoretical purity or intellectual ease, a necessary competence when devising approaches to real-life problems.

Finally, familiarizing students with different research traditions trains them to be self-reflective on their own relationship with the subjects they study or the groups whom they will, in the future, direct their policies at. While classical social theories are based on a positivist epistemology assuming a clear distinction between the researcher and the object of study, some ethnographic perspectives question such separation. Being exposed to these latter favours the adoption of an emic approach by students, who are stimulated to develop their analyses based on concepts and categories that are relevant and meaningful to their subjects and a certain degree of empathy with them. This is particularly important when dealing with cultural diversity, as different worldviews interact with different life-worlds which co-exist in the same societal arenas creating new chances but also raising new types of conflicts.

In sum, different explanatory paradigms stimulate the cognitive, ethical and emotional capabilities that are necessary to act upon the (culturally diverse) world to make it more inclusive. They feed a healthy scepticism *vis-à-vis* too simplistic understandings of culture-related social issues as well as quick-fix recipes to address them, which we think is crucial. As a teaching team, we therefore cherish multidisciplinarity. Our approach fits well the philosophy of Tilburg University, an institution which has historically been engaged in societal issues, despite increasing research performance pressures which tend to favour specialization over societal relevance.

Interactive Didactics: Including Students in Learning Processes

A second cornerstone of the Master's is its interactive didactics. This teaching approach is highly valued in the Dutch educational system. Graduate students not only have to acquire knowledge but also the capacities to critically elaborate such knowledge and communicate it to others. To facilitate learning these skills, all modules in the programme include a combination of lectures, seminars and working groups. Similarly, grading is based on different types of collective and individual assignments ranging from written tasks during the semester to written exams, debates based on scientific literature and presentations. Also the Master's thesis process is interactive. Students are required to actively engage with a specific topic related to the organization of cultural diversity both through the existing literature and by carrying out empirical research. The thesis follows a classical research cycle, from drafting a theoretical concept, to the formulation of research questions addressing understudied aspects in existing literature, designing and carrying out the empirical research, and writing and revising the final text. Yet differently from elsewhere, students start out at the beginning of the year working as a group and only gradually pass on to working on a more individual basis, always with the support of a teacher. The more collective initial phase is meant to favour dialogue and exchange among students before they engage with their own research.

We are aware that it is not always easy to find a healthy balance between transmitting content and letting students develop competences, using more top-down and bottom-up approaches, and allowing autonomy while still guiding processes. While consensus is sought on the big lines, each instructor maintains some autonomy in his or her teaching style. Students are therefore likely to be exposed to a variety of teaching approaches. This is again useful for them because it fosters the development of various skills and familiarizes them with different ways to relate to one another and to the teacher.

The fact that the students themselves are a diverse group reinforces this dynamic. Interactive didactics force them to dialogue with others and to develop, to some extent, a common language. It constantly exposes them not only to different ideas but also to different ways of doing things, requiring them to negotiate styles which mediate between different needs and habits. These processes are sometimes guided by teachers yet often also occur outside the classroom, in teams carrying out specific projects.

Because interactive didactics highlight both teachers' and students' identities more than traditional ex-cathedra education, they further reveal how illusionary the clear-cut distinction between science and politics, still upheld in many Bachelor programmes, actually is. The first reaction of students to a critical analysis of dominant ethnicist discourses is to relegate such an analysis to an act of politics, not science. Yet, students need to be aware that what they will think and do, as diversity 'experts', will always have a political dimension, and to develop ways of dealing with it. The inquiry with potential employers of future graduates conducted before designing the programme actually indicated that they expected our graduates to be able to analyse diversity-related issues taking into consideration underlying interests and power relations, and considered this a basic skill graduate students should acquire in the Master's. The challenge is to recognize the political dimension of the social sciences without reducing the latter to the former. It is about being aware of one's political role and being able to deal with political conditions and implications, while being guided by sound analysis and knowledge as academically trained experts. As educators working within a critical paradigm, our goal is to endow these young intellectuals with a critical edge so that they can contribute to building an inclusive, culturally diverse society.

Collaborations with Societal Actors: Including Organizations in the Learning Process

The third pillar of our Master is its close collaboration with private, non-profit and public organizations working on cultural diversity. Contacts with the 'real world' during the programme through guest lectures, field visits and fieldwork for the Master's thesis, aim at helping students confront theory with practice and put both in perspective. Again, this principle intends to stress the juncture between science and action. Confronted with the complexity of real-life situations, we hope students will become aware that social engineering just does not do, and that they need to critically interpret situations and engage with field actors' own perspectives, if they want to make a difference (see Ball 1995, p. 263).

While in the Tilburg academic context multidisciplinarity is possible and interactive teaching methods appreciated, a teaching approach that encourages confrontation with practice is considered somewhat more problematic. Such engagement is quickly associated with the development of too 'applied' knowledge. The university rather emphasizes theoretical knowledge, together with training in scientific methods and academic skills, the backbone of all curricula. Quantitative methodological courses represent the main mechanism of student selection in the Bachelor programmes.[4] At the same time, scientific personnel is advised to carry out applied research only in so far as it can lead to publications in leading international scientific journals, the most important criterion for evaluations and promotions.

Of course, these principles are not specific to our university. Yet, in Tilburg they are more than managerial principles, they are at the very heart of the university identity. The strong emphasis on high 'scientific' standards in teaching and research entails the risk of encouraging us to keep a distance from real-life 'practice'. This emphasis is not unrelated to the fact that Tilburg University is a small, young university specialized in disciplines such as economics, law, social sciences and the humanities. Until 1986 it was a higher vocational school offering post-secondary education mainly in economics. In order to build a strong academic identity and solid reputation, it emphasizes high scientific standards, as US business schools did in the early 20th century to gain legitimacy within academia (Perriton 2007 based on Locke 1993).

We believe that university education should not be completely severed from real-world practices and confined to the ivory towers. It is fundamental that students of cultural diversity learn how to relate with other actors. They need to become aware of their own role in society, now as students but later also as 'experts' and policymakers, and learn how to negotiate relations with actors fulfilling other roles. This is because they will not just be asked, in their future positions, to design and implement policies and actions. They will above all need to understand other actors' logics, interests and positions, in order to build shared processes to make decisions and implement them. These more relational and process dimensions are not mere instruments. They are in themselves powerful tools of inclusion, of making everybody feel an 'insider' within a community (see Pelled et al. 1999), someone whose needs and opinions are taken seriously.

While classical academic curricula teach students mainly to engage with ideas and concepts, contact with the field gives them a feeling of the importance of social processes to achieve sustainable solutions to social problems. Further, our classroom experience tells us that this contact helps students question both theory and practice. In general, students who come back from the field are either very positive of the practices they have witnessed or utterly negative. This is because their theoretical education stimulates them to think in extremes, as theoretical thinking stresses internal coherence. Yet practices are less 'pure' than theory. They do not follow grand, clear-cut principles, they are more often a 'matter of degree' than a 'matter of order' (Perelman and Olbrechts-Tyteca 1969; Zanoni and Janssens 2004). Through interactive classroom practices, such as debates, students who are overly positive are encouraged to go back to theory to question practices, while students who are overly negative, because they do not see theory properly applied, are encouraged to reconsider the advantages of practical, hybrid, consensus-based solutions. Both need to keep interrogating existing knowledge yet in a constructive way.

SUCCESS FACTORS OF THE MASTER'S PROGRAMME

It is certainly too early – after only a year of experience with the programme – to evaluate the programme in its entirety. However, the first cohort of students has evaluated the programme in overall positive terms, and the idea and the design have already received some recognition within our university. In November 2007, the university board honoured our efforts with the yearly university educational innovation prize.

We see several key factors that contributed to getting the university apparatus to approve the programme. First, there was a committed team of scholars who agreed on the need of such a programme in the current Dutch context and who were willing to invest time and energy into it. Their motivation is particularly praiseworthy, as the time they have put into the programme was not accounted for in official time allocation procedures, within a university context where research is by far the most important evaluation criterion. Second, we had the support of a top manager, the Dean of the Faculty of Social and Behavioural Sciences, who believed in the relevance of the topic of cultural diversity for society and organizations. His political role was key also because he became, in the course of the development of the programme, Dean of the other faculty involved, the Faculty of the Humanities. Third, once we had a preliminary idea about what the programme would look like, we were able to mobilize a group of about 40 students who expressed their interest in the programme and wanted to be informed about its progress. This signalled to the university that there was a potential student public for it.

Fourth, we were patient. It took quite some time to build consensus among the parties involved – the Faculty of Social and Behavioural Sciences, the Department of Organization Studies and Babylon – and let them realize the advantage of the collaboration. During the development of the programme, the Faculty of Social and Behavioural Sciences realized that it could serve as the first experience in developing specialized Master's, in line with official faculty policy. The Department of Organization Studies within the faculty saw it as an opportunity to diversify its Master's programmes. Finally, Babylon could profile itself with its own Master's programme. While all parties could claim the Master's as their own, the costs of launching it could be spread across two faculties and six departments. Finally, the collaboration could succeed because the coordinator played a facilitating role between the parties and managed the programme in all its aspects. As a member of both the Organization Studies department and Babylon, he could mobilize people and resources throughout the process. These factors all concurred to take the programme where it is today and may serve as an illustration for colleagues that intend to embark on similar projects.

Next to the consolidation of the programme, we see two main challenges for the near future. First, it is our ambition to make the programme truly inter-national by attracting more foreign students and encouraging students to conduct their Master's thesis research abroad. Coming from and/or investigat-ing different societal contexts facilitates putting specific discourses and soci-etal problems into perspective. Second, we want to recruit a substantial number of Dutch students with an ethnic minority background. In the first cohort, only three students had this demographic profile. As mentioned above, we believe that these students can play a particularly important role in build-ing a more inclusive Dutch society.

SEIZING THE MOMENT

The Master's in Organization of Cultural Diversity represents one of our personal strategies to make our profession more rewarding to us, as 'tempered radicals' within the academia (Meyerson and Scully 1995). It is one of those 'practices at the interstice' (Sweet 1998) through which we both comply with a number of demands in the academic environment yet also put forward our ideas of a more just, less exclusive society.

Paradoxically, the current tensions of ethnic diversity in Dutch society, which we regret, were actually a necessary condition for the launch of our programme. They have created a demand for diversity-related competences which we could use to justify the new programme even in these times of continuous rationalizations of the educational offer. We could grab this oppor-tunity by drawing from a market logic, one we often ourselves oppose in the academic environment (see Lawrence and Sharma 2002). Also, by launching a programme on a specific issue, the organization of cultural diversity, we went along with the trend of specialization of graduate education to meet labour market demands (see Buchbinder 1993), of which we are ourselves rather critical. We see these two aspects as most problematic, yet colleagues reading this piece might identify additional signs of compliance we may have overseen.

Yet we cannot help but also see the advantages of our co-optation. Aside from our main ambition – training the new generation of professionals with a critical approach to rather than technicians of cultural diversity – we also see additional potential advantages. For instance, by targeting foreign students and students with a minority background and stimulating contacts with the field, we hope to develop networks including not only public and private organiza-tions, but also ethnic minority communities and organizations in the Netherlands and abroad. Our increased visibility as a community of scholars is likely to increase the impact of our ideas in the public arena as well as our chances to raise funds for diversity-related research. Getting to know students with a foreign or minority background interested in diversity-related issues will stimulate increasing their number among junior researchers and possibly, in the longer run, senior academics including professors. To date these groups remain heavily underrepresented in academic ranks.

While compromising is often an uncomfortable position (Meyerson and Scully 1995) it might be also inevitable if one wants to have some degree of impact in one's direct environment. Total assimilation into the university system would mean us losing ourselves on the way, which we want to avoid. However, neither are we ready to pay the high price of marginalization, to have our voices totally silenced. While we certainly do not claim to have the final answers to the question of how to promote a more inclusive society or even only give sense to our daily work as academics, these are strategies that have, until today, worked for us.

NOTES

1. Dutch official classification distinguishes 'autochthonous' from 'allochthonous' people. The latter have at least one parent born abroad or are themselves born abroad. Among them, a distinction is made between those born in so-called Western and those born in so-called non-Western countries. The latter make up 1.7 million, or 10.8 per cent of the total population (CBS 2004); only they are the object of public discussion.
2. For similarities with Sweden and Norway, see Omanović (2006) and Wikan (2002) respectively.
3. See denunciations by Human Rights Watch (*Trouw* 9 April 2003), the Council of Europe on 26 January 2006 (*de Volkskrant* 28 October 2006), the European Court of Human Rights (*de Volkskrant* 12 January 2007), and the national Ombudsman (TV documentary *Zembla* 21 May 2006).
4. Qualitative methods have only recently received more room in the curricula. Paradoxically, while they are thought to be more difficult to apply for students than quantitative methods, they are not used as 'selection courses'.

REFERENCES

Alghasi, Sharam, Thomas H. Eriksen and Halleh Ghorashi (eds) (2009), *Paradoxes of Cultural Recognition: Perspectives from Norway and The Netherlands*, Aldershot, Hampshire: Ashgate.

Aronowitz, Stanley (2000), *The Knowledge Factory: Dismantling the Corporate University and Creating True Higher Learning*, Boston: Beacon Press.

Ball, S.J. (1995), 'Intellectuals or technicians? The urgent role of theory in educational studies', *British Journal of Educational Studies*, **43** (3), 255–71.

Barth, Frederik (1969), 'Introduction', in Frederik Barth (ed.), *Ethnic Groups and Boundaries: The Social Organization of Cultural Difference*, Oslo: Universitetsforlaget, pp. 9–38.

Baumann, Gerd (1999), *The Multicultural Riddle: Rethinking National, Ethnic, and Religious Identities*, New York and London: Routledge.

Berry, J.W. (2001), 'A psychology of immigration', *Journal of Social Issues*, **57** (3), 615–31.

Berry, J.W. (2005), 'Acculturation: Living successfully in two cultures', *International Journal of Intercultural Relations*, **29** (6), 697–712.

Boyce, G. (2002), 'Now and then: Revolutions in higher learning', *Critical Perspectives on Accounting*, **13** (5/6), 575–601.

Buchbinder, H. (1993), 'The market oriented university and the changing role of knowledge', *Higher Education*, **26** (3), 331–47.

CBS (Centraal Bureau voor de Statistiek) (2004), *Allochtonen in Nederland 2004*, Voorburg, Heerlen: CBS.

Entzinger, Han (2003), 'The rise and fall of multiculturalism: The case of The Netherlands', in Christian Joppke and Ewa Morawska (eds), *Towards Assimilation and Citizenship: Immigrants in Liberal Nation-States,* Houndsmills: Palgrave Macmillan, pp. 59–86.

Featherstone, Mike (1995), *Undoing Culture: Globalization, Postmodernism and Identity*, London: Sage.

Flax, Jane (1990), *Thinking Fragments: Psychoanalysis, Feminism, and Postmodernism in the Contemporary West*, Berkeley, CA: University of California Press.

Geertz, Clifford (1973), *The Interpretation of Cultures*, New York: Basic Books.

Geuijen, Karin (2004), *De Asielcontroverse: Argumenteren over Mensenrechten en Nationale Belangen*, Tilburg PhD Dissertation, Amsterdam: Dutch University Press.

Giroux, H.A. (2006), 'Academic freedom under fire: The case for critical pedagogy', *College Literature*, **33** (4), 1–42.

Gullestad, Marianne (1996), *Everyday Life Philosophers. Modernity, Morality, and Autobiography in Norway*, Oslo: Scandinavian University Press.

Heath, Anthony and Sin Y. Cheung (eds) (2007), *Unequal Chances: Ethnic Minorities in Western Labour Markets*, Oxford: Oxford University Press.

Lawrence, S. and U. Sharma (2002), 'Commodification of education and academic labour: Using the balanced scorecard in a university setting', *Critical Perspectives on Accounting*, **13** (5–6), 661–77.

Litvin, D.R. (1997), 'The discourse of diversity: From biology to management', *Organization*, **4** (2), 187–209.

Locke, Robert R. (1993), *Management and Higher Education since 1940*, Cambridge: Cambridge University Press.

Meyerson, D.E. and M.A. Scully (1995), 'Tempered radicalism and the politics of ambivalence and change', *Organization Science*, **6** (5), 585–600.

Omanović, Vedran (2006), *A Production of Diversity: Appearances, Ideas, Interests, Actions, Contradictions and Praxis*, Gothenburg: PhD dissertation, Gothenburg University.

Pelled, L.H., G.E. Ledford and S.A. Mohrman (1999), 'Demographic dissimilarity and workplace inclusion', *Journal of Management Studies*, **36** (7), 1013–31.

Perelman, Chaim and Lucie Olbrechts-Tyteca (1969), *The New Rhetoric: A Treatise on Argumentation*, London: University of Notre Dame Press.

Perriton, L. (2007), 'Really useful knowledge? Critical Management Education in the UK and the US', *Scandinavian Journal of Management*, **23** (1), 66–83.

Said, Edward (1994), *Representations of the Intellectual*, New York: Vintage Books.

Saul, John R. (1997), *The Unconscious Civilization*, Melbourne: Penguin.

Siebers, H. (2004), 'The management of multiculturalism: Coming to terms with the multiplication of experienced difference', *International Journal on Multicultural Societies*, **6** (2), 300–321.

Stolcke, V. (1995), 'Talking culture: New boundaries, new rhetorics of exclusion in Europe', *Current Anthropology*, **36** (1), 1–13.

Sweet, S. (1998), 'Practicing radical pedagogy: Balancing ideals with institutional constraints', *Teaching Sociology*, **26** (2), 100–111.

Wikan, Unni (2002), *Generous Betrayal. Politics of Culture in the New Europe*, Chicago and London: The University of Chicago Press.

Zanoni, P. and M. Janssens (2004), 'Deconstructing difference: The rhetoric of human resource managers' diversity discourses', *Organization Studies*, **25** (1), 55–74.

3. Moving towards Inclusive Excellence in doctoral studies

Mary Ann Danowitz and Frank A. Tuitt

Universities, as organizations, are continuously challenged to create an inclusive environment for a multiplicity of identities including race-ethnicity, sexual orientation, ability, gender and religion (Cox 2001). A key element of an inclusive university environment is the curriculum. It is a locus and transmitter of values (Rudolph 1977), a contract with students and a statement of intentions about what knowledge is to be offered to prepare graduates for the labor market and society (Meil 1996). Due to the curriculum's importance, connectedness to faculty values and identity and subjugation to faculty authority and expertise, the majority of curricular change is small and nuanced (Arnold 2004). Yet these changes can also produce a significant shift in mission and priorities, especially at the departmental or academic program level.

In this chapter we focus on a successful case of diversity management: a strategic change to incorporate diversity and inclusiveness into a PhD program in the United States. Specifically, we delineate three types of changes: strategic administrative actions, curricular changes and pedagogical changes. The authors – Mary Ann Danowitz and Frank Tuitt – were hired in 2004 and 2005, respectively, to transform a course-based graduate program in the area of higher education to meet the needs of the 21st century. Using critical race and feminist perspectives and personal reflections we (Danowitz, a female White full professor and feminist; Tuitt, a Caribbean American Black male assistant professor and an emerging critical race scholar) describe our experiences at the University of Denver and how they led to changing practices in the graduate program. First, we sketch the broader social realities of the program by considering the changing landscape and demographics of US higher education and society, focusing on students and members of academic staff and the university setting. Second, we place our case in the context of the current discourse on Inclusive Excellence in US higher education (Association of American Colleges and Universities (AACU) n.d.). Third, viewing curricular innovation as a form of diversity management we describe the curricular and pedagogical change process from the perspective of teachers who recognize the value of using our own lived experiences as critical components of the educational process. Finally, we discuss the implications for improving practice.

SOCIAL REALITIES

Educational achievement and skill levels are declining in the United States while it is experiencing sweeping demographic shifts (Braun et al. 2007). According to the US Census Bureau (2004) by 2010 34.9 per cent of the US population will be part of an ethnic minority. Blacks (including people of African and Caribbean descent) will make up 13.1 per cent of the population, Latino/as 15.5 per cent, Asians 4.6 per cent and all other races 3.0 per cent. Much of the population growth will come from immigrants and their US-born children (Passel and Cohen 2008). This browning of high school graduates in the United States suggests that colleges and universities will need to transform their educational practices to meet the needs of an increasingly diverse student body. This will also require that colleges and universities prepare graduates who have skills to work with individuals from diverse backgrounds, especially underrepresented groups who have been subjected to discrimination.

Unfortunately, US higher education has yet to align its practices with demographic shifts. This may be seen in that predominantly White institutions of higher education[1] have failed to develop adequate responses to the access and achievement gaps facing students of color.[2] For instance, African Americans constitute nearly 13 per cent of the US population; however, they earned only 8.7 per cent of the total degrees awarded in 2004–2005 at the bachelor's level, 8.5 per cent at the master's level and 5.5 per cent at the doctoral level (Cook and Cordova 2007). The challenge of underrepresentation of students of color becomes even more acute in the case of people of color among the faculty members. For example, Blacks and Latinos make up 5.6 per cent and 3.4 per cent, respectively, of the faculty in institutions of higher education (US Department of Education 2006). Thus, it is important to focus on policies that may improve the educational system and narrow the achievement gap (Braun et al. 2007), because it is morally right and because there is an urgent need to ensure the competitiveness of the US economy by creating the most qualified and skilled labor force.

The situation in Colorado is particularly critical because of its low high school graduation rates (Metro Denver Economic Development Corporation 2008). Moreover, students of color in cities, who mostly come from lower income families, find the challenges of making the transition from high school to higher education especially difficult. For example, in 2002 only 43 per cent of the students of color in Denver public schools graduated from high school and only 9 per cent of them completed a four-year college degree (Lee 2006).

The state also has poor funding support and is ranked 48th (out of 50) in state and local financing of higher education per full-time student (Metro Denver Economic Development Corporation 2008).

Although the most pressing inequities in educational opportunities and achievement in the United States occur along the lines of race and ethnicity, gender inequities persist within higher education. The progression of women in education is similar to most European nations: women account for 52 per cent of bachelor (first) degree recipients; however, beginning with doctoral recipients the percentage of women decreases at each step of the academic hierarchy. In research universities the percentage of women decreases from 46.9 per cent of doctoral students, to 35.9 per cent of assistant professors, to 30.2 per cent of associate professors, to 15.8 per cent of full professors (Glazer-Raymo 2007). Thus, women of color face multiple and intertwined challenges and forms of discrimination.

INCLUSIVE EXCELLENCE

In 2005, the AACU called for higher education institutions to approach diversity through Inclusive Excellence, a comprehensive and innovative approach linked directly to the mission of higher education. US universities had mainly approached diversity issues in a fragmented manner. The AACU's approach was to challenge US postsecondary institutions – that, since their founding in the American colonies in the 17th century have been predominantly populated by White male students – to consider how to involve the entire academic community to merge inclusivity with excellence (Milem et al. 2005). From a management perspective, the AACU made a business case for diversity in higher education by connecting teaching, one of the primary functions of universities to student diversity learning outcomes. The underlying assumptions of Inclusive Excellence are that teaching, research and service – the three main missions of higher education – must be linked to diversity. This is necessary if universities are to educate diverse students who will become the workforce and to prepare all students to work effectively in such a labor market. To help institutions frame and monitor their efforts to promote and achieve Inclusive Excellence, Williams et al. (2005) proposed four areas of emphasis: access and equity, campus climate, diversity in the curriculum, and student learning and development. Although our efforts in the Higher Education PhD program attended to all four dimensions, in this chapter we focus on diversity in the curriculum and student learning and development.

In theory, higher education embraces the idea that what students study, the content of their courses and the manner in which those courses are taught have significant implications for what and how students learn and develop. For example, diversifying the curriculum helps transform graduate and professional schools into more inclusive environments (Williams et al. 2005). Using diverse content and perspectives lets students know that their perspectives may be welcomed as well, especially if the content aligns with students' interests (Tuitt 2003). Unfortunately, even in cases where the curriculum is diverse, faculty members often continue to use traditional modes of instruction (Banks 1991), which serve to exclude rather than include students (Tuitt 2003). Accordingly, Inclusive Excellence calls for the integration of diverse perspectives and inclusive practices that embody multiple student identity groups. This involves a focus on student intellectual and social development by utilizing student-centered and inclusive curriculum and pedagogy, as well as the purposeful development and utilization of educational resources to create a welcoming classroom environment that attends to the cultural differences of learners to enhance teaching and the learning environment. In short, through an Inclusive Excellence framework educators utilize a range of teaching/learning strategies that help students see how they can promote equity and ask questions, examine assumptions and question cultural myths regarding the social order and their place in it (Smith-Maddox and Solórzano 2002).

THE PHD PROGRAM: STRATEGIES AND THE IMPLEMENTATION OF INCLUSIVE KNOWLEDGE AND PEDAGOGIES

Using our own experiences in a feminist reflective fashion (Deem 1996), we focus on the developments in the professional PhD program around race, gender, and inclusive values, knowledge and pedagogy. The setting, the University of Denver, is a private research university enrolling approximately 4500 undergraduates and 5000 graduate students. It is located in the state capital, Denver, which has a population of about 51 per cent people of color. In 2004 the College of Education, our academic unit, had approximately 600 graduate students taught by 27 full-time faculty members and a larger number of part-time adjunct faculty members. Two full-time faculty members were Black, two Latino and one Latina. Most faculty members were women. There were no staff members of color and fewer than 11 per cent of the students identified as racial/ethnic minorities. Most of the students were professionals studying part time, thus some of the programs were viewed as a form of professional development.

At the time of writing this chapter, I (Danowitz) had been appointed six years earlier with the mission of transforming the doctoral program so that it could prepare students for the future. I had developed curricula and supervised PhD students for two decades and my research has a strong feminist orientation, often examining issues of access and equity in universities. I interpreted the task of developing a higher education program as an opportunity for curricular and pedagogical reform, in order to prepare students who would be committed and able to provide leadership for highly diverse organizations. To bring about this reform, strategies and tactics were necessary to lay the groundwork for the changes and to implement the change process. One of the first activities was to fill a faculty position by hiring a junior colleague.

The dean, Ginger Maloney, a visionary committed to learning across the life span, wanted the College of Education to become more responsive to equity and diversity issues; she was receptive to my research and teaching. When finalizing my appointment, we agreed that I would become the chairperson of a search committee to hire another faculty member in higher education. The committee would recommend a candidate or candidates to the dean, who then would make the final appointment (with concurrence of the chief academic officer). I knew that the appointment of a new colleague would be one of the salient strategic decisions affecting my role and the future of the graduate program. He or she would be a crucial partner in the transformation process and together we would be the two principal faculty members directing PhD students.[3] Our arrival at the University of Denver would also signal a change in direction to members of the University and the national network of the profession. The strategic change process began with a revision of the position description and posting it in academic publications throughout the US along with my contacting senior scholars working on diversity and asking them to recommend junior colleagues for the job. The position description was explicit about important characteristics and qualities. It stated, 'We seek a colleague with a demonstrated line of research and a commitment to teaching that includes ethnicity and race in relation to postsecondary education.' We did not include gender as a preferred area of research because our higher priority was race and ethnicity, however, we looked carefully at candidate's sensitivity to gender issues.

I (Danowitz) also recommended that the dean make changes in the search committee membership. This was the second strategic decision, which was intended to ensure there would be members sensitive to diversity and inclusivity, and with whom I could develop personal relationships and with whom the program might develop alliances in the future. Having successfully assembled a diverse search committee, representing key constituencies, we set out to find a candidate with whom I could partner to transform the program.

This is where I (Tuitt) entered the picture. I graduated from the Harvard Graduate School of Education in 2003. In my search for a faculty position, two things were especially important to me: being able to work with a diverse group of faculty and students who were committed to access and equity in education; and working for an institution that had an explicit commitment to diversity and excellence. When I first saw the job description for an assistant professor of higher education at the University of Denver, I remember thinking, 'wow, this position is perfect for me!' It described the institution's desire for a faculty member who was committed to multicultural issues as it related to teaching and learning in higher education, which just happened to be what my research in general and my dissertation in particular was all about.[4] Having recently worked as a research assistant for the Harvard National Campus Diversity Project.[5] I was keenly aware of the disconnect between espoused intentions and theory and practice. It was important for me as a Black male to know that my research and scholarship on access and equity would align with the mission of both the college and the program.

STRATEGIES AND SUBSTANCE OF CHANGE

The College was organized into seven more-or-less autonomous programs or departments. Each program was expected to generate enough money from student tuition fees to pay for its faculty salary expenses. Thus, there was pressure on the programs to maintain or increase the number of students enrolled. In the area of curriculum, the College Program Planning and Review Committee held the authority to approve or veto new academic programs, specializations and courses. Changes in course names and descriptions were subject only to an administrative review focusing on form rather than substance.

We strategically decided to innovate incrementally by graphing (Nag et al. 2007), bringing new knowledge and pedagogical approaches from outside the University and inserting them into the existing curricular structures. This enabled us to reduce the amount of internal stakeholder involvement that would be required for approval in order to avoid potential resistance and to expedite the process so the change could go into effect for the next incoming student group.

MISSION

The Higher Education program is one of more than 213 graduate programs offering this specialization in the US (Association for the Study of Higher Education 2008). A loosely coupled organization of program directors meets annually to discuss curricular matters, but there are no external requirements or standards for a higher education PhD specialization. All are course-based programs requiring a thesis or dissertation for completion. The program at the University of Denver, like many others, developed in the 1960s with the mass expansion of universities and colleges in the United States and the need for individuals trained in research and administration of higher education. They follow a traditional structure (with some variation) of required courses including the history of higher education, curriculum and instruction, students and clientele, administration and organizational theory. Students then choose advanced courses for their area of expertise. A few doctoral programs, usually those in urban areas, include diversity. Students studying higher education are predominantly mature adults holding administrative or faculty appointments in higher, adult and continuing education organizations.

After analysing the institutional and larger higher education environment, we began the curricular reform by changing the mission of the graduate program to include multiculturalism and diversity:

> The Higher Education Program's mission is to prepare professionals for administrative and teaching leadership roles in postsecondary institutions, public and private agencies of higher education and training and development settings in a multicultural and changing world. Colleges and universities throughout the world face multiple challenges in this new century associated with decreasing governmental funding, managerialism, globalization and increasing cultural diversity. These institutions and the larger systems of which they are a part need responsible and effective administrative and faculty leaders who can guide various internal and external constituencies to new solutions to social, political and economic challenges. (University of Denver, 2004)

Thus, we defined a specific market niche for the doctorate. We explicitly recognized critical issues in higher education in the United States and especially in Colorado. This also distinguished our program from others. To the best of our knowledge, there were only a couple of other programs in which multiculturalism or diversity were a defining value. We also assumed that the majority of students would be women in the growing sector of midlevel managerial positions (Danowitz Sagaria and Agans 2007).

CURRICULUM

To bring the new mission to life we began by examining our course offerings and content and made several changes to assist our students' understanding of education and its technologies of teaching and managing through the lenses of power, inequality, race and ethnicity, class and gender. We changed our introductory higher education course from a mainstream historical approach to a social, political and economic contextualization of education. This introduced students to critical perspectives (for example, Pierre Bourdieu, Michael Apple and Lois Weiss) and changes in class, access and disenfranchisement in postindustrial nations. It also brought theory to life by encouraging students to use critical theory to analyse their own identity formation related to gender, race, ethnicity and class in a major paper. Recognizing that this would be difficult for some students, we brought our engaged pedagogy to life by incorporating our own perspectives and experiences into our teaching by sharing our own examples of how our multiple identities were influenced by our race, class and sexual orientation; this modeling often occurred by sharing personal narratives to help students see how they might make connections between their own experiences and material they were reading.

We reframed a course from learning organizations to diversity in organizations. The former included the processes and benefits of becoming a learning organization (for example, Peter Drucker, Chris Argyris and David Garvin). The reframed course introduced students to the theory and practice of enhancing cultural diversity in organizations (for example, Taylor Cox, Daryl Smith and Jeff Milem). We also added elective courses including ones on women in higher education globally and critical race theory in education (Table 3.1).

We were able to make the aforementioned changes through a technical revision process (minor changes related to course title and content) in order to lay the foundation for our most significant initiative – changing our concentration from 'Teaching and Learning' to 'Diversity and Higher Learning'. We wanted to be explicit about our focus and values. This concentration offers a four-course sequence on enhancing diversity, access and equity in organizations. It provides a critical theoretical and practical understanding of the impact of race, ethnicity, gender, sexual orientation, religious affiliation and other social identities on organizational and individual learning for careers in multicultural affairs and diversity management, curriculum development, university instruction and administration, consulting, or training.

Table 3.1   Course changes

2001–2002	2003–2005
Current Issues (Historical Foundations) II	Social and Political Context of Education
Learning in Organizations	Diversity in Organizations
Design and Administration of Adult Programs	Design and Administration of Multicultural Programs
	Women in Higher Education Globally
	Critical Race Theory in Education

CHANGES IN PHILOSOPHY AND PEDAGOGICAL PRINCIPLES

We also made a conscious effort to become more inclusive in the content offering and competencies we expected from our students. First, we established the principle that our courses would address diversity in real and meaningful ways – diversity would not merely be an 'add-on'. This approach embraces the idea that education should be used for social and political change. Thus, we challenge students to use the knowledge they acquire to promote equity and social justice for society in general and marginalized groups and communities in particular. For example, in the Design and Administration of Multicultural Programs course students had the option of either conducting a case study of an existing program or organization seeking to promote equity and social justice, or designing a multicultural program that addresses inequities in education. In both cases students were encouraged to share their assignments with those individuals and institutions that could directly benefit from the work.

Second, we embraced a principle of engaged pedagogy (hooks 1994). This reflexive, experiential and critical approach aligns with womanist, feminist and critical values and pedagogies. An underlying assumption of the pedagogy is that one's own experience is central to understanding and developing knowledge. It emerges from the idea that the personal is political (from the second wave women's movement of the 1960s) and recognizes that personal and private matters are highly political and are shaped by power relations between men and women.

The pedagogical approach in our courses established the basis for recognizing and distinguishing various kinds of racism and inequalities, and contributed to students seeking methodologies consistent with their values for their dissertations. It also created dissonance for some of our students by asking them to critically question and identify underlying assumptions of traditional quantitative methods, which they had been socialized to accept as truth. For example, students struggled to accept how narratives of lived experiences (their own and others) could be powerful tools for understanding oppression and discrimination. Some, usually practicing administrators, who had not deeply queried their racism, sexism, or the influence of their class experiences, were encouraged to confront these issues in a reflective fashion. This became especially challenging and disturbing to some White students who had not previously acknowledged their White privilege and/or racism. Sexism also became a topic of discussion in the classroom – men and women questioned their implicit assumptions and language use. Moving from the personal to the organizational and then to broader social, political and economic contexts, students came to think about how their work settings reduce or reproduce inequalities.

As professors we modeled and attempted to make our hidden curriculum more apparent. For example, we developed an orientation (induction) program for our PhD students based on the book *Teaching to Transgress* (hooks 1994), to begin the formal socialization process preparing students for engaged pedagogy. During this event, we were explicit about our intention to provide doctoral training that would challenge students to interrogate their existing beliefs, values and worldviews. Furthermore, we wanted to model personal engagement with radical and transformative perspectives and alert them to the type of deep reflective work in which they would be expected to engage. To that end, Tuitt shared a personal narrative concerning a fictional conversation he has with bell hooks, an important member of his intellectual family. During the presentation we asked students to imagine that this conversation centers around two important questions: What is my responsibility as a teacher as it relates to teaching in a manner that respects and cares for the souls of my students? and What are my students' responsibilities related to engaging in education as a practice of freedom?

During this presentation we asked the higher education faculty and students to consider the following (we used the words of bell hooks [1994]):

Keep in mind that to educate as a practice of freedom is a way of teaching where anyone can learn. Many of today's students want a meaningful education, one where their professors will not offer them information without addressing the connection between what they are learning and the impact it can have on their overall life experiences. Hopefully, your students are at the University of Denver because they are passionate about something and want to make a positive difference in this world. Please encourage them to follow their passions and use it as a source of motivation for learning.

In addition to being meaningful, education should be exciting. It is rare that any professor, no matter how eloquent, can generate through his or her actions enough energy to create an exciting classroom. Excitement is generated through collective effort. Your classroom should be an exciting place, never boring. And if boredom should prevail, have in your teaching repertoire a variety of pedagogical strategies that can intervene, alter, or even disrupt the boring atmosphere.

Even though you have a doctorate from Harvard, you must resist the temptation to present yourself as the all powerful and all knowing – and that you and only you have control over the learning process. Please be advised that everyone (professor and students) influences the learning process. Consequently, you must genuinely value everyone's presence. These contributions are resources. Used constructively, they enhance the capacity of any class to create an inclusive and transformative learning community.

One way to avoid having a professor centered teaching and learning process is to make your classroom a democratic setting where everyone feels a responsibility to contribute. In this regard it will be important for you to establish a dialogical relationship between you and your students where you affirm your students' presence and their right to speak in multiple ways on diverse subject matters. In this dialogical professor-student relationship everyone brings to the classroom intellectual and experiential knowledge from previous encounters that can only strengthen the learning environment.

Your students must enter the classroom with the conviction that it is crucial to be an active participant and not a passive consumer or empty vessels waiting for you to impart your wisdom and expertise. They must own their education. Although professors are here to teach, ultimately, students are responsible for what they learn.

In general, we wanted to set the tone for each student's academic journey in our PhD program. Many of our students responded with excitement and anticipation because from the very beginning of their doctoral education they saw that we were intent on delivering on our program's mission to prepare and train transformative intellectuals who would become agents of change. Alternatively, a few students expressed anxiety related to how their own personal beliefs and values might be challenged.

Recognizing that our students bring significant life experiences with them, we sought to leverage their experiences with the understanding that it would be critical for the overall learning process (see Carnell 2007 and hooks 1994). Thus, we encouraged our faculty to engage in a pedagogy and curriculum that leveraged the experiences of the students both as individuals and as a community of learners and created a setting for them to reflect and act. The course activities and assignments we chose attempted to balance personal reflection with the team learning. In the Diversity in Organizations course that Tuitt taught, students were evaluated on five activities: class participation, analytical reflection, an individual paper, a group case study paper and a group case study presentation. The first three activities focused on individual experiences and contributions; the last two emphasized teamwork in multicultural settings. Moreover, the assignments highlighted integration of theory with practice. For example, students are expected to write one- to two-page analytical reflections that integrate personal experiences and readings in their weekly journals. Likewise, group case studies require students to research actual organizational efforts to enhance diversity through the lens of diversity change models and other course readings.

In another course, the introductory PhD seminar Social and Political Context of Education, we examine the role of social institutions and analyse how they perpetuate and challenge classism, racism, sexism and homophobia. Students are expected to write a 12–15 page educational autobiography, using theory to reflectively analyse how a dominant institution or institutions such as education and religion, or how ideologies, viewpoints, norms and expectations influenced their relationships and identity. The instructor treats the autobiography confidentially and during the last class session students may elect to read a passage or a couple of paragraphs from their autobiography. All students have chosen to read. I (Danowitz) sometime read from a narrative about how and why I, a lesbian (who was formerly married), consider the Catholic Church my spiritual home, although it does not accept homosexuality. This enables me to teach reflexive analysis with my life and tends to break down stereotypical perceptions that lesbians and gays do not belong to traditional and patriarchic religious groups and shows how someone can be a member and activist in an organization they hope will change.

Expecting our students to move from theory to practice and from practice to theory in an environment embracing Inclusive Excellence can inspire students to become more engaged in research for the public good (Bowen and Bok 1998). This has resulted in two significant outcomes. First, many students have chosen to write their comprehensive examination paper (their major academic work preceding the dissertation) on topics associated with Inclusive Excellence including: a transformative and inclusive leadership framework for white college administrators; predominately white institutions' impact on Hispanic students; US student athletes' sexual identity formation; and pluralistic mentoring empowerment. Second, many students began to view their academic work and sustained personal engagement with underrepresented communities as an opportunity to transform how people view the world and their role in it. Thus, it changed the way they have chosen to engage in their professional roles.

IMPLICATIONS FOR PRACTICE

Chen and Van Velsar (1996) claim that a commitment from leaders is integral to successfully diversify and transform organizations. They propose, 'the diversity leader develop the capacity to be an open-minded, continuous learner, a relationship builder and a people developer' (p. 299). In our experience, implementing diversity management in the curriculum we were able to make significant changes by being strategic, intentional, creative and personally engaged. These changes have resulted in College, University and community recognition for its commitment to diversity and equity. For example, the dean frequently spoke about our program in public settings and recently the University of Denver Center of Multicultural Excellence awarded Tuitt the Profiles of Excellence Outstanding Faculty Award for our program's efforts to promote Inclusive Excellence.

Overall, we believe that the practices and experiences we have described provide a framework for other graduate programs that wish to become more inclusive and relevant to changing societal and economic needs. This framework calls for a careful examination of the content (what) and the pedagogy (how) used to train future scholars and practitioners to ensure that organizations move away from a change model where diversity efforts are often challenged to lower standards and instead embrace the tensions that are an integral part of the organizational learning process (Smith 1996). Strategically, the framework calls for an assessment of the organizational context, policies, procedures and politics (Danowitz et al. 2009) to create allies to bring about curricula change and to reduce resistance.

Furthermore, our experience suggests that through a conscious effort to engage student resistance in teaching and learning and by supporting the growth of all community members, it is possible to overcome a history of inequality and a failure to address diversity. However, to be successful, program leaders must be academic change agents and develop a 'diversity change infrastructure that is holistic, multidimensional and focused on making a real difference' (Williams et al. 2005, p. 13). Only when programs focus on the intellectual and social development of their students, engage in the purposeful development and utilization of resources, attend to cultural differences, create a welcoming community and embrace all of its diversity to enhance student and organizational learning, can they move towards Inclusive Excellence (Williams et al. 2005).

NOTES

1. Universities and colleges that historically have served White students and which currently enroll 76+ per cent White students.
2. In this chapter, we use the terms people of color and students of color to describe individuals who are of African American, Asian American, Latino and/or Native American descent.
3. A third tenure-track faculty member in the program was serving as associate dean of the College with reduced teaching and advising responsibilities. There also were approximately eight adjunct faculty members contracted to teach one or two courses each year.
4. The title of my dissertation is 'Black souls in an ivory tower: Understanding what it means to teach in a manner that respects and cares for the souls of African American graduate students.'
5. http://gseacademic.harvard.edu/~ncdp/

REFERENCES

Arnold, G.B. (2004), Symbolic politics and institutional boundaries in curriculum reform: The case of National Sectarian University. *Journal of Higher Education*, **75** (5), 572–93.
Association for the Study of Higher Education (2008), Higher education programme data base. Unpublished report. East Lansing: Michigan State University.
Association of American Colleges and Universities (n.d.), Making Excellence Inclusive. http://aacu.org/inclusive_excellence/index.cfm, accessed 22 January 2009.

Banks, J.A. (1991), *Teaching strategies for ethnic studies.* Boston: Allyn and Bacon.

Bowen, W.G. and Bok, D. (1998), *The shape of the river: Long-term consequences of considering race in college and university admissions.* Princeton, NJ: Princeton University Press.

Braun, H., Kirsch, I., Sum, A. and Yamamoto, K. (2007), *America's perfect storm: Three forces changing our nation's future.* Princeton, NJ: Educational Testing Service.

Carnell, E. (2007), Conceptions of effective teaching in higher education: Extending the boundaries. *Teaching in Higher Education,* **12** (1), 25–40.

Chen, C.C. and Van Velsar, E. (1996), New directions for research and practice in diversity leadership. *Leadership Quarterly,* **7** (2), 285–302.

Cook, B.J. and Cordova, D.I. (2007), *Minorities in higher education 22nd annual status report: 2007 supplement.* Washington, DC: American Council on Education.

Cox, T., Jr. (2001), *Creating the multicultural organization.* San Francisco: Jossey-Bass.

Danowitz, M.A., Hanappi-Egger, E. and Hofmann, R. (2009), Exploration and exploitation in organizational change: Developing and implementing a diversity management curriculum. *International Journal of Educational Management,* **23** (7), 590–603.

Danowitz Sagaria, M.A. and Agans, L.J. (2007), Career patterns in higher education. In Barbara Bank (ed.), *Gender and education: An encyclopaedia.* London: Praeger, pp. 635–42.

Deem, R. (1996), Border territories: A journey through sociology, education and women's studies. *British Journal of Sociology of Education,* **17** (1), 5–19.

Glazer-Raymo, J. (2007), Gender equality in the American research university: Renewing the agenda for women's rights. In M.A. Danowitz Sagaria (ed.), *Women, universities and change: Gender equality in the European Union and the United States.* Basingstoke, UK: Palgrave Macmillan, pp. 161–78.

hooks, b. (1994), *Teaching to transgress: Education as the practice of freedom.* New York: Routledge.

Lee, C. (2006), *Denver public schools: Resegregation, Latino style.* Cambridge, MA: Civil Rights Project at Harvard University.

Meil, A. (1996), Curriculum that matters: Origins of what ought to be. *Educational Forum,* **60**, 340–43.

Metro Denver Economic Development Corporation (2008), *Toward a more competitive Colorado.* Retrieved April 4, 2008, from http://www.metrodenver.org/files/documents/news-center/research-reports/TMCC_III_FullStudy.pdf.

Milem, J.F., Chang, M.J. and Antonio, A.L. (2005), *Making diversity work: A researched base perspective.* Washington, DC: American Association of Colleges and Universities.

Nag, R., Corley, K. and Gioia, D. (2007), The intersection of organizational identity, knowledge and practice: Attempting strategic change via knowledge grafting. *Academy of Management Journal,* **50** (4), 821–47.

Passel, J.S. and Cohen, D. (2008), *US population projections: 2005–2050,* Retrieved April 4, 2008, from http://pewhispanic.org/files/reports/85.pdf.

Rudolph, F. (1977), *Curriculum: A history of the American undergraduate course of study since 1636.* San Francisco: Jossey-Bass.

Smith, D.G. (1996), Organizing for diversity: Fundamental issues. In C.V. Turner, M. Garcia, A. Nora and L. Rendon (eds), *Racial and ethnic diversity in higher education.* New York: Simon and Schuster, pp. 532–42.

Smith-Maddox, R. and Solórzano, D.G. (2002), Using critical race theory, Paulo Frere's Problem-posing method and case study research to confront race and racism in education. *Qualitative Inquiry*, **8** (1), 66–84.

Tuitt, F.A. (2003), Afterword: Realizing a more inclusive pedagogy. In A. Howell and F.A. Tuitt (eds), *Race and higher education: Rethinking pedagogy in diverse college classrooms*. Cambridge, MA: Harvard Educational Review, pp. 243–68.

University of Denver (2004). *Higher education PhD handbook.* Denver, CO: University of Denver College of Education.

US Census Bureau (2004), *US Interim projections by age, sex, race and Hispanic origin.* Retrieved April 4, 2008 from http://www.census.gov/ipc/www/usinterimproj/natprojtab01a.pdf.

US Department of Education (2006), *Digest of education statistics, 2005 (NCES 2006–030), Table 224.* Washington, DC: National Center for Education Statistics.

Williams, D.A., Berger, J.B., and McClendon, S.A. (2005), *Toward a model of inclusive excellence and change in postsecondary institutions.* Washington, DC: Association of American Colleges and Universities.

4. From a bottom-up movement to a top-down strategy: reframing responsiveness to gender equality in an Austrian university

Regine Bendl and Angelika Schmidt

INTRODUCTION

We, Regine Bendl and Angelika Schmidt, are tenured associate professors at the Department of Management at the Wirtschaftsuniversität Wien (Vienna University of Economics and Business). Angelika is in the Institute for Change Management and Management Development and Regine is in the Group for Gender and Diversity Management. We have lived most of our academic and professional lives at Wirtschaftsuniversität Wien (WU). It is where we graduated and submitted our dissertations. Regine passed her Habilitation[1] in 2004 and Angelika is completing hers. Since the 1990s we have been feminist activists involved and the integration of gender equality at the WU. It is from the latter experience that we developed and approach the following guiding question for this chapter: What were the processes of inclusion of equal opportunity and gender and diversity issues at the WU like and how did we experience them? While various accounts have documented university change processes towards gender equality from an organizational perspective (see Pellert and Gindl 2007; Danowitz Sagaria and Van Horn 2007) our story is a further contribution in understanding inclusivity efforts from an activist perspective (see also Katila and Meriläinen 1999 and 2002).

We tell our story about the successful implementation of equal opportunity and gender and diversity initiatives at WU attending to the mobilization from the bottom-up, the changing roles of activist participants as well as the feminist collective's changing role and relationship to the formal university management. We map this process in four phases. In the grass-roots collectivist action (1990–1993) we describe how it all began, how crucial it was to have an activist pioneer and how the first financial support enabled the development of important actions and activities. In the second phase of formalizing activism (1994–1997) we write about how the involvement of more activists necessitated formalization and created friction over feminist aims and practices as institutionalization progressed. In the third phase, mainstreaming gender equality (1998–2002), we chronicle gender mainstreaming's acceleration of the inclusion process of gender and diversity in research and teaching and how it began to undermine the feminist collective's position. Lastly, in losing political edge through formal recognition (2002 to the present) we emphasize two processes: the integration of gender equality as a top-down strategy with financial sponsorship and the near dissolution of the feminist collective. Thus, success is an ambiguous notion depending on the context and perspective. Finally, we offer a conclusion with our personal remarks.

Since we have been involved in most of the mobilization efforts for inclusion of equal opportunity and gender and diversity issues, we are not disinterested researchers, analytical excavators or historians. Rather we see ourselves as storytellers embedded in relationships with others persons and the WU itself. According to Wolfram Cox and Hassard (2007), we are representing the past because the different points in the inclusion process do not refer to homogeneity, linearity or independency of events but to heterogeneity of processes, structures and persons as well the plurality of chronological codes, which are constructed and reproduced differently depending on the interpreters or story tellers of the past. Based on participant observation and the analysis of internal memos, protocols and publications, and official reports of the WU and the Ministry of Science, we identified these four phases for the inclusion process. As we will show, this inclusion process refers to an ambiguous notion of success as we are also highlighting the collective's changing role in relationship to formal university management structures. Altogether, however, these four phases enable us to highlight the central dynamics, character and course of the internal organizational movement towards gender equality and diversity. However, we hope that these phases can also offer a lens to guide the action of others (Benford and Snow 2000) and to reflect current developments towards gender equality at other universities.

Our story is located in a changing context. In the 1980s there was a second wave of feminism in Austria and advocacy for gender equality began at the universities. In the early 1990s the establishment of Working Committees on Equal Treatment and Equal Opportunity Plans for Women introduced a legal framework for gender equality and feminist action. Austria's joining the EU in 1995 and the expectation that it would implement the EU Directive on Gender Mainstreaming generated more backing for initiatives to make universities more inclusive. Other reforms of the legal framework of Austrian universities began triggering structural changes in the 1970s. These continued through 2002 with a new university act, which introduced managerial structures and granted full autonomy to universities including authority for staffing and budgetary decisions. With this power shift from the ministry to the university came a revised and leaner organizational and a governance structure with responsibility for the integration, oversight and monitoring gender related matters.

REGINE'S STORY ON GRASS-ROOTS COLLECTIVIST ACTION (1990–1993)

For me, the first phase of grass-roots collectivist action was mainly about passion for gender equality and the importance of having a pioneer who was both a leader and role model. It was also about setting first claims for equality and financial support. The spirit and actions of one woman, Renate Buber, shaped and drove this phase. Today I consider her as the pioneer of collective feminist action at the WU. Renate Buber was a member of the first generation of female faculty. When I became her colleague at the Institute of Retailing and Marketing in 1991 she already had been working for many years as researcher and member of several committees at the WU: therefore, she knew the organizational structures and processes well and would tell stories about female faculty members who had been subjected to discrimination.

Renate Buber gained support from the Austrian university-wide network of Contact Women and gathered younger female researchers, like me, as well as more experienced ones, administrators, interested students and feminist activists for collective action. She shared much of her knowledge with us and devoted a great deal of time introducing equal opportunity to WU persons and committees in decision-making roles. It was Renate Buber's extraordinary effort that brought about two powerful and effective structures for lobbying for equality and inclusion, the informal Working Group for Women in Research and Teaching at the WU and the formal Commission for Equal Opportunities. Also, due to her initiative and a reluctant university administration the Group on Equal Opportunities was established in compliance with the Law of Equal Opportunity. These legal changes and Renate Buber's efforts resulted in the implementation of the first voluntary official Equal Opportunity Plan for Women at the WU. The developmental process of this plan was dynamic and intensive and for the first time we, the feminist collective, could officially negotiate our claims with the WU decision makers. By establishing data collecting at the WU this plan was an important step towards monitoring gender equality.

Informed by Renate Buber's ideas, spirit, strength, experience and courage, we planned collective actions and strategies to inform and influence the official WU committees like the Working Group for Equal Opportunities and the Commission for Equal Opportunity. Our work was familial and collaborative. We used informal contacts, frequent communication and immediate feedback to develop and carry out our activist agenda.

Some of us gained positions on WU committees, which enabled us to employ an effective combination of informal and formal strategies and tactics to accomplish our aim of gender equality and inclusion. This informal style of management was successful, because no one outside the informal Working Group for Women in Research and Teaching knew exactly who supported us, what our goals were, what we planned to do; thus, how powerful 'all those women' really were. Usually between three and twelve activists attended the meetings of the informal Working Group for Women in Research and Teaching at the WU. Attendance depended upon individual interest and self-assessment of possible adverse career consequences. Our fears were justified when the WU did not renew the employment contracts of highly engaged members.

Joining this grass-roots group was important to me for several reasons. As a member of a bottom-up movement, I could share a vision to improve the situation in terms of careers, representation and agency for myself and also, more importantly, for subsequent generations of female researchers. As part of a network, I could establish new relationships with other female researchers and work in a familial atmosphere characterized by support and appreciation. Some friendships continue today. The glue that still holds us together is a shared commitment to equal treatment and equal opportunity for women at universities. As a young researcher it was also intriguing and rewarding to learn about power, organizational structures, processes and informal networks.

We embarked on many activities at this phase. With special funds from the Ministry of Science some of us began offering classes on women's and feminist issues. Teaching one of those courses, the role of women in further education, was a milestone in my career as researcher in that I published my first text based on this course (Bendl 1991). Furthermore, we organized the first further personal development seminars exclusively for female researchers. For example, in 1992 I organized the first seminar on communication skills for women with funding from the WU.

Due to Renate Buber's efforts working with the Rector and the Governor of the Austrian National Bank, the Dr Maria Schaumayer Scholarship for Habilitation was created. This grant offered female researchers financial support to write their Habilitation. The scholarship continues today and nearly 20 female researchers have benefited from it.

Another collective action, which continues today is the WU Women's Lecture, which we first organized in 1990.[2] We wanted to create a space for female researchers to present their research results because we considered women's and feminist issues important for organizational and economic research. We welcomed discussions among researchers from various disciplines at the WU along with other women from other state institutions or profit organizations. I was able to obtain corporate sponsorship for the WU Women's

Lecture for several years. In 1991 we published this first WU Women's Lecture for public distribution (Bendl et al. 1991) and established a book series, which has continued under various editors and produced the 17th volume in conjunction with the 25th WU Women's Lecture.

Our bottom-up movement experienced a crisis when our pioneer unexpectedly resigned from the (informal) leader position of the informal Working Group for Women in Research and Teaching, as the Head of the official Commission on Equal Opportunities and as a member of the official Group on Equal Opportunities. In my opinion, Renate Buber's decision to withdraw was prompted by the continuous pressure from our new boss and not by her desire to engage exclusively in research and teaching. She withdrew completely from feminist activism and research for many years. In the late 1990s she again organized another WU Women's Lecture (published in Buber and Ernst 1999) on career paths of women in academe.

More than astonished about her decision and very sad about having lost a comrade-in-arms I went on with my feminist engagement. Other activists took over Renate Buber's positions and we continued working in her spirit, as she had influenced most of us over the years. Today this pioneer phase is history, perhaps better called 'herstory' and represents the time when feminist grass-roots activism took hold at the WU and activists positioned themselves for further engagement. This early time of feminist engagement is well documented although conversations with young female colleagues indicate that they do not know about it. However, as a feminist and a tenured member of the WU, I will never tire from telling this pioneer story and keeping herstory alive. Telling the story acknowledges Renate Buber's pioneering role for the collective and her important influence as a role model who taught me the basics of feminist activism. Second, sharing her story and the first phase of feminist grass-roots activism helps to work against oblivion, which is one of the main, if not the greatest, foes of gender equality.

ANGELIKA'S STORY ON THE FORMALIZATION OF ACTIVISM (1994–1997)

While all the important structures supporting gender equality were set up in the first phase, the second phase, formalization of activism, can be characterized by the involvement of more activists, which triggered the need for more formalization and created friction about feminist aims and practices as the institutionalization of gender equality continued. The phase began when Renate Buber withdrew from committees and suspended her public activism. At this time I was beginning my career as a young researcher and was encouraged to join a forum where I could work with my former teachers. I had been a member of the female student group attending the WU Women's Lecture and now I had the opportunity to discuss feminist issues in another institutional setting. Being a member of the next generation of the feminist collective, one of my memories are the mythical stories about Renate Buber's withdrawal.

The meetings of the Working Group for Women in Research and Teaching appeared well organized but soon a new formal division of labour was established. More new actors became involved, more regular meetings were held, planning functions were shared, a closed mailing list was developed and a homepage was created. Responsibility for organizing the meetings rotated until 1995 when Ulla Ernst took over. I found her background and approach as a feminist philosopher from the Institute of Information Technology to the situation and developments at the WU new and stimulating. I soon shifted from a life narrowly focused on intellectual, economic and political issues to being fully engaged in the Working Group for Women in Research and Teaching at the WU.

As women's participation in WU committees increased, within the meetings of the Working Group for Women in Research and Teaching we clarified our expectations for gender equality and women's issues and crafted our political positions for the formal and informal WU structures. The bottom-up process remained the defining principle of activism, however, differentiation and reorganization in our activist group began. For example, we changed the form of the WU Women's Lecture from a weekly lecture to a one- or two-day workshop. This then evolved into an international two- or three-day platform for national and international researchers to discuss women's and feminist topics in order to stimulate the international exchange of ideas among practitioners, politicians and researchers. I was involved in organizing the WU Women's Lecture and editing a volume on economy, power and fear (Ernst et al. 1997).

Apart from these community-building aspects of the WU Women's Lecture, we also benefited from the teaching opportunities financed by the Ministry of Science. We were given the chance to bring in our research into our teaching, which generated more student interest. Interdisciplinary work increased. Experimental team-teaching cultivated more cooperation, which spawned research and publications.

In the Working Group for Women in Research and Teaching we created an inspiring atmosphere, although our meeting locations moved among different institutes as we did not have an official meeting room. However, the positive atmosphere charged us to go on claiming equal opportunity and advancing our careers by attending conferences, networking nationally and publishing in Austrian outlets. Despite all our activism, the Ministry of Science's first report on equal opportunity for women at universities in 1996 (Bundesministerium für Wissenschaft, Forschung und Kunst 1996) showed clearly that women were still largely underrepresented at the WU. Therefore, we expanded our activities to include more networking and exchange of information with other universities (for example, the Interuniversity Coordination Centre[3] and Group on Equal Opportunities at the Ministry of Science). Ulla Ernst especially inspired us to participate in these groups as she knew many activists throughout Austria from her involvement in the feminist movement and her previous activities as researcher at the University of Vienna.

As the activity level of the working group increased, conflicts began over the trade-offs between equality and difference among the group members. We had several discussions centring on the following questions about how to obtain managerial and secretarial support for our actions: What structure would be most effective for reaching the goal of inclusion? Should we establish an association with its own legal structures independent from the university structures with no chance of WU funding? Or, should we advocate for a coordinating centre within the formal WU organizational and funding structures? Some of us drafted a document on setting up an official association in order to give more functional power to the movement. However, there was little agreement about such an incisive structural change, which prompted most of those who had worked on the document to withdraw from the Working Group for Women in Research and Teaching. The remaining activists including myself and members of the official committees (Commission for Equal Opportunities and the Group on Equal Opportunities) began advocating for a coordinating position. Finally, the WU obtained financial support from the Ministry of Science and we could define aims and job descriptions for this coordination centre. After five years of negotiation and preparation the Rector implemented a Coordinating Centre with an employee based in the Personnel Department.

OUR JOINT STORY ON MAINSTREAMING GENDER EQUALITY (1998–2002)

Austria joined the European Union in 1995. This triggered an increase in public discourse on gender equality and the introduction of Gender Mainstreaming in 2000 (see Council of Europe 1998). These developments also influenced the inclusion process of gender equality at the WU. On the one hand, in this third phase Gender Mainstreaming supported the collective's claim for gender equality by placing expectations on WU decision makers. On the other hand, the newly implemented Coordination Centre took over work which had previously been done by the Working Group for Women in Research and Teaching. However, feminist activists and members of the different committees began to diverge on the desired goals and how to reach them.

The Coordination Centre became a hub for further networking activities.[4] Although the implementation of the Coordination Centre fostered integration of different actors and mirrored a kind of consolidation in the integration of equal opportunity and gender and diversity issues, it also contributed to weakening the cooperative spirit of action among us activists. Individuals began to cooperate with the staff member of the Coordination Centre instead of cultivating cooperative action amongst the activists. Thus, differentiation among our roles, status and power increased and subtle tensions became more explicit. Additionally, different interests among the members of three committees (Working Group for Women in Research and Teaching at the WU, Group on Equal Opportunities and Coordination Centre) became visible.

The critical event of divergence among our interests as activists was the revision process for the Plan for Equal Opportunity for Women. It was agreed that we should renew our advocacy for the professorship for gender and diversity, but the divisive question was, what perspective should we take? The position of the 'realists' among some activists was that the Coordination Centre and the future Professorship should become one entity, with the professor also being responsible for coordinating action (Coordinating Centre as part of the Professorship). The Head of the Group on Equal Opportunities for Women[5] favoured this position as she was of the opinion that this strategy would make the Professorship more attractive to the Rector and, thus, would improve the chances of implementation. The fundamentalists, the group to which the staff member of the Coordination Centre and we both belonged, argued that such a move would weaken the inclusive forces and our feminist collective. Thus, we voted for maintaining the Coordination Centre as part of the Personnel Department and creating an academic unit with a professorship focusing on research and teaching (Coordination Centre and Professorship as separate units).

In our retrospective view the revised Plan for Equal Opportunity for Women, which adopted the realist perspective and linked the Coordination Centre with the proposed Professorship for Gender and Diversity in Organizations, further disunited and weakened our activist agenda. The whole process made clear that differences grounded in personal antipathy or closeness to powerful male decision makers could splinter our feminist activism. The process also unveiled that our engagement was not only about inclusion and structural changes but also about our own power positions in the female network and within the WU. As a result, several more activists refocused on their career and missed meetings of the Working Group for Women in Research and Teaching at the WU. Although we both had supported the fundamentalist perspective, which had not been included in the revised Plan for Equal Opportunities, we continued working for inclusion.

Despite these internal power struggles among the activists, the integration of women's, gender and feminist perspectives progressed and differentiation increased. More gender-oriented courses in more disciplines were offered. The WU began financing these courses and integrated them in the regular study programme. Students started to write diploma and dissertation theses on women's, gender and feminist topics and we activists began to attend relevant international conferences and develop our international networks. The feminist collective with the support of the Coordination Centre made the WU Women's Lecture an even more professional event. Angelika was involved in organizing two symposia on women and poverty in 1999 and 2003 (Heitzmann and Schmidt 2001, 2004).

Two other signs of inclusion of gender and diversity issues were the renewed advocacy for the Professorship on Gender and Diversity in Organizations and the development of a working group to design a new programme, a competence field[6] for the WU curricula. We both worked in autonomous teams with proponents lobbying the WU study commission for this new field of study. At that time, however, efforts were unsuccessful. The proposal was denied based on the official WU position that only a full professor can be responsible for a competence field. But at that time no full professor was available to provide leadership and assume responsibility.

All in all, despite the splintering of unity due to changing administrative structure and internal power struggles, our feminist collective achieved an important goal: the University established a Professorship for Gender and Diversity in Organizations with responsibility for a competence field.

OUR JOINT STORY ABOUT LOSING POLITICAL EDGE THROUGH FORMAL RECOGNITION OF GENDER EQUALITY (2002 TO THE PRESENT)

The new University Act 2002, which introduced managerial structure to Austria's universities, was a double-edged sword for us as activists and our goal of inclusion of equal opportunity and gender and diversity issues at the WU. On the one hand, the University management, the rectorate, became responsible for the inclusion of equal opportunities and gender and diversity, which triggered a formal top-down policy and action approach to gender equality and related matters. On the other hand, the direct governmental 'cut-through' in equality issues by the Ministry of Science was lost due to the shift from democratic participation to managerial decision-making processes at the universities. In other words, we activists lost our supporting invisible hand. Some committees were eliminated or replaced by others like the Commission for Equal Opportunities. We both served on that Commission, which administered the Dr Maria Schaumayer Scholarship for Habilitation. Now the Vice

Rector for Research and External Affairs administers the Dr Maria Schaumayer Scholarship for Habilitation and another new one established to promote excellent[7] young female researchers. This change reduced the opportunity for activists – researchers, professors and students – to participate in the decision-making process for awarding the Dr Maria Schaumayer Scholarship and created a less transparent process coordinated by a senior manager. Unfortunately, the lack of transparency in University decision-making processes, which we successful challenged in earlier phases of activism, is re-emerging today. All and all, these kinds of changes have reduced our possibilities or duties for political representation and we have shifted our activist efforts to our academic work of research, international conference presentations and publishing in highly ranked journals.

We both consider this phase as the most radical for the changes in feminist action and university structures. As a consequence of the new managerialism and increasing public discussion and expectation to incorporate Gender Mainstreaming, the Rectorate implemented equal opportunity as a long-term strategy and supports it with financial commitments. The Professorship for Gender and Diversity in Organization, for which we had advocated together with so many other activists for several years, was implemented in 2002 and once again a further education (professional development) programme tailored for women was offered. This time, the Personnel Department and not female activists have organized and delivered the programme.

The establishment of the Professorship of Gender and Diversity in Organizations was accompanied by the new academic unit Group for Gender and Diversity Management in the Department of Management.[8] This led to the development and implementation of a Competence Field in Gender and Diversity Management in the study programme of business administration (see Danowitz et al. in press), which soon was followed by the Department of Economics' implementation of a Competence Field in Feminist Economics. These innovations have led to an increase in diploma/master theses, doctoral dissertations, and advanced studies on gender and equality topics at the University. Regine submitted the first Habilitation on gender in the field of business administration at the WU (Bendl 2005). In other words, it now became officially possible to specialize in the gender and diversity area.[9]

The Coordination Centre still exists only on paper. The staff member of the Coordination Centre was reassigned from the Coordination Centre to the Personnel Department. Although the professorship was implemented seven years ago, the realist position linking the Coordination Centre to the Professorship (the position which we both have opposed so strongly) still has not been realized. The Professor for Gender and Diversity in Organizations still considers the coordination and administration functions for gender equality beyond the scope of an academic unit. She argues that this combination dilutes research and teaching efforts and places demands on an academic unit to coordinate and provide support services above and beyond what is expected of all other WU academic units – and we both share this opinion. The Rector has been unwilling to reinstall the Coordination Centre as part of the administration and the attempts of the Working Group for Women in Research and Teaching to reestablish the Coordination Centre have fizzled out. As the Ministry of Science no longer has an invisible hand in these types of internal university decisions due to the University Act of 2002, there is no longer external support for our activist agenda.

Altogether, the University Act of 2002 which established managerial governance had unanticipated consequences for us activists. The implementation of inclusion as a top-down strategy led to a deeper crisis among us activists, which produced a retreat or a hibernation (see Barry et al. 2007). The change from a bottom-up movement to a top-down strategy for inclusion also led to a near dissolution of the informal Working Group for Women in Research and Teaching at the WU. Our activist meetings have become more than infrequent and our informal exchanges only take place sporadically (with only those who accompanied the inclusion process from the beginning and belong to our generation).

With the establishment of the Professorship for Gender and Diversity in Organizations and the Group for Gender and Diversity Management our principal objects of desire and struggle have been realized. Theoretically, today research and teaching on gender and diversity can take place in any of the University's academic units. In comparison to the situation in which we began our bottom-up collectivist action, current structures stimulate individual development and careers. However, despite Gender Mainstreaming and gender equality as a top-down strategy, these developments still take place at the margin of the university. Gender Equality still has not reached the centre of the WU.

CONCLUSION

Our story shows that in the last two decades the strategy of inclusion has been transformed from a bottom-up movement to a top-down strategy. Gender equality and equal opportunity have become an official strategy of the WU. These modifications are rooted in changes in the supportive structures for inclusion. The importance of the Working Group for Women in Research and Teaching at the WU as a symbol and evidence of a feminist bottom-up movement has disappeared due to the introduction of the managerial university. The official decision makers, Rector, Vice Rector for Research and External Affairs and Professor for Gender and Diversity in Organizations along with the Head of the Group on Equal Opportunities are now the key actors for the anti-discrimination and inclusivity agenda and action. The trade-off for formal legitimacy and incorporation has been an erosion of wide democratic participation and activism.

Our story also demonstrates that the feminist collective at the WU was successful in realizing its goals for the inclusion of gender and diversity issues in the study plan and research as well as for the first Professorship for Gender and Diversity in Organizations at a German speaking university of economics and business. This inclusion process occurred in conjunction with an evolution from feminist bottom-up (grass-roots) activism to an official institutionalized top-down guardianship. All in all, we both consider this development as a success story for inclusion and innovation for the WU. At the same time, we are very aware that feminist activism seems to have fallen into deep hibernation. We have no experience about how to deal with these new inclusive structures which, as the non-installation of the Coordination Centre shows, still can be directed against women's and feminist interests or that advocate for women's equality and interests only as long as they do not interfere with managerial (which are still predominantly male-oriented) interests.

Organizational change is highly environmentally dependent on tensions between progress and regression (Lewin 1963 [1947]). In our Austrian case, there were many helping forces. The activism at the WU began as part of second wave feminism and it came in the wake of legal changes which supported feminist activism in Austria and throughout the European Union. There were also interested female students, highly intrinsically motivated administrative and academic staff, a supporting Ministry of Science with many committed feminist administrators and EU policies endorsing inclusion as well as an emerging international research community engaged in women's/men's/feminist/gender and diversity issues. The hindering forces were many, including male decision makers who attempted to preserve an organizational culture which supported their male norms and control, or, in other words, patriarchy. However, despite all these counter forces, the WU has made positive and significant moves towards gender equality in inclusion over those years.

EPILOGUE

While we are aware that we have contributed to the process of change of our university towards more inclusion, we also know that our experiences as activists during these years have changed us. In this sense, we come to the conclusion that advocating for inclusion of equal opportunity and gender and diversity issues represents an irreversible process for both organizations and the people in them. Persons have the power to change organizations and organizations have the power to influence persons. The WU is not the same, nor are we after all those years. What did we give and what did we gain from our engagement? We not only spent much of our time on activism. As equality flagships (see Cunnigham et al. 1999) we were also at times confronted with debasement, aggression and hostility. At times it was very demanding as well as difficult to be true to our own interests and decisions. We were, however, also greatly rewarded. Over the years we have met many intelligent, courageous and strong, as well as sensitive and caring women, who were both comrades-in-arms and sources of personal and professional support. Some long-lasting friendships developed and we were part of a collective that continues to nourish and strengthen our spirits as researchers and teachers today.

What we have learned most from our activist experiences over the years is that the personal is political. In other words, we learnt from scratch what it meant to be the other and to be subjected to discriminating structures and processes. As we were empowered to be politically active, we developed an understanding of how to recognize and oppose discriminating human behaviours and organizational logics – for ourselves and for those who come after us.

NOTES

1. The Habilitation is an extensive thesis, which assistant professors have to write after their doctoral thesis in order to gain tenure and become associate professors at Austrian Universities.
2. The organizers were: Regine Bendl, Renate Buber, Andrea Grisold, Ruth Simsa.
3. German terminology: Interuniversitäre Koordinationsstelle.
4. Brigitte Parnigoni, splitting her time between Coordination Centre and the Personnel Department, was responsible for the centre's activities.
5. Hildegard Hemetsberger-Koller.
6. German terminology: Kompetenzfeld 'Frauen und Wirtschaft – gender studies'.
7. The introduction of the term 'excellence' is based on the current EU discourse on excellence. Since that time the Rectorate set up several initiatives to support 'excellence' at the WU.
8. Edeltraud Hanappi-Egger was appointed as the Chairholder for the Professorship for Gender and Diversity in Organizations.
9. After having worked in the Institute of Retailing and Marketing for ten years, Regine moved to this newly established academic unit in October 2002.

REFERENCES

Barry, Jim, John Chandler and Elisabeth Berg (2007), Women's movements: Abeyant or still on the move, *Equal Opportunities International*, **26** (4), 352–69.
Bendl, Regine (1991), Frauen und Weiterbildung, in Regine Bendl, Renate Buber and

Andrea Grisold (eds), *Wenn zwei das Gleiche tun, ist das noch lange nicht dasselbe. Frauen, Männer und Wirtschaft*, Schriftenreihe Frauen, Forschung & Wirtschaft: Band 1, Wien: Service Fachverlag, pp. 107–28.

Bendl, Regine (2005), *Revisiting Organization Theory: Integration and Deconstruction of Gender and Transformation of Organization Theory*, Frankfurt am Main: Peter Lang Verlag.

Bendl, Regine, Renate Buber and Andrea Grisold (1991, eds), *Wenn zwei das Gleiche tun, ist das noch lange nicht dasselbe. Frauen, Männer und Wirtschaft*, Schriftenreihe Frauen, Forschung & Wirtschaft: Band 1, Wien: Service Fachverlag.

Benford, Robert D. and David A. Snow (2000), Framing processes and social movements: An overview and assessment, *Annual Review of Sociology*, (26), 611–31.

Buber, Renate and Ursula Marianne Ernst (1999, eds), *Frauenwege: an einer Wirtschaftsuniversität zwischen Politik und Wissenschaft*, Schriftenreihe Frauen, Forschung und Wirtschaft: Band 8, Frankfurt am Main: Peter Lang Verlag.

Bundesministerium für Wissenschaft, Forschung und Kunst (1996), *Frauenbericht*, Wien.

Council of Europe (1998), *Gender Mainstreaming: Conceptual Framework, Methodology and Presentation of Good Practices*, Final Report of Activities of the Group of Specialists on Mainstreaming, EG-S-MS, 98/2, Strasbourg: Council of Europe.

Cunningham, Rosie, Anita Lord and Lesa Delaney (1999), 'Next steps' for equality?: The impact of organizational change on opportunities for women in civil service, *Gender, Work and Organization*, **6** (2), 67–78.

Danowitz Sagaria, Mary Ann and Pamela S. Van Horn (2007), Academic Excellence and Gender Equality at Ohio State University, in Mary Ann Danowitz Sagaria (ed.), *Women, Universities and Change. Gender Equality in the European Union and the United States*, New York: Palgrave, pp. 179–95.

Danowitz Sagaria, Mary Ann, Edeltraud Hanappi-Egger and Roswitha Hofmann (2009), The development and implementation of a diversity management curriculum. Organizational change through exploration and exploitation, *International Journal of Education Management*, **23** (7), 590–603.

Ernst, Ursula M., Luise Gubitzer and Angelika Schmidt (1997, eds), *Ökonomie M(m)acht Angst*, Schriftenreihe Frauen, Forschung und Wirtschaft: Band 7, Frankfurt am Main: Peter Lang Verlag.

Heitzmann, Karin and Angelika Schmidt (2001, eds), *Frauenarmut*, Schriftenreihe Frauen, Forschung und Wirtschaft: Band 11, Frankfurt: Peter Lang Verlag.

Heitzmann, Karin and Angelika Schmidt (2004, eds), *Wege aus der Frauenarmut*, Schriftenreihe Frauen, Forschung und Wirtschaft: Band 14, 2, Auflage, Frankfurt: Peter Lang Verlag.

Katila, Saija and Susan Meriläinen (1999), A serious researcher or just another nice girl? Doing gender in a male-dominated scientific community, *Gender, Work and Organization*, **6** (3), 163–73.

Katila, Saija and Susan Meriläinen (2002), Metamorphosis: From 'nice girls' to 'nice bitches': Resisting patriarchal articulations of professional identity, *Gender, Work and Organization*, **9** (3), 336–54.

Lewin, Kurt (1963 [1947]), Gleichgewichte und Veränderungen in der Gruppendynamik, in Kurt Lewin (ed.), *Feldtheorie in den Sozialwissenschaften*, Bern: Hans Huber Verlag, pp. 223–70.

Pellert, Ada and Michaela Gindl (2007), Gender Equity and Higher Education Reform, in Mary Ann Danowitz Sagaria (ed.), *Women, Universities and Change. Gender*

Equality in the European Union and the United States, New York: Palgrave, pp. 61–72.

Wolfram Cox, Julie and John Hassard (2007), Ties to the past in organization research: A comparative analysis of retrospective methods, *Organization*, **14** (4), 475–97.

PART II

Setting examples and reworking pedagogy

5. Teaching diversity in a 'conservative' state: using who I am and empirical evidence to contradict erroneous perceptions

Myrtle P. Bell

I am an African-American, female, Christian, heterosexual professor who teaches diversity at the University of Texas at Arlington (UT-Arlington), a large public school in the state of Texas, USA. Most of the students at UT-Arlington are from working class backgrounds and many are the first in their families to attend college. The student body is diverse in race and ethnicity, with 48 per cent White, 14 per cent Latino, 14 per cent Black, 11 per cent international students, 10 per cent Asian and 1 per cent Native American students.[1,2] Because of the university's very successful wheelchair basketball team, the 'Movin' Mavs', and strong support programs for students with disabilities, there is a significant portion of students with disabilities on campus. There are support systems, networks and social groups for students from various racial and ethnic backgrounds, sexual minorities, students with disabilities, and many other groups. Overall, the diversity in the student body creates a wonderful and rich environment for learning about diversity first hand and creates a unique norm of diversity rather than homogeneity, at least among the students.

It is in the context of diversity as the norm that I have been formally teaching diversity at UT-Arlington since 1997. However, I have taught diversity informally nearly all my life, having grown up in the southern portion of the USA, in the heart of the Civil Rights movement, and having attended very segregated (White) schools throughout high school and college (see Bell 2009). For my first formal diversity work, UT-Arlington is a unique university and setting for teaching diversity. Texas is a state that is noted for being 'conservative', with a population that professes veneration of 'family values', 'religious values' and 'patriotism'. On the surface, such values are not necessarily negative but they can easily be distorted to translate into racist, sexist, heterosexist and, more recently, anti-Muslim behaviors.

In this chapter I discuss my use of research and US Census data in teaching diversity in a positive, effective manner that exposes my students to the lives and experiences of others who are different from them in some manner. Because of space constraints, I limit my discussion to teaching in three areas: (1) working women, (2) religion and sexual minorities and (3) Arab-Americans and Muslims. I chose these three areas from a host of other possibilities because they are most useful in examining how I use who I am to effectively teach diversity in my context.

CONTEXT MATTERS

In comparison to the racial and ethnic diversity of the student body at UT-Arlington, the population in the state of Texas and the USA overall is considerably less diverse, with 74 per cent, 14 per cent, 12 per cent and 4 per cent, White, Hispanic, Black and Asian students, respectively (American Community Survey 2006). The university faculty is even less diverse than the state, with some departments being more than 90 per cent White and/or 90 per cent male (although this is changing slowly). I am often the first Black professor and sometimes the only woman professor that students have had, which students often point out. I use my solo status as a learning point about sex segregation of jobs and the dearth of women professors compared to the bounty of women teaching kindergarten, elementary school and high school – all lower wage, lower status positions in education that women typically occupy. I compare those to the higher wage, higher status professoriate that is typically occupied by men particularly in colleges of business (see Bell 2007, p. 262). Once noted, students clearly and easily see the stark differences, having experienced them throughout their education, even though they may not have recognized the sex segregation at the time. Another learning point is that many of the women and racial and ethnic minorities teaching in the college of business at my university are adjunct professors, contracted on an as-needed basis, or graduate students, rather than tenure-track professors. The women who are tenure-track professors are considerably more likely to be assistant or associate professors than full professors, which is evidence of the glass ceiling in academia.

Although this changes with hiring and turnover each year, and the university is making significant progress in increasing faculty diversity, for periods during my years in academe I have been the only or nearly the only Black woman with tenure on campus, in the college of business and in the department of management. At the time of this writing, I am the only Black person in the department of management and one of two in the college of business. In 2009, I was promoted to Full Professor, and became the only woman Full Professor in the history of the department, the only Black Full Professor in the college and the only Black woman Full Professor on campus. As a token

(Kanter 1977), I am fully aware that I may be viewed with skepticism as a professor at all, and particularly as one teaching diversity (Andre 1993; Gallos et al. 1997). I know I may be viewed as speaking for many other non-dominant group members. I know that if I 'step out of line' in classes or in class requirements and control I may be the target of backlash via complaints to administration or low teacher evaluations. More positively, I also know that I am viewed as a role model and mentor for many students of color and women, who are happy to see someone like them in a professorial role, which makes my position important for large numbers of students whom I may never formally teach. Also, for different reasons, my existence is positive for Whites and men who may have never had a woman of color as a professor.

It is in this context that I have been teaching diversity to both graduate and undergraduate students for more than a decade, having first taught a 'Women in Organizations' course when another female professor unexpectedly left the university. In teaching diversity, one of my primary goals is to open students' eyes to misconceptions about others who are different and to help dispel and expel many inaccuracies that are widely held. In a context that is often skeptical of and sometimes very negative towards people of diverse backgrounds (that is, non-White, non-Christian, or outsiders of various sorts[3]), I use empirical research and data to help change attitudes, beliefs and, hopefully, behaviors. The courses are 'elective' courses, so those who are interested in diversity issues enroll by choice, which makes them more receptive to the topic than other students might be. Even so, those self-selected students come to class with attitudes and beliefs shaped by living in an environment that is often unfriendly to different others.

As part of the course, and my efforts toward contradicting erroneous beliefs and stereotypical attitudes, students learn that most women with small children work outside the home; that most Arab-Americans are Christian (and that those who are not Christian are unlikely to be terrorists); that employers seem to prefer White men with a criminal record to Black men without one (Pager 2003); that older workers (often thought to be technologically inept and unwilling to learn) and people with disabilities have similar or better performance, absenteeism and turnover to younger workers and those without disabilities (Job Accommodation Network 1999); that Blacks, Asians and Latinos receive lower returns on their investments in education than Whites; and that no federal laws in the USA prohibit people from being fired for being gay, lesbian, or overweight (see Bell 2007). Empirical research and data help convince students that things they have learned from the media or have 'always believed' are not necessarily accurate. Students discuss these beliefs, often with supporting anecdotal evidence, which I contrast with empirically substantiated results. At the same time the evidence and data are presented, I make a point not to discount what students have seen or been led to believe

(Stewart et al. 2008). Anecdotal evidence is acknowledged, but is also contrasted with empirical evidence and data that involve many hundreds or thousands of individuals, and these large numbers help students see the veracity of the evidence.

As an example, in a recent course, one White female student provided an example of how her husband was negatively affected by a 'quota' system for hiring minorities. Quotas are rigid numbers of proportions of women and minorities that employers are required to hire as part of affirmative action programs, and are generally illegal in the USA, despite common misperceptions that they are required by law. When such comments are made, I discuss the fact that quotas are largely illegal in the USA – they are only legal when imposed by a judge in cases of blatant and persistent discrimination, and judges are reluctant to impose them (Bell 2007). We discuss common misunderstandings about affirmative action, how they are formed, and why they may be so pervasive. We also discuss the negative outcomes for individuals and organizations when quotas are used or are perceived to have been used and focus on the ways that affirmative action should be used effectively and legally to reduce underutilization of women and minorities in certain jobs. I encourage students to share that quotas are largely illegal when they hear them equated with affirmative action, whether at work, at home, or other venues, and give them the information with which to do so.

I emphasize the existence of different identities that may be dominant and valued in one context and non-dominant and devalued in another context, making diversity relevant to everyone. For example, although I am Black and female, which are both non-dominant groups, I am a Christian in the USA, a dominant group. Because I infuse theories and evidence about stereotyping, aversive racism, similarity effect and social identity, students learn how such processes can affect people's opportunities and outcomes. Each semester students indicate they feel more equipped to understand difference and to work to effect change in their work and home lives. It is rewarding and encouraging when students who were enrolled many years earlier send e-mails with examples of how they recently shared some of what they learned so many years before or used it in their own decision making.

WORKING WOMEN

A common perception among many White, heterosexual students and some students of color is that most women do not work outside the home, particularly women with small children. 'Soccer Mom' and 'Stay-at-Home-Mom' are common terminology, and this terminology pervades many people's views of women and their (lack of) commitment to work. In contrast to perceptions of

White women, however, many erroneously perceive women of color, particularly Black women, to prefer welfare (that is, government support) to working. Some students believe that Hispanic women are less likely to be employed because of strong cultural traditions and male dominance in Hispanic communities. Many of these perceptions are shaped and reinforced through media representations, often of women at the very ends of the wealth and poverty extremes. Some wealthy women may choose not to work, and some very poor women may be unable to afford quality childcare to work, although neither is the norm for most American women. Even so, in the 'Bible Belt' in which I live and work, many believe that women should not work outside the home if at all possible. Women's roles, for many, are perceived to be wife and mother, exclusively. Despite religious beliefs, the media, and other sources of misperceptions, among students at UT-Arlington anecdotal evidence of their having working mothers, grandmothers, aunts, siblings, wives, or being working mothers themselves helps support what data show: a majority of women, including women with small children, of all racial and ethnic backgrounds, are employed outside the home.

The US Census bureau reports that 74 per cent of all men participate in the workforce, compared with 60 per cent of all women. Thus, while it is true that women's participation rates are less than men's, the majority of all women are employed. Women without children and women with graduate degrees (reflecting their investments in their educations and their ability to afford quality childcare) participate at the same rates as all men: 74 per cent. Students are also unaware that nearly 20 per cent of women past childbearing age do not have children (US Census Bureau 2001); any fears of children negatively affecting the propensity of that group of women to work are clearly unfounded. Most importantly, most women who are mothers of small children are employed; nearly 60 per cent of mothers of children under age five are employed outside the home.

Overall, in the past three decades, the labor force participation of women with minor children (under age 18) has increased from 47 per cent to 72 per cent (US Department of Labor 2004a). Women with younger children are also employed; over 60 per cent of women with children under three are employed. About 74 per cent of women with graduate degrees and children less than one year old are employed. Women who are single parents are more likely to be in the workforce than men; 79 per cent of single mothers work outside the home. These high rates of employment are in stark contrast to media and political representations of single mothers as being unemployed and create fertile discussion and learning opportunities in class.

Discussion of facts versus fiction and misperceptions versus realities about working women helps shed light on how perceptions shape and limit opportunities for working women. Students' experiences with managers who ask about their marital status or children or who look at the ring finger on their left hands also underscore the problems working women face. I sometimes share some of my personal experiences with stereotypical perceptions about working women's propensity to leave the workforce, including in the interview for my first job after I completed my MBA. The hiring manager, a young married White man, asked why a 'pretty young girl' like me was still single. Some students express their view that the statement was one of sexual harassment, which provides a good segue to learning about sexual harassment but is not an accurate assessment of the reason for the question. Instead, the question probably reflected concerns that I would soon marry and leave the workforce (Bell 2009). As an African-American, I knew no women of working age who did not work outside the home. The overwhelming majority of Black women, including those with small children, are employed. When teaching about women's participation in the workforce, data showing that African-American women participate at higher rates than White, Asian and Hispanic women (US Department of Labor 2004b), support my perceptions and create opportunities for learning and debunking stereotypes. In the USA, 62 per cent, 60 per cent, 59 per cent and 57 per cent of Black, White, Asian and Hispanic women, respectively, participate in the workforce. In addition, because I am a working mother who has worked continually since my children were born, this also provides a living example to dispel the stereotype of mothers not being employed. Through me, students are able to see that working with small children can be possible and, I hope, fulfilling. As a Black working mother, in particular, I also have helped dispel the stereotype that Black women prefer welfare to work.

RELIGION AND SEXUAL ORIENTATION

Another area in which I have used who I am to teach diversity is regarding religion and sexual orientation. The intersection of sexual orientation and religious diversity is a key concern in a largely religious state in an area that is part of the 'Bible Belt' and where the great majority of the population is Christian. As a Christian, I use my own perspectives to help students who are struggling with understanding and 'tolerating'[4] sexual minorities. Many Christian churches speak against homosexuality, but it is important to note that some churches embrace homosexuals and are not anti-gay. At the beginning of class I introduce and give students some information about my background, including the fact that I profess the Christian faith. As appropriate, I repeat that I am a Christian during the semester. This creates a bond between me and other Christians, as we are both members of the 'in-group' of Christians in Texas and the USA (Tajfel 1978). Thus, my being a Christian creates a level of credibility about my views of Christian beliefs and attitudes toward sexual minorities. It also indicates to students that people can be Christian while also being against discrimination against sexual minorities.

When beginning the discussion of a fairly common perception that Christians are anti-gay, I mention how this disturbs me, as a Christian person who is not anti-gay. I then say that I was pleased to learn from empirical research that it is not Christians, per se, who are anti-gay, but religious fundamentalists from various religious backgrounds. I provide multiple references of studies in this area for those who are interested in further examination of the research (for example, Altameyer and Hunsberger 1992; Duck and Hunsberger 1999; Laythe et al. 2001).

In addition, we cover two legal cases that demonstrate differences in behaviors of Christians toward sexual minorities and different organizational treatment of the two Christian men (Bell 2007). In the USA legislation (Title VII of the Civil Rights Act) prohibits religious discrimination against employees, but does not prohibit discrimination against sexual minorities or require employers to make efforts to treat them inclusively. In one case, an employee, Richard Peterson, was vehemently opposed to gays, and posted religious sayings condemning homosexuality in his workspace at Hewlett-Packard (H-P). After months of trying to reason with Peterson about the display of large- sized, religious sayings targeting homosexuals, H-P fired him. Peterson sued H-P, alleging religious discrimination. The courts ruled that H-P's well-planned, thoughtful diversity program (through which they promoted inclusiveness and respect for people of different races, ethnicities, ages, sexual orientations, and other areas) was evidence of their commitment to diversity and that they had not discriminated against Peterson (Bell 2007). Peterson could have posted religious sayings in his workspace, as long as they were of reasonable size and visible to and intended for his own use, rather than being visible to and used to make a statement about and to others.

In the second case, a Christian employee, Albert Buonanno, who was not anti-gay, was terminated by his employer, AT&T, for refusing to sign a statement that he would 'value' others' lifestyles. Buonanno sued AT&T, alleging religious discrimination. In contrast to the H-P case, the courts ruled that Buonanno's rights had been violated and that AT&T could have made an exception to the policy that required all employees to sign such a statement. Title VII requires employers make reasonable attempts to accommodate people's religious beliefs, without 'undue hardship' and allowing Buonanno to mark out certain portions of the statement would have been reasonable (see Bell 2007 for further details of these cases).

In our class discussions, I emphasize that these two cases clarify people's rights to have their beliefs about various sexual orientations, but that their actions at work toward people can be prescribed by organizations. Exhibiting hostile behavior under the guise of religious beliefs, regardless of the religion, is not acceptable. Even so, when organizations have a diversity policy that prohibits discrimination against sexual minorities, care must also be taken not to trample on people's religious rights. At times during class students express concerns that the rights of people with strong religious beliefs about non-heterosexual behavior are ignored. I use the AT&T case as a clear example of why organizations should not trample on the rights of such people to have their beliefs and how they may avoid doing so while also protecting sexual minorities. As a Christian, I am also a known counterexample to those who believe that Christians will abhor employees who are gay male, lesbian, bisexual, or transgender. I also provide an example to those who believe that Christians' rights to hold to their religious teachings about non-heterosexual behaviors are trampled by organizations in the name of diversity that this does not necessarily have to be the case.

At times during class, we also discuss religious organizations that are inclusive toward sexual minorities, recognizing that there is diversity within the Christian faith. As mentioned earlier, even among Christians in a 'Bible-Belt' state, there is diversity of beliefs about sexual orientation. Although it is not directly relevant to teachings about religion and sexual orientation, I discuss other diversity issues relevant to religious organizations. In some religions (not limited to Christianity), women are not allowed to lead or pastor churches. In other religions, when allowed to pastor, the 'stained glass ceiling' in which women pastors are assigned to smaller, less prestigious organizations often exists (Purvis 1995; Sullins 2000). In a recent course, one student's mother was a pastor, and this student confirmed the idea of the stained glass ceiling with specific evidence about her mother's experiences.

Another key diversity issue among religious organizations is that most religious organizations are racially homogeneous (Schaefer 2002). Most people worship with people who are similar to them in race; heterogeneity is not the norm among churches. Discussions about the existence of diversity issues within religious organizations emphasize the importance of recognizing the breadth and depth of diversity and differences within all organizations and the need to avoid assuming homogeneity among individuals within organizations.

ARAB-AMERICANS AND MUSLIMS IN THE USA

As mentioned in the previous section, Federal law in the USA prohibits religious discrimination in employment, except for a narrow subset of strictly religious organizations operating only for religious purposes (for example, churches). As such, it is generally illegal in the USA to discriminate against people because of their religious beliefs or practices. After the terrorists acts of September 11, 2001 in the USA, in October, 2001, employers and unions, both covered by Title VII, were encouraged to be 'particularly sensitive' to discrimination against or harassment of persons who are, or are perceived to be, Muslim, Arab, Afghani, Middle Eastern, or South Asian (for example, Pakistani, Indian) (Bell 2007). Despite these warnings, since that time, religious discrimination charges with the US Equal Opportunity Commission have increased, and have not returned to their pre-9/11 levels.

Anti-Arab sentiment and discrimination is a particularly delicate area of diversity learning in the USA. There are about 3.5 million Americans who have some Arab heritage and 80 per cent of them are American citizens but less than one quarter are Muslims (Arab American Institute 2008). When we cover Arabs in our study of religious diversity, students are very surprised to learn that most Arab-Americans are not Muslims and that most Muslims in the USA are not Arab-Americans (Profile of the US Muslim Population 2001). In fact, 34 per cent, 27 per cent, 15 per cent, 10 per cent and 14 per cent of American Muslims, respectively, are Asian, African-American, White, Hispanic and other racial/ethnic origins (American Religious Identification Survey 2001). Students frequently ask 'Why don't we know this?' or 'Why doesn't the media talk about this?'. Such questions lead into the role of politicians and the media in spreading or stopping stereotypes, division, fear and hate and the need to learn, investigate and think for oneself.

I also discuss how although only 24 per cent of Arab-Americans are Muslims (Arab American Institute 2008), those who do follow Islam should not be construed as terrorists. Followers of Islam, as with many other religions, generally eschew violence. We discuss the law relevant to religious discrimination in the USA, Title VII of the Civil Rights Act of 1964, which prohibits discrimination in employment on the basis of race, sex, national origin (country of birth) and religion. Prior to class discussions, many students are unaware of the prohibitions against religious discrimination. Title VII also requires employers to make reasonable accommodations to allow people to observe their normal religious practices, another unknown point to most students. Media reports of Muslims being fired for wishing to pray during their prescribed times are useful in teaching that point. Initially, some students express concern that some groups would be allowed time off to pray at work. A discussion of frequent break times for smoking, coffee, snacks, or simply visiting with co-workers that occurs throughout workdays, contrasted with restrictions on time away from work for prayer, helps students understand the apparent anti-Muslim sentiment in denial of break time specifically to pray. As there are often students enrolled who have strong Christian religious beliefs (that do not necessitate specific prayer times), this helps bring understanding of commitment to one's religious beliefs, and empathy when people are denied the right to observe them.

We also discuss the diversity of beliefs within religious groups regarding many topics of interest to both Islam and Christianity. When students bring up issues of male dominance and lack of opportunities for women by Muslims, I bring up the stained glass ceiling in most Christian churches (discussed earlier), again emphasizing that male dominance is not unique to one particular religious faith. When discussing racial profiling, in which police and law enforcement officers target Black, Hispanic and sometimes Asian citizens for arrest and harassment (that is, 'driving while Black' or 'driving while brown'), I bring up the concept of 'flying while brown' that has occurred in the USA post 9/11. Racial profiling against those who appeared to be Arab increased significantly in the USA after 9/11, and several instances of people being removed from aircraft were reported in the news (for example, Polakow-Suranksy 2001). Research about people's views about racial profiling indicates that most Americans are uncomfortable with profiling, but are also uncomfortable about flying with Middle Easterners, helps students understand how fear can make people behave in ways that are inconsistent with their expressed beliefs. Because the students at UT-Arlington are so diverse, in many classes, there are Black, Hispanic, Asian and Middle-Eastern students who share their personal experiences with racial profiling and we can agree about the problems it causes.

In sum, I believe that as one who is not anti-Arab or anti-Muslim in a time when many (of various backgrounds) in the USA are, my position of presenting empirical evidence and contrasting views is an important, inclusive and, based upon the responses of my students, effective practice. A diversity of topics and an open mind help students see that similarities exist and differences are acceptable.

REFLECTIONS ON TEACHING DIVERSITY WITH PERSONAL EXPERIENCE, EMPIRICAL EVIDENCE AND DATA

My experiences as a Black, working, heterosexual Christian mother, and the experiences of the students at a diverse university, combined with empirical evidence, are invaluable in teaching and learning about diversity. Experiences and evidence help in our discussions of organizational measures to prevent discrimination against and increase equity for other non-dominant and traditionally devalued workers. Upon reflection of the positive reactions and success of the course, it appears that the coupling of experiences with evidence is a unique tool in teaching diversity. Since most people are aware of the stereotypes and misperceptions about certain groups, using them in teaching about diversity seems natural. The personal evidence provides validation of students' lives and experiences at times (for example, women work) and contradiction in others (for example, not all Christians are anti-gay), but in both cases, empirical evidence helps build credibility. The evidence also provides students with information they can use to teach diversity to family, friends and co-workers, and ways in which to investigate and validate or invalidate information for themselves in the future.

When discussing aspects of teaching diversity to those considering becoming diversity professors or adding a diversity course, I emphasize that teaching diversity is more difficult than teaching other courses, but it is also considerably more worthwhile (Gallos et al. 1997). I believe that our unique position as subjects, but also teachers, makes infusion of our personal backgrounds and experiences a critical aspect of positive diversity learning. When coupling personal experiences with empirical evidence and data, sometimes even the most suspicious and perhaps even hostile of students begin to understand and appreciate difference. Over a decade of teaching diversity formally and a lifetime of teaching diversity informally, I have found it to be the most rewarding of occupations.

NOTES

1. Fast Facts, http://www.uta.edu/uta/overview, accessed 15 March 2008.
2. I acknowledge that there are problems with these categorizations, for example, Hispanics can be Black (for example, Afro-Cubans), and that they are US-centric. Discussions of these problems and the social constructions of race are important learning points in teaching diversity and inclusion.
3. As an example, a once popular bumper sticker displayed on some vehicles said 'If you ♥ New York, take 30 East'. This (30 East) is a major highway out of the state, and this bumper sticker mocks the 'I ♥ New York' slogan.
4. The word 'tolerance' is commonly associated with teaching about diversity (for example, 'teaching tolerance'), but itself is a word with negative connotations, a point we also discuss in class. For example, Webster online defines tolerance as '1: capacity to endure pain or hardship, 2 a: sympathy or indulgence for beliefs or practices differing from or conflicting with one's own b: the act of allowing something, 3: the allowable deviation from a standard; 4a (1): the capacity of the body to endure or become less responsive to a substance (as a drug) or a physiological insult especially with repeated use or exposure *developed a tolerance to painkillers* (2): relative capacity of an organism to grow or thrive when subjected to an unfavourable environmental factor' http://www.merriam-webster.com/dictionary/tolerance, accessed 29 September 2008.

REFERENCES

Altameyer, B. and Hunsberger, B. (1992), 'Authoritarianism, religious fundamentalism, quest, and prejudice', *The International Journal for the Psychology of Religion*, **2**(2), 113–33.

American Community Survey (2006), Fact Sheet 2006, http://factfinder. census.gov/servlet/ACSSAFFFacts?_event=&geo_id=01000US&_geoContext=0100 0USpercent7C04000US48&_street=&_county=&_cityTown=&_state= 04000US48&_zip=&_lang=en&_sse=on&ActiveGeoDiv=&_useEV=&pctxt=fph&p gsl=040&_submenuId=factsheet_1&ds_name=ACS_2006_SAFF&_ci_nbr=null&qr _name=null&reg=nullpercent3Anull&_keyword=&_industry=, accessed September 30, 2008.

American Religious Identification Survey (2001), The Graduate Center, the City University of New York, Exhibit 13, http://www.gc.cuny.edu/faculty/ research_briefs/aris/key_findings.htm, accessed October 3, 2005.

Andre, R. (1993), 'Diversity curricula in the business school', *Journal of Education for Business*, **68**(5), 313–16.

Arab American Institute (2008), http://www.aaiusa.org/arab-americans/22/demographics, accessed March 13, 2008.

Bell, Myrtle P. (2007), *Diversity in Organizations*, Mason, OH: South-Western (Cengage).

Bell, Myrtle P. (2009), 'Effects of the experience of inequality, exclusion, and discrimination on scholarship', in Mustafa Özbilgin (ed.), *Equality, Diversity, and Inclusion*, London: Palgrave.

Duck, R.J. and Hunsberger, B. (1999), 'Religious orientation and prejudice: the role of religious proscription, right-wing authoritarianism, and social desirability', *The International Journal for the Psychology of Religion*, **9**(3), 157–79.

Gallos, Joan, Ramsey, V. Jean and associates (1997), *Listening to the Soul and Speaking from the Heart: The Joys and Complexities of Teaching about Workplace Diversity*, San Francisco: Jossey-Bass.

Job Accommodation Network (1999), *Accommodation Benefit/Cost Data*, Morgantown, WV: Job Accommodation Network of the President's Committee on Employment of People with Disabilities.

Kanter, Rosabeth (1977), *Men and Women of the Corporation*, New York: Basic Books.

Laythe, B., Finkel, D. and Kirkpatrick, L.A. (2001), 'Predicting prejudice from religious fundamentalism and right-wing authoritarianism: A multiple-regression approach', *Journal for the Scientific Study of Religion*, **40**(1), 1–10.

Pager, D. (2003), 'The mark of a criminal record', *American Journal of Sociology*, **108**, 937–75.

Polakow-Suransky, S. (2001), 'Flying while brown', *The American Prospect*, **12**(20), November.

Profile of the US Muslim Population (2001), *American Religious Identification Survey, Report No. 2, October, 2001*, The Graduate Center, The City University of New York, http://www.gc.cuny.edu/faculty/research_briefs/aris/key_findings.htm, accessed March 10, 2005.

Purvis, Sally B. (1995), *The Stained Glass Ceiling: Churches and Their Women Pastors*, Louisville, KY: Westminster John Knox Press.

Schaefer, Richard T. (2002), *Racial and Ethnic Groups* (8th edition), Princeton, NJ: Prentice-Hall.

Stewart, M.M., Crary, M. and Humberd, B.K. (2008), 'Teaching value in diversity: On the folly of espousing inclusion, while practicing exclusion', *Academy of Management Learning & Education*, **7**(3), 374–86.

Sullins P. (2000), 'The stained glass ceiling. Career attainment for women clergy', *Sociology of Religion*, **61**(3), 243–67.

Tajfel, Henri (1978), 'Social Categorization, Social Identity and Social Comparison', in Henri Tajfel (ed.), *Differentiation Between Social Groups*, London: Academic Press, pp. 61–76.

US Census Bureau (2001), http://www.census.gov/Press-Release/www/2001/cb01-170.html, accessed January 22, 2008.

US Department of Labor (2004a), 'Women in the Labor Force: A Databook', Report 973, Table 6, http://www.bls.gov/cps/wlf-databook.pdf, accessed December 16, 2004.

US Department of Labor (2004b), Bureau of Labor Statistics, 'Civilian labor force participation rates by sex, age, race, and Hispanic origin, 1982, 1992, 2002, and projected 2012', (Table 4.1 Civilian Labor Force by Age, Sex, Race, and Hispanic Origin, 1992, 2002, and projected 2012).

6. Doing difference with graduate management students: methods used to develop inclusive practices

Sandra Billard

There is much theorizing in my various areas of interest – action research, inclusive teaching practices and gender relations in organizations – about the importance of listening to voices from the periphery, and of valuing and including difference for effective learning, organizational research and practice to occur. There is little direct examination though of *how*, at the micro-structural level, this might be practically achieved. My aim in this chapter is to show how respecting difference and inclusion can be taught to business school students in courses that are not explicitly created to tackle these issues and where issues like diversity management or gender equality are not part of the course syllabus. By reflecting on the teaching strategies employed in one particular academic situation – a year long action learning and action research programme that students undertake as part of their Masters of Business Management at a regional Australian university – I seek to contribute to an exploration of the kinds of practical interventions, strategies and methods that can be used to facilitate effective 'doing' of difference.

THE TEACHING CONTEXT

One of the most important developments in management learning has been the realization that learning occurs best when it is directly related to real work, to 'doing' or to action. 'Action learning' is based on this understanding. 'Action research' is based on a similar premise that taking action to change or improve a situation, and working collaboratively on this within a system, will result in sounder and more useful understandings and insights. Participants involved in projects utilizing these approaches typically deeply engage the client systems within which they are located. With an emphasis on the integration of theory with practice, action learning and action research are innovative and positive approaches to learning and research in complex and changing environments.

For more than 15 years the School of Business at the University of Ballarat has been fostering such successful action learning and research projects in regional Australian organizations through its Master of Business Management (MBM) programme. This programme is one of a handful of such graduate business programmes in Australia. Recent research (Riley 2005) identifies that whilst action learning can be seen in a variety of academic programmes in Australia only 6 of 47 MBA providers were assessed as delivering programmes with a strong action learning base.

Students in the MBM programme at Ballarat usually study part time over three to four years whilst working full time. The first two-thirds of their studies include core and elective units in areas such as organization theory and behaviour, managerial skills, creativity, change, strategy and general research methods. The final third of the programme, covering the action learning and action research component of the MBM, is then undertaken over a whole academic year. In this part of the programme each student negotiates, undertakes and reflects on a significant change-oriented project in their particular organizational situation. At the same time they meet regularly as a group in what is called a 'learning set', to further challenge and support each other's learning and development of effective managerial practice. The set process is supported by the programme co-ordinator/facilitator.

Typically, in any year, the number of students undertaking this final year-long project component of the MBM is quite small – between four and seven students. In terms of their profile, the students work in manufacturing, government, health, education and community sectors; and they work for themselves, for small and medium-sized enterprises and for multinationals. Mainly they are already middle to senior level managers facing complex challenges and responsibilities in their work roles. They range in age from their 20s to 60s (but are mostly in their late 30s and 40s) and are most often Australian domestic students rather than international students. Over the years the programme has been running, there has been an increase in the participation of women, but men still make up the majority of students in most class groups.

Not surprisingly, the different backgrounds, situations and aspirations of the MBM students lead to great variety in the focus and scope of their projects. A sample of the project topics from recent years give an indication of this diversity: 'Non-profit service delivery: managing high numbers of part-time staff to improve service quality'; 'Attaining a shift in mindset around hazardous manual handling tasks in a food manufacturing organization'; 'How do we adapt problem-based, web-assisted learning to better engage our students?'; 'Developing a strategy for the support of Country Fire Authority brigades directly impacted by major fires'.

GETTING STARTED WITH ACTION RESEARCH

The intended MBM projects are varied but students have in common that they are all fairly well novices in relation to action learning (AL) and action research (AR) when they start their project year – and like novices in other situations they can feel excited about, yet also overwhelmed by, the complexity and demands of the work they are going to be undertaking. At the first workshop of the year a typical response of students is to want limits installed and rules or guidelines to follow: 'What are the parameters in applying AL?'; 'How exactly do I present this so my organization signs on to me doing AL?' As one student reflected in her journal, 'I observed and personally experienced lots of uncertainties as to whether we will grasp what the project involves ... there were lots of expectations for guidance from the lecturer and anxiety to grasp everything immediately'.

How do I respond to these stated – and unstated, but no less pressing – requests? As a teacher in a graduate management programme my deepest motive is to contribute to more effective management in organizations and to create the conditions for students to develop into more reflective practitioners and be managers who are inquiring, inclusive, learning-oriented and ethical in their actions. As an action research educator I have found that it is ultimately most valuable if students can consider their university-based learning space as an action research space – for facilitating their learning about being effective action learners and action researchers. The university-based learning space can be seen as being in parallel with the kinds of project spaces students might be seeking to establish and maintain in their own organizations and communities over the coming year. Consequently, within this university space the ways that we relate and talk to each other and the kinds of activities we engage in are all multifaceted sources of potential learning – touchstones – for the students as novice action researchers and action learners.

A 'teaching as action research' strategy is congruent with many action research approaches, be it co-operative inquiry (Heron and Reason 2001), educational (Kemmis and McTaggart 1988, 2000) or feminist grounded (Maguire 1987, 2001; Lather 1991; Fine 1994; Treleaven 1994; Weiner 1994) action research. Such an approach means that in getting the students started there is a double focus on developing both understanding and action (Fine 1994), for 'we get deeper information about the nature of our realities when our prime concern is to develop practical skills which change these realities' (Heron 1996, p. 114). At the same time a strong emphasis is also placed on validating people's perceptions of their reality, reflexivity, relational methods, analyses of gender and power relations, and on links being made between the micro and macro, and the personal and the political (Maguire 1987, 2001; Lather 1991; Treleaven 1994, 2001; Weiner 1994).

ACTION RESEARCH AND DIFFERENCE

Attending to issues of power, respecting difference and inclusive practices are vital for effective action learning and action research. A fundamental assumption in feminist and many other forms of action research is that it is necessary to have significant participation in an investigation by those affected by a situation or problem. Reciprocity in researcher–researched and facilitator–participant relationships is typically advocated (see for example, Reason 1988). The challenge, however, from a feminist perspective, is to develop 'practice which is attentive to issues of exclusion and committed to developing the conditions under which many voices can speak and be heard' (Bordo 1990, p. 140).

Engaging with and valuing difference is not only important in terms of women and men from diverse cultural and work backgrounds needing to all feel included and able to contribute to and benefit from the activities undertaken. Being able to effectively appreciate and work with difference is also central to the students' learning and development as novice action researchers. This is because action research is change oriented. Kemmis and McTaggart (1988) have articulated in some detail the kinds of changes being sought.

> In action research we look for changes in three different aspects of individual work and the culture of groups: changes in the use of *language and discourses* – the actual ways that people identify and describe their world and work; changes in *activities and practices* – what people are actually doing in their work and learning; and changes in *social relationships and organisation* – the ways people interrelate ... and the ways their relationships are structured and organised. ... Action research is concerned equally with changing *individuals*, on the one hand, and, on the other, the *culture* of the groups, institutions and societies to which they belong. The culture of a group can be defined in terms of the characteristic substance and forms of the language and discourses, activities and practices, and social relationships and organisation which constitute the interactions of the group. (1988, pp. 15–16, original emphasis)

Action research is thus focussed on change and in change processes it is not sufficient to work with only 'common denominator' data. It is critical to pick up information on silences, and the marginal and contradictory aspects of situations as well. As many feminist and change researchers and practitioners have argued (see for example, Lather 1988; Dick 1989; Martin 1990; White and Epston 1990; Alvesson and Billing 1992; Engestrom 1993, 1999; Cumming and Holvino 2003), it is from these non-conformist sources that change often develops.

Consequently, in my teaching of management students, I choose to draw strongly in both content and process on action research approaches that explicitly look beyond the common denominator and recognize the significance of outlier data. To be able to use such approaches to action research, students need to develop their peripheral vision (Bateson 1994) and their capacity to pick up contestations in language, activities and relationships that go against the grain of the dominant discourses and characteristic enactments in any given situation (Kemmis and McTaggart 1988). In this context it can be appreciated that for students learning about action research processes and seeking to consciously change their situations, it is especially important for them to be attuned to, rather than fearful of, difference.

Beyond a broad 'teaching as action research' strategy, I have observed over several years of practice that there are particular micro-strategies and methods that can be especially enabling for developing experiential, presentational, propositional and practical knowing (Heron 1996) about difference and inclusion. Critically, the four different ways of knowing extend

> beyond the primarily theoretical, propositional knowledge of academia. *Experiential knowing* is through direct face-to-face encounter with person, place or thing; it is knowing through the immediacy of perceiving, through empathy and resonance. *Presentational knowing* emerges from experiential knowing, and provides the first form of expressing meaning and significance through drawing on expressive forms of imagery through movement, sound, music, drawing, painting, sculpture, poetry, story, drama, and so on. *Propositional knowing* 'about' something, is knowing through ideas and theories, expressed in informative statements. *Practical knowing* is knowing 'how to' do something and is expressed in a skill, knack or competence. (Heron and Reason 2001, p. 183, original emphasis)

The micro strategies that can be useful for developing these different forms of knowing in relation to difference include perspective-making and perspective-taking activities (Dixon 1996), the use of playful processes like drawing, stories and metaphors, engaging in critical reflection on process and, most importantly, using modest structures that are based on ethics of respect, care, democratic participation and choice (Billard and Herbert 2006). The remainder of this chapter will explore how these interventions have worked for students to expand their arenas of action and reflection.

BAMBOO SCAFFOLDING

The first meeting of the group is a two-day start-up workshop. From the beginning of our work together I try to introduce a range of modest structures that have been likened to bamboo scaffolding (Billard and Herbert 2006). These frameworks are intended to be light and flexible, yet robust; and, most importantly, they are designed to be attentive and responsive to different local circumstances and needs as well as to emergent conditions, rather than being overly restrictive and smothering of generative learning and negotiation. Over the two days I introduce some of my core ideas and principles for how we might work together – notions of adult learning, going around the action research cycle (of planning, acting, observing and reflecting), having choice and taking responsibility, valuing the personal, valuing reflexivity, the importance of recognizing and including different perspectives, and taking risks. I regard it as important for the participants to experience what it is like to work together utilizing these principles, to be able to reflect on their experiences and to decide for themselves whether and how they might apply these principles themselves. The intention is that such touchstone experiences act as visions of what can be – of more inclusive and generative relationships, activities and language use.

To illustrate how such modest structures might operate I will look at one thread of activities relating to the first stages of the students' negotiation of their projects for the year. The scope of the AL/AR project work and its associated presentations, reports and dissertation is generally broader, deeper and more complex than any work previously undertaken in their studies (and possibly also more far reaching than anything previously undertaken in their work lives). This can be very exciting, challenging and daunting for students as they arrive to start their action learning studies.

Early in the first session students are provided with an overview of critical activities in the year long programme and asked to share their initial burning questions about the programme. All of the questions and observations generated are first recorded on chart paper and then later returned to for discussion at opportune times in the group's subsequent work. Also very early in the session, students are given space for expression of their initial ideas for their projects. A few questions seeking clarification or elaboration may be asked of students but as the facilitator of a beginning group/set process I do not make evaluative judgements about the suitability of the topics at this early stage. Rather, I facilitate the students engaging in a range of activities that enable them to better build their own understandings of their work and the value of the perspectives and questions of others.

A semi-structured approach to group questioning and knowledge building can be helpful at this beginning stage. As an example, students use a checklist of questions from Winter and Munn-Giddings (2001) as a starting point, and work in pairs or trios to interview each other about their project ideas. In this way they start exploring in greater depth and breadth the basic purpose of their proposed work, who else could be affected, their assumptions about the situation, and how they might try to make the work collaborative. At the same time they build their relationships with each other, and practise their questioning and reflection skills within the group. A brainwriting activity is also undertaken as an aid to further divergent exploration of potential project areas. For this activity each student writes at the top of a large sheet of paper their project topic as they currently conceive it. These sheets are then hung up on the walls around the room. In groups of two or three, students move around the room, consider each topic, and add questions or comments to assist the topic owners in thinking differently about their question.

The combination of containers for their work and opportunities for expression and divergent exploration seems to help mediate initial anxieties that might otherwise be paralysing, and to assist the students to be present and engaged in the unfolding processes and stepping stones of the AL/AR Methodology unit. As one student, Alice (a pseudonym), later commented in her journal:

> reasonably early in the session we all put forward our ideas for our action learning projects and it was a relief for me to 'get mine out'. I had been agonising in silence over the appropriateness of the project over the holidays. It was interesting to see that the others were also unsure of their projects ... Throughout the session we revisited our projects with various activities which assisted us to delve deeper into the issues. Asking questions in a triad proved useful, as did the written comments contributed [in brainwriting] by all of the group members. These activities prompted me to continue questioning myself [and] I can now see a slightly different issue to what I first came up with. (Alice's journal, Visit 1)

PERSPECTIVE-MAKING AND PERSPECTIVE-TAKING

One of the challenges for any group, but more critically for an action learning or action research group, is to create ways for everyone to be able to satisfactorily understand their own perspectives and to be able to express these. Our effectiveness as action researchers depends on this, for as John Heron argues 'autonomous preference precedes authentic co-operative choice. In any negotiation preceding a co-operative choice, each agent needs to identify and state his or her preferences, and where relevant their underlying values, otherwise real co-operation is not possible' (1996, p. 17).

The importance of women feeling safe to express themselves, have a voice, express emotion and be heard, has been frequently discussed in the feminist literature (see for example, Lewis 1992; Tarule 1992; Buzzanell 1994; Treleaven 1994, 2001). Less attention has been given, though, to how these outcomes might be negotiated in practice in a mixed gender relational context. The commonly discussed understandings of democratic dialogue, active listening, or speaking freely, that appear in the organizational learning literature (see for example, Isaacs 1993; Schein 1993) are also deficient in this respect. They often leave gender and other power inequities unproblematized and unattended to in their conceptualizations of how new understandings are developed, participation is negotiated, or decisions are made in groups.

The initial step in what can be termed 'perspective making' is for people to first understand, identify or develop their perspectives. In the work of the

AL/AR students this process is assisted by providing participants with trigger questions to consider, time to work alone before there is discussion with others, and the development of reflective skills through journal writing. Paired, small group work and semi-structured activities then help to some extent in creating safer spaces for the expression of everyone's ideas and in contesting some of the potential patterns of dominance and silence within a group. I have observed, though, that activities which incorporate 'perspective taking' (Dixon 1996) are particularly effective in allowing all participants' voices to be heard and acknowledged.

Nancy Dixon describes perspective taking as 'paraphrasing the ideas and arguments of others ... It is the ability to comprehend and voice how the situation appears from another's standpoint' (1996, p. 19). Importantly, it is the speaking of the other's perspective – rather than just the listening – that is considered by Dixon to play a critical role in the creation of new understandings. As I see it the act of speaking in this situation moves a person from 'just looking' primarily from their own perspective still, to putting on, even if for only a moment, the other's shoes. And so through this act of speaking in perspective taking, people can have an experience of an enlarged vision, seeing a situation not just from their own standpoint, but also from other perspectives.

The emphasis in Dixon's discussion of perspective taking is primarily on the speaker role within the process. However, I consider there can be an equally powerful dynamic at play when people are in a listener role. Especially for people who have experienced marginalization, domination and silencing in their interactions with powerful others, it can be very empowering to listen to someone else trying to represent your views, and to feel that there has been a commitment by the other to hearing you. So perspective taking can be affirming of both self and others.

In the work of the AL/AR students, there can be opportunity for many of our activities to include a perspective-making and perspective-taking approach. For example, after students have led a presentation and learning activity at Visit 2 on the role of the set in action learning, it can be appropriate to further explore issues around students' hopes and concerns relating to how we would like the set to work together. We might initially talk in pairs about our thoughts and feelings, and then in a structured 'round' we all represent our partner's views back to the whole group. We then discuss the issues and perspectives that have emerged in a more informal way in the large group, paying attention throughout the process to areas of difference and surprise as well as areas of agreement.

Voicing the ideas and arguments of others as well as one's own ideas, and listening to oneself as well as others, creates a significantly enlarged space for expression and understanding and subsequent actions. Rather than differences necessarily being fearful or threatening – and therefore fought, self-censored, or smoothed over in our work together – participants become more positive about identifying and actively exploring differences in experiences and views. This enlarged space gives us all greater capacity to work effectively on the content and process of our inquiry and learning. Students have frequently made observations in their journals about the flow on value in this kind of space:

> Visit 2 provided some great conversation and thinking space … Another important and emerging aspect of the group dynamic is the value of seeing people consider your project in a positive way – thinking through your scenario, putting effort into their considered comments. The dynamic is such a contrast to the normal competitive learning environment where people are often a little reluctant to share, communicate and contribute to the work of others. I was buoyed by the feeling of thinking I had some potentially useful thing to contribute to the work of others – exploring, questioning, fleshing out other projects … throughout the day I actually felt an ability to 'keep with the moment' and be an effective listener. (Felix's journal, Visit 2)

The perspective-taking approach is effective in allowing for, and facilitating, the different work that had to be done by differently situated people in the group such as women and men. In the initial stages, the challenge for some men in the group, for example, can be to learn to listen, be more responsive and acknowledge the perspectives of others. And the challenge for some women in the group can be to express and better understand their own perspectives. Thinking of a perspective-taking process promotes the notion that everyone had something to do, to stretch for, and that it is also an undertaking that could be collaborative rather than adversarial. The method is involving of all participants, enhances our basic skills in listening, expression and participation, and develops powerful experiential knowings about difference within the group. These experiences also provide a meaningful base for reflection by participants, and nourish the further development of other forms of knowing about difference.

OTTERS, STARLINGS, PELATONS

Identifying preferences and exercising choice can be very exciting and enabling. It can also be very challenging, risky and anxiety provoking, especially when the wider organizational or societal culture is one that actively discourages the exploration of feelings and values, and we are not particularly skilled at identifying and expressing ourselves in such a way. When anxiety levels are uncomfortably high there can be a strong and restricting pull towards order and closure.

Early in the initial workshops, to help mediate possible anxiety and maintain necessary space for expression, inclusion, choice and generative action, I typically introduce and use processes that might variously act as 'safety nets' for students. At the same time that these processes act as possible safety nets they also operate as springboards for learning – learning about ourselves and learning from and valuing others in the group. Importantly, these processes facilitate group members being better able to look at, and work with, the emotional and other challenges being faced in our action learning work. They are not intended, and nor in the main do they act, to smooth over or distract us from these challenges. The processes used include a variety of playful verbal and non-verbal techniques such as drawings, photography, dramatic representations, story telling and metaphors.

Alice's reflections at the end of her project year give some insight into the potential usefulness of such processes.

> There have been many occasions where I spoke up at the risk of appearing silly and have been stretching myself to participate. I appreciate the luxury of this forum and I took advantage of every meeting that we had … I enjoyed our meetings and the calm, yet stimulating, atmosphere. One exercise that I particularly enjoyed was the Metaphor exercise. On two occasions we imagined ourselves and the set as an animal or a vehicle. Although I had a previous experience in using metaphors, this exercise assisted me to expand my view of the set and myself, in a way that I would not have otherwise dared to explore. (Alice's final report)

The playful exercise Alice refers to involves set members individually identifying then sharing metaphors and underlying reasons for their choices in the group. The activity is not only fun, it also yields enormously rich and imaginative understandings about the various preferences of students – understandings that often surprise and delight people as we reflect further on the metaphors and their meanings to us. This particular activity, thinking of ourselves and the set as an animal or vehicle for the journey we are embarking on, is also quite regularly reintroduced by set members and used to help reflect on our effectiveness as a learning set and how we might try to change ourselves to better achieve our evolving visions. Along with drawings, photographs, and stories and metaphors from other activities, the variously imagined set animals or vehicles (for example, a flock of starlings, a pelaton, a middle-aged labrador, a Mini Minor, sea otters, a colony of ants) are frequently mentioned in our work together and contribute significantly to group culture.

Using metaphors and symbols and other aesthetic forms of presentation to express views and feelings often helps students to surface understandings that are important to them but that they have not necessarily been conscious of or able to articulate. In this way presentational knowing emerges from experiential knowing (Heron and Reason 1997) and provides a source for further reflection – both individually and collectively – and subsequent development of propositional understandings about issues and practices of significance to students in their broader situations.

The stories, metaphors and nonverbal methods help facilitate more creative and curious approaches to the action learning and action research work. Such play allows people to not only better identify preferences and interests, but also to let go of these and experiment, and to be more spontaneous and flexible in their thinking and actions. Looking back on their project year students often express great appreciation that they have learned the value of being curious and inquiring and many observe that the set has provided them with a safe space for trialling new behaviours and processes. As Zoe reflected at the conclusion of her action learning year, wondering whether she had observed or learnt anything significant:

> I learnt how inquisitive I am and how I love learning ... I have truly become more creative, my capacity to think in different dimensions has increased significantly. The learning I have experienced ... has succeeded in heightening my awareness of my own learning style and that of others. It is a significant step to take when one learns that and to feel comfortable in practising the art of 'walking a mile in someone else's shoes'. This is a heady experience that I have had as an outcome of this project. (Zoe's final report)

In this sense the university-based action learning and research space can create a new space for participants, one that is an interstice, somewhat akin to Winnicott's (1971) notion of transitional space. Within this space participants can safely play and experiment; expose, express and (re)invent themselves; and recognize themselves and others. Susan Long has also emphasized how action research requires settings which participants feel are safe to experiment in. She argues that 'gradually, then, members are able to learn and to take their learnings beyond the transitional space into their organisation work proper' (1998, p. 8). Felix's reflections in his final report are pertinent to these points:

> It was particularly important for the university set to provide a degree of comfort and confidence, because it allowed me to maintain an adequate degree of confidence when entering into the workshops within the organization. For me, this illustrated the concept of the 'learning environment' and the role of more subtle elements in creating such a space (i.e. participant attitudes, feeling a sense of permission to speak freely, witnessing others struggle, seeing people free of pretence and asking questions freely). The contrast of this environment to many other so-called learning environments became evident quite early. Whereas in other environments an awkwardness, feeling of deficit or sense that 'I should know' often dominates, the university set environment was experiencing quite a speedy evolution. Participants were experiencing an ever-increasing ability to let their guards down and ask/think aloud the questions and thoughts that may otherwise remain in

their head. ... [In my organizational project] I learned that facilitating effective problem solving/exploration techniques and putting in an effort to create an appropriate atmosphere are not just techniques for solving problems. They're mediums through which to build positive, open and effective relationships with people. If people feel confidence in the process, if they feel listened to, if they feel welcomed, wanted and valued, then their contribution will be more forthcoming and constructive. The ongoing benefit for my practice will be if I refuse to leave behind a commitment to these things and ensure they follow me into future practice. (Felix's final report)

CONCLUDING THOUGHTS

Activities that involve perspective making and perspective taking and play are very helpful in developing strong experiential and presentational understandings about difference and multiplicity in our own and others' viewpoints. In addition these experiences provide touchstones for developing conceptual or propositional understandings on these issues. And as students' inquiries and understandings evolve, such activities also increasingly act as spaces for practising different language, activities and relationships that reflect learnings about difference and inclusion.

The opportunity to do difference differently, to do changed gender or power relations and try different participatory processes plays a critical part in the learning of novice action learners and researchers. In the relatively safe space of the university-based learning set, participants can enact, experiment with, practice and reflect on what is being talked about, and aspired to, in terms of more inclusive participation processes and practices. Changing our own language, modes of action and social relationships then leads us to try and also change interactions in other communities and organizational systems to which set members belong. Through all of this the dynamic between experience and reflection, and the interweaving and interdependence of evolving propositional, practical, presentational and experiential kinds of knowing are critical. The cyclical method of action research also allows for ongoing changes in consciousness and experience to inform each other, and for changes in intentional practice, understandings and systems to develop over time and in different situations.

As has been outlined in this chapter, some activities and processes are seen to significantly assist inclusive practices and the doing of difference for people in the group. These include activities that facilitate the expression, recognition and affirmation of self and others, ones that reinforce participants' experiences of choice and self responsibility in their involvement in their learning and research, and activities that develop participants' constructive engagement with rather than fearing, smoothing over or dismissing difference. The methods used within the University of Ballarat's action learning and action research programme appear to help 'nurture those places where worlds meet' (Bordo 1992, p. 166) and to encourage the development of effective understandings and practices across differences. I hope that the explication of these methods within this chapter will also contribute to understandings of how, at the microstructural level, we might practically achieve valuing of difference in teaching and broader organizational practices.

REFERENCES

Alvesson, Mats and Yvonne D. Billing (1992), 'Gender and Organization: Towards a Differentiated Understanding', *Organization Studies*, **13** (12), 73–102.

Bateson, Mary C. (1994), *Peripheral Visions: Learning Along the Way*, New York: Harper Collins.

Billard, Sandra and Anne Herbert (2006), 'A Suggestion about Using Action Research for Understanding Organisation as it Happens', Paper presented at Second Organization Studies Summer Workshop: 'Return to Practice: Understanding Organization as It Happens', Mykonos, Greece. Accessible at http://www.egosnet. org/journal/os_summer_workshop_2006.shtml.

Bordo, Susan (1990), 'Feminism, Postmodernism, and Gender-scepticism', in Linda J. Nicholson (ed.), *Feminism/Postmodernism*, New York and London: Routledge, pp. 133–56.

Bordo, Susan (1992), 'Review Essay: Postmodern Subjects, Postmodern Bodies', *Feminist Studies*, **18** (1), 159–75.

Buzzanell, Patrice M. (1994), 'Gaining a Voice: Feminist Organizational Communication Theorizing', *Management Communication Quarterly*, **7** (4), 339–83.

Cumming, James A. and Evangelina Holvino (2003), *CGO Briefing Note No. 19, Enhancing Working across Differences with the Problematic Moment Approach*, Boston: Center for Gender in Organizations, Simmons School of Management.

Dick, Bob (1989), *Delphi as a Dialectical Process: Generating Agreement out of Disagreement*, Chapel Hill, Queensland: Interchange.

Dixon, Nancy M. (1996), *Perspectives on Dialogue: Making Talk Developmental for Individuals and Organizations*, Greensboro, NC: Center for Creative Leadership.

Engestrom, Yrjo (1993), 'Developmental Studies of Work as a Testbench of Activity Theory: The Case of Primary Care Medical Practice', in Seth Chaiklin and Jean Lave (eds), *Understanding Practice: Perspectives on Activity and Context*, Cambridge and New York: Cambridge University Press.

Engestrom, Yrjo (1999), 'Expansive Learning at Work: Toward an Activity Theoretical Reconceptualisation', Changing Practice Through Research, Changing Research Through Practice Conference, Surfers Paradise, Australia: Centre for Learning and Work Research, Griffith University, Brisbane, Australia.

Fine, Michelle (1994), 'Dis-tance and other Stances: Negotiations of Power inside Feminist Research', in Andrew Gitlin (ed.), *Power and Method: Political Activism and Educational Research*, New York: Routledge, pp. 13–35.

Heron, John (1996), *Co-operative Inquiry: Research into the Human Condition*, London: Sage.

Heron, John and Peter Reason (1997), 'A Participatory Inquiry Paradigm', *Qualitative Inquiry*, **3** (3), 274–94.
Heron, John and Peter Reason (2001), 'The Practice of Co-operative Inquiry: Research "with" rather than "on" People', in Peter Reason and Hilary Bradbury (eds), *Handbook of Action Research: Participative Inquiry and Practice*, London, Thousand Oaks and New Delhi: Sage, pp. 179–88.
Isaacs, William N. (1993), 'Taking Flight: Dialogue, Collective Thinking, and Organizational Learning', *Organizational Dynamics*, **22** (2), 24–39.
Kemmis, Stephen and Robin McTaggart (eds) (1988), *The Action Research Planner* (3rd edn), Geelong, Australia: Deakin University Press.
Kemmis, Stephen and Robin McTaggart (2000), 'Participatory Action Research', in Norman K. Denzin and Yvonna S. Lincoln (eds), *Handbook of Qualitative Research* (2nd edn), Thousand Oaks, CA: Sage, pp. 567–605.
Lather, Patti (1988), 'Feminist Perspectives on Empowering Research Methodologies', *Women's Studies International Forum*, **11** (6), 569–81.
Lather, Patti (1991), *Getting Smart: Feminist Research and Pedagogy with/in the Postmodern*, New York: Routledge.
Lewis, Magda (1992), 'Interrupting Patriarchy: Politics, Resistance and Transformation in the Feminist Classroom', in Carmen Luke and Jennifer Gore (eds), *Feminisms and Critical Pedagogy*, New York and London: Routledge, pp. 167–91.
Long, Susan (1998), 'Action Research, Participative Action Research and Action Learning in Organisations', *Management Paper Series*, Centre for Organisational and Strategic Studies, Swinburne University of Technology. Vol 1, February.
Maguire, Patricia (1987), *Doing Participatory Research: A Feminist Approach*, Amherst, MA: Centre for International Education, University of Massachusetts.
Maguire, Patricia (2001), 'Uneven Ground: Feminisms and Action Research', in Peter Reason and Hilary Bradbury (eds), *Handbook of Action Research: Participative Inquiry and Practice*, London, Thousand Oaks and New Delhi: Sage, pp. 59–69.
Martin, Joanne (1990), 'Deconstructing Organizational Taboos: The Suppression of Gender Conflict in Organizations', *Organization Science*, **1** (4), 339–59.
Reason, Peter (ed.) (1988), *Human Inquiry in Action: Developments in New Paradigm Research*, London, Newbury Park, Beverly Hills and New Delhi: Sage.
Riley, Chris J. (2005), *A Case Study Analysis of the Rationale for Incorporating Action Learning into Australian MBA Programmes*, Unpublished PhD thesis, Gibaran Business School, South Australia.
Schein, Edgar H. (1993), 'On Dialogue, Culture and Organizational Learning', *Organizational Dynamics*, **22** (2), 40–51.
Tarule, Jill M. (1992), 'Dialogue and Adult Learning', *Liberal Education*, **78** (4), 12–19.
Treleaven, Lesley (1994), 'Making a Space: A Collaborative Inquiry with Women as Staff Development', in Peter Reason (ed.), *Participation in Human Inquiry*, London: Sage, pp. 138–62.
Treleaven, Lesley (2001), 'The Turn to Action and the Linguistic Turn: Towards an Integrated Methodology', in Peter Reason and Hilary Bradbury (eds), *Handbook of Action Research: Participative Inquiry and Practice*, London, Thousand Oaks and New Delhi: Sage, pp. 261–72.
Weiner, Gaby (1994), *Feminisms in Education: An Introduction*, Buckingham and Philadelphia: Open University Press.

White, Michael and David Epston (1990), *Narrative Means to Therapeutic Ends*, New York and London: W.W. Norton & Company.
Winnicott, Donald W. (1971), *Playing and Reality*, London: Tavistock.
Winter, Richard and Carol Munn-Giddings (2001), *A Handbook for Action Research in Health and Social Care*, London and New York: Routledge.

7. Gender in education: an inclusive project

Ulla Eriksson-Zetterquist

INTRODUCTION

In 1998–1999, when I was a doctoral student in Organizational Studies, Eva-Maria Svensson, PhD in Law, and I managed a project called 'Gender in Education' at the School of Business, Economics and Law[1] at the University of Gothenburg (hereafter HGU).[2] The Swedish Ministry of Education and Research financed the project that aimed at increasing knowledge about gender in teaching situations at HGU.

There was considerable interest in the project by the media as well as by our colleagues who, in various ways, committed to its goals and ideas. A year after the project's conclusion, an evaluation reported that the most visible result of the project was that gender inequality had become an issue on the agenda in some HGU departments.

In this chapter, my aim is to describe general and personal experiences from efforts working with gender inclusion in an academic environment. The case exemplifies how the issue of gender in education needs to be locally situated in the university sub-cultures in order to relate to practice. First, I provide a brief overview of the context of the project.

Increasing gender equality has been a political goal in Sweden since the beginning of the 1960s when a national government report stated that men and women should have equal roles and responsibilities in work life, society and child rearing. According to the report, gender equality, besides advancing democratic principles, would also help solve the country's labour shortage and would increase gross national product. The 1970s debate in Sweden on gender equality resulted in the passage of the 1980 Swedish Act Concerning Gender Equality Between Men and Women.

Swedish government policy, inspired by these democratic, economic and political ideas, has created work conditions such that Sweden often scores very high in international comparisons of gender equality. However, despite these impressive international scores, the Swedish labour market is still not gender inclusive. Although 79 per cent of women and 84 per cent of men between the ages of 20 and 64 are employed, the Swedish labour market remains gender-segregated since women work primarily in public administration (75 per cent are women) as opposed to private companies (40 per cent are women).

In education, Sweden has actively promoted equal opportunities for women. In particular, since the 1970s there have been various attempts to encourage women to pursue degrees in science and, since the 1990s, the Swedish Government has tried to stimulate equal interest in science among school age girls and boys. While statistics from the early 1990s on show that more women than men have a university degree, today the majority of students in science education are men while the majority of students in the humanities and the social sciences are women. At the turn of the millennium, only 25 per cent of the students in Swedish university science courses were women. It is typical that top managers in Swedish industry have engineering degrees so the relatively few numbers of women pursuing engineering and other scientific courses of study is considered problematic. If there is to be gender inclusion in industry management, the government policies state that more women need to earn engineering and science degrees. Thus, because of the gender inequality in work and in higher education, the Swedish Government has allocated resources for the purpose of increasing the awareness of gender equality at the universities.

In 1995 the Swedish Ministry of Education issued a call for projects on gender in education. The Ministry stated in their document, 'Mapping and evaluation of gender equality projects in universities and colleges', that university gender equality work was an integral part of the Government's general equality programme. The Government's premise was that a focus on gender equality in the universities would increase gender-related knowledge as well as promote greater gender inclusion among male and female students.

The Swedish National Agency for Higher Education has also stated that students studying Economics, Business Administration and Law, who are expected to take key positions in society, are especially lacking in knowledge of gender equality. Therefore, to advance the Agency's work, the Swedish Government gave it the special assignment[3] of supporting projects designed to develop course modules on gender as well as gender equality in courses in Economics, Business Administration and Law.

Our project was conducted at HGU. In 1999 HGU had seven academic departments and a research institute: Economic Geography, Economic History, Informatics, Statistics, Business Administration, Economics, Law and the Gothenburg Research Institute (GRI). At the time of our project, in general the proportion of male to female students in the bachelor programmes was gender-equal, with the exception of the bachelor programmes in Law, with 60 per cent women students, and Informatics, with 30 per cent women students. Business Administration, which employed more teachers than any other department, was divided into four sub-groups: Accounting, Organization, Marketing and Finance. As GRI is an externally financed research institute that offers no undergraduate courses, we excluded it from the Reference Group (see below) as a study object in our 'Gender in Education' project.

FROM IDEAS TO LOCAL PRACTICE

In 1995 the Swedish Ministry of Education approved a grant application for a project aimed at mainstreaming gender thinking among the HGU faculty. After internal discussions on how to proceed, Eva-Marie Svensson, who had recently been awarded a PhD degree in Law with gender as a special interest, and me, being a doctoral student in organization studies with gender as a special interest, were selected as project leaders because of our special interest in gender issues.

As we wanted as many participants as possible in the project, our first step was to seek support from the HGU Faculty Council, the HGU Dean and the HGU Department Heads. According to the instructions from the Ministry of Education, we were required to offer the programme to all HGU faculty members. Our starting point was to educate the permanent teaching staff about gender issues in education. We were concerned that such a goal might be unrealistic since faculty members had little extra time because of full-time workloads and, furthermore, based on our previous research on gender equality issues, we knew that some of them did not find these issues especially urgent or interesting. How could we attract other colleagues in addition to those who were already interested and/or engaged in these issues? The Faculty Council had planned a course for the faculty on supervising HGU doctoral students but allowed us to use that course's scheduled time slot to present our 'Gender in the Education' project. For us, this action indicated the Faculty Council's support of our project.

In addition, the Faculty Council and Eva-Maria Svensson created a Reference Group that was composed of two Faculty Council members and a representative for the Department Heads. The Department Heads were also tasked with encouraging their faculties to participate in the project. With this organizational support, we launched the 'Gender in Education' project in 1998. In its final version, the project consisted of two parts: a series of seminars for all faculty members and a series of four workshops each for the six Departments and the four Business Administration Department sub-groups.

We invited ten groups of teachers to take part – four from the Business Administration Department and one group each from the other six Departments. Eight groups immediately reported their interest, but Marketing (from the Business Administration Department) and the Informatics

Department declined to participate. The non-participants said they were
involved with 'concurrent internal change processes'. The Informatics
Department was busy with major organizational issues (it would later become
part of the IT-University at the University of Gothenburg) and Marketing was
busy with internal reorganization.

THE SEMINARS

Our next step in the project was to invite well-known scholars from different
disciplines to speak at seminars. We believed that these scholars, in presenting
various topics related to gender and education, would lend legitimacy to the
project. In total, we held seven seminars during the period between the Fall of
1998 and the Spring of 1999.

In the first seminar, after Göran Bergendahl (the new HGU Dean) introduced the project, Ulla Holm (f[4]), PhD in Practical Philosophy and Professor
of Gender Studies from the Department of Gender Studies at the University,
presented gender research, gender concepts and attitudes towards science.
While either Eva-Maria Svensson or I could have given this lecture, we invited
Ulla Holm because we believed her credentials as a philosopher from an external faculty would impress our colleagues and would encourage their participation. However, Holm's philosophical perspective confused them and failed
to provoke their curiosity about gender issues. In retrospect we realized that it
would have been better to present the gender issues from perspectives more
familiar to the faculty, namely, business, economic and legal perspectives.

This initial setback had negative consequences for the rest of the seminars.
After the first seminar, which 110 people attended, typically only 20–40
people attended each of the remaining six seminars. Nevertheless, the next
four speakers continued to present gender-related topics: Mats Alvesson (m)
(see Alvesson and Billing, 1997), former faculty member and author, on
gender and culture in organizations; Sue Rosser (f), American anthropologist
and guest professor in the Department of Gender Studies, on the use of different approaches to feminism in research projects; and Christine Wennerås (f)
and Agnes Wold (f) (1997), Associate Professors of Medicine, on their
research on gender prejudice that led to changes in the Swedish Research
Council[5] for Medicine. Wennerås and Wold described the bias in the Council's
system of funding postdoctoral fellowship applications where nepotism and
sexism influenced peer review scores. As a result of their research, the
Medicine Council members were replaced. In addition, this Council as well as
others began to fund gender issue research projects.

At the fifth seminar Mats Furberg (m), Professor Emeritus of Theoretical
Philosophy, lectured on gender and knowledge. In his conclusion, he stated:

> Two things are so obvious that they are almost embarrassing to mention. The first is that there is no reason to believe that women have more or less knowledge than men. The second is that there is every reason to believe that men have neglected knowledge areas in which more women than men are interested.

At the time, Eva-Maria Svensson and I were extremely impressed by this statement. It is interesting to note, however, that ten years later, Furberg's remarks no longer have such an impact on me, which shows how gender equality has become a much more mainstream issue.

Ninni Hagman (f), an expert on gender equality, presented the sixth seminar on sexual harassment in academia, and Barbara Czarniawska (f), HGU Professor of Management Studies, presented the seventh seminar on how to conduct research on gender equality in organizations. Eva-Maria Svensson and I expected that these topics, plus the presence of Barbara Czarniawska, would greatly interest our colleagues, but again these lectures had relatively few attendees. Although we did not question our colleagues on why they did not attend the seminars, we speculate that they may have been overwhelmed with other teaching and research demands or may have simply had little interest in the seminar topics.

As the third step in the project, we focused on the variety in disciplinary cultures related to mainstream gender issues in the different educational areas at HGU. For that purpose, we developed a workshop model that we could use for the participating departments at HGU. In addition, we prepared a reading list of articles and books that provide a conceptual basis for the issues identified in the workshop model.

THE WORKSHOPS

The workshops, which included discussions of subject-specific issues, were offered separately to the six Departments and the four Business Administration Department sub-groups. By structuring these discussions as internal workshops we could discuss gender in relation to each learning subject and could attend to the local culture of each Department or Department sub-group. We could also focus on the specific experiences the participants had had in meetings with their students. At the beginning, we offered a preliminary plan for the workshops with four different themes focusing on different aspects of gendering. Our intention was to present a guide to the workshop participants that they could use to identify the most important issues for their disciplinary field or circumstances at the department or sub-group.

Initially, in the first introductory workshop sessions, we presented our concept of the 'Gender in Education' project, the preliminary workshop plan and our reading list. The issues brought forward in the preliminary workshop model were as follows:

1. Making gender visible by identifying possible problems. Questions teachers may ask themselves: What is the gender of the course literature authors? How are men and women presented in that literature? Are assignments and examinations gender neutral? What kinds of male/female experiences are used as examples? How is language used and does it in any way prejudice men or women? Do men and women choose different subjects for study? Are there gender differences in grading? What is the gender of students entering doctoral programmes?
2. Examining the 'culture of teaching'. Does this culture favour certain students? How can different teaching methods support the majority of students? How can quiet or passive students be supported?
3. Scrutinizing the relationships between teachers and students. How do teachers interact with female and male students? How are teachers treated by female and male students? How are problematic situations with challenging students best handled?
4. Drawing conclusions from the seminar series. What postulates can be formulated for the future?

The reading list that we prepared was distributed to each participating Department and Department sub-group concerned. The material discussed different aspects of gender in education and suggested ways to develop the issue in the instructional context. These readings, which were representative of the few available texts at the time being discussing gender in education, were chosen as we found them thought provoking and practice-oriented. They also revealed the great variety in the issues related to gender in education. In addition, as the suggested books and articles were academic texts,[6] they also gave legitimacy when showing how other academicians discussed similar issues.

After presenting our preliminary workshop plan two or three times at the first workshops, we then decided to change our procedure. We became aware that the Departments and the Department sub-groups had different approaches to the issues, different experiences and different problems. As a result, the first workshop was changed to a brainstorming session that led to a schedule for the next three workshops. Thereafter, at the second workshop, most Departments and Department sub-groups chose to conduct a spreadsheet practice that provided an overview of the education they offered. We took notes at all workshops, which were then transcribed and sent to all participants. Subsequently we analysed these transcriptions and presented the analysis in our final report on the project (Eriksson-Zetterquist and Svensson, 2002).

In order to present examples of issues that arose at the workshops, I will outline the issues brought forward at the brainstorming workshops and the subsequent spreadsheet practice workshops. A typical workshop began with an opening from the Department Head who introduced us and the purpose of our project. Then Eva-Maria Svensson spoke about gender in education with a focus on gender research and the background for the workshops. She presented relevant key issues: 'man as norm', feminist research as a critique of traditional research and doubts about objectivity as an ideal. She also stressed that a gender perspective includes more than working for equal opportunities for men and women.

We then invited workshop participants to share their reflections in brainstorming sessions where they could present their ideas including those on subject-specific issues. These sessions provoked, for example, discussions on whether social class was a more important issue than gender *vis-à-vis* discrimination and inequities. Other reflections concerned whether 'women are a privileged group in this Department' and whether the learning culture is perceived by female students as masculine. In one workshop, participants discussed the philosophical notions underlying the project and questioned why the gender issue that is a matter of subjectivity was valid here and yet is not in other areas.[7] Our perception was that in this workshop there was certain amount of latent hostility towards the issue of gender and towards the project itself. Participants in other workshops, however, were more straightforward and agreed that 'gender does matter, but we do not know how'.

Another thought brought forward in the workshop discussions was stated by one participant as: 'There is a risk of bias when we focus on gender'. Some departments required faculty to attend the workshops. Still others asked for such an approach arguing that 'the workshop should be compulsory to avoid just preaching to the choir'. Some departments took a student perspective claiming that 'it is not appropriate to talk about gender with various members of the student body' or 'it is important that our student assignments avoid introducing stereotypical ideas about gender'. It was also evident there was a concern about whether 'it is more important to fight for justice than for gender' as the open discussion of positive and negative views on gender in education revealed. By the seminar's conclusion, we had received both positive and negative ideas about gender in education.

It was also evident in the workshops described that gender was a controversial topic. Some faculty members were quite reluctant to discuss gender issues either among themselves or with students; for them, class issues, the focus of their research in the 1970s and 1980s, were more important. In the workshops where gender was prioritized over class issues, however, I did not observe this same hostility to the discussion of gender issues. Rather, participants were curious about gender in education issues and were willing to explore those issues. One example of such an approach came from the

Business Administration sub-group in Finance who concluded: 'We have about 20–25 per cent women employees as teachers and PhD students. How does this influence our subject? We believe that men emphasize the content of our subject. Men appear to be more traditional while women develop the subject.' Yet another example came from the Business Administration sub-group in Accounting who asked: 'Is economic and rational thinking a masculine construction? Would such thinking have been different if women had developed it?'

A wide variety of issues thus emerged from the workshops. Some faculty members revealed their prejudices about, or ignorance of, gender issues; others posed stereotypical questions about women and mathematics and about women and their analytical abilities.

Since the brainstorming sessions related to gender issues and the internal department cultures sometimes created tension among the participants, we found our dual leadership presence advantageous. While one of us led the discussion, the other could reflect on the ideas expressed and could conceive of solutions to the difficult situations that arose. Additionally, we could share our observations from two points of view when we later reflected on the workshops.

As we needed a gender perspective on the courses offered by the six Departments and the four Business Administration Department sub-groups, we designed a spreadsheet exercise with the assistance of the participants. As explained above, this exercise was used in the second workshop. The spreadsheet had vertical rows for the courses and horizontal columns for the gender distributions of the students, the literature authors, the teachers and the course managers. In order to examine the inclusion of gender in education, additional columns indicated the presence or absence of gender issues in lectures, literature, assignments and examinations. Each course was listed by row.

The original spreadsheets were lost through computer malfunction. Below, based on our workshop notes, I have constructed Table 7.1 as an illustration of a partial spreadsheet used in the workshops. Course managers provided the data. As Table 7.1 reveals, the details about the courses as provided by the course managers varied significantly. By comparing this information, we could observe the different managers' understanding of and commitment to the task of identifying gender aspects in the courses. An empty box suggested that the course manager had not really committed to providing the information requested.

Designing and completing the spreadsheets required considerable effort, but the results were very interesting. For instance, we could see from the 'gender in content' column that some course literature had gender issue content but only a half page or so. We also learned that women were mostly responsible for the undergraduate courses, while men were more responsible

Table 7.1 Workshop spreadsheet

Course	Literature	Author gender	Gender in content	Gender in exercises	Teachers	Comment
Basic course 1	5 books	Appears to be male	Lit 1: half page discussing discrimination, ethnicity, gender Lit 4: details about home help/cleaning Lit 5: distribution of income: the young vs. the elderly	Marginal: Discussions of female labour	There used to be some female teachers but not any more	In previous literature one chapter was written by women
Course 2		Male	Book 2: half page discussing women in the labour market	No		Gender aspects in financial plan
Course 3	Collection of readings		No gender perspective			Possibility of using other data to enlighten the issues. Gender issues for this

Table 7.1 continued

Course	Literature	Author gender	Gender in content	Gender in exercises	Teachers	Comment
						topic are brought forward in doctoral education
Course 4	1 book	2 males	Nothing			
Course 5		Male		Nothing about gender	Women faculty manage the exercises	*

Notes: * In this course the percentage of women students was as follows: Spring semester 1998: 50%; Fall semester 1998: 43%; Spring semester 1999: 72%. The results from the exams: Men: failure 33%; pass 37%; pass with distinction 30%. Women: failure 17%; pass 69%; pass with distinction 14%.

for the graduate courses. For the most part, male authors wrote the course literature although in some cases author gender was obscure (authors use first name initials only or have first names that are not gender specific).

We also found many positive instances of gender equity in education. As one of our goals in the project was to highlight such positive instances of gendered courses (in other words gender in education is not an eccentric, feminist notion), we accepted all positive examples, no matter how minimal the level of gender inclusion. In this way we hoped to emphasize aspects of the gendered existence and to raise its awareness among the faculty members. In the long run, we hoped this emphasis would provide positive reinforcement and would promote work with the gender issue in future courses.

We found that the workshop format, in which we, the workshop leaders, and the faculty members met, allowed us to handle spontaneous issues immediately as they arose. In addition, the discussions in the workshops led to insights by everyone involved. As the workshops progressed, with evidence of both positive and negative outcomes of how gender affected education, we saw how our strategy of emphasizing the positive outcomes had good effects. We could report positive results in an environment where academics often expect criticism. Furthermore, we ourselves were both surprised and encouraged by the instances of gender we found. Emphasizing the positive became a survival strategy for us.

EVALUATING THE PROJECT

A project such as 'Gender in Education' is difficult to evaluate, especially from a quantitative perspective. One qualitative evaluation approach is to present summaries of the final discussions by the participating departments. Therefore, in this section I describe departmental results from the different academic disciplines and cultures in the project. In addition, I present some quantitative data related to the project's results that are based on our seminar and workshop notes and the final project assessments.

The majority of the teachers and researchers in the Statistics Department were men although the one professor and the Department Head were women. Beginning in the 1990s, both genders were used in assignment examples[8] as it was assumed that male/female students could more easily understand the material if the examples used gender identification. The Statistics faculty had also analysed the evidence collected by Wennerås and Wold (1997) on gender prejudice in research funding. Thus the Statistics Department exemplified how easily gender can be included in teaching and, in addition, how favourable gender inclusion is to the learning situation.

The majority of the teachers and researchers in the Business Administration sub-group of Accounting were men, although two associate professors were women and the majority of the students were women. The Accounting sub-group mentioned gender issues in education in relation to professional status as concern. Given the situation where women in the working world of accountancy receive (and allegedly willingly accept) lower salaries than men, the future professional status of accountants was a topic of discussion. As low salaries may undermine occupational status, the issue was how to avoid diminishing the status and prestige of the subject discipline of Accounting. A suggestion was made that women students should be taught the skills of salary negotiation.

The professional status issue was also applicable to the local situation of the HGU researchers, for example, in the Economics Department. In this Department, the faculty listed many positive examples of support given to women undergraduates and to women doctoral students. Eighteen of the Department's 50 doctoral students were women. However, in response to concerns over the high drop-out rate among women doctoral students, the Department had invited their women doctoral students to discussions of their programme. In these meetings, the women students shared their experiences with each other and with the professors in attendance. The students claimed that because the Department was too 'masculine', many women were deterred from applying to the programme. Also, they complained about a lack of role models: there were no women professors in the Department.

We found a quite pragmatic local application of gender in education issues in Environment Studies, which is part of the Economics Department. Here the format for the internal seminars had changed from informal discussion to formal seminars in which a chairperson managed the speaking times so that everyone had a chance to speak. In this way, both the women and the shyer men could express their opinions more readily. The participants reacted positively to the structure of these formal seminars.

In general, applicable to all participants, the reflections and learnings from our project varied. There were differing personal experiences in academia and differing reflections on what may happen when people learn more about gender in working life. These responses from the faculty members show that projects, such as 'Gender in Education', need to be locally situated. Owing to the partic-ular circumstances of each project environment, it is impossible to standardize the processes.

In general, there was considerable internal and external interest in the project. Although attendance at the seminars declined after the first seminar, which 110 persons attended, 137 persons attended the workshops. Attendance seemed in part the result of the internal seminar culture of each Department. Some Department Heads made attendance more or less compulsory for everyone. In other Departments, the participants were either mainly doctoral students or mainly teachers. The Economics Department, for instance, invited only teachers to the workshops and required them to give the Economics Department Head a written explanation in case of absence(s). External interest in the project was evident by the media coverage. The Gothenburg University Journal (*GU-Journalen*, 99.2), the magazine Gender (*Genus*, 1/99) and the Gothenburg University TV channel reported on the project. A book by Fredrik Bondestam (2005) presented an overview of projects such as 'Gender in Education'.

In June 1999 we conducted an evaluation of the project using an email survey addressed to all faculty members at the seven HGU Departments (approximately 300 people). We received 76 answers. Of these 76 respondents, 46 had participated in the project. Of the 30 respondents who did not participate, 23 respondents replied that they had no time, 3 replied they were uninterested and 4 did not reply. Of the 46 responding participants, 32 persons rated the seminars 'good' or 'very good'; many expressed appreciation of the discussions and said they provoked interesting reflections.

Our email survey asked if and how the project had affected the participants' pedagogy. Most respondents answered that they could not pinpoint direct effects but that they felt they had become more aware of how gender influenced learning. However, some respondents said that they had changed their teaching style after the workshops. In addition, some Departments reported that they had created working groups to develop a gender perspective in their curricula, and some Departments even scrutinized their course literature from a gender perspective.

In 2000 we conducted a follow-up evaluation of the project's results. We sent an email survey to the HGU Department Heads, Study Directors and the gender equality ombudspersons. We contacted 21 persons but received only 3 responses. These responses indicated the Departments handled gender issues in teaching mostly through informal discussions. According to the respondents, they noted no direct results from the project.

Our perception is that these follow-up evaluations do not fully reflect the effect of our project on gender in education. Because of the relatively low number of responses to our email surveys, we can draw few conclusions about the local situation in the various departments. We believe our notes from the workshops provide a better and more nuanced view of the project's effects since they describe the specific insights reached by the Departments. This was confirmed by our observation that faculty members, in the seminars and workshops, began to reflect on issues of gender equality in education. To that end, we believe our project had a positive effect.

CONCLUSIONS

In reflecting on the 'Gender in Education' project a decade later, my concerns about the project's success have decreased. In these ten years, similar projects have been conducted in Sweden, and we ourselves have received requests to repeat our project at other universities. Many books and articles about gender in education have been published in Sweden as well. The most positive effect of our project is perhaps the fact that my colleagues still remember and comment favourably on it. In some sense, we feel we were pioneers in initiating a discussion concerning gender in education.

Regarding the factors behind the project's success, we state that organizational support we received was crucial. The Swedish Ministry of Education's financial support attested to the importance of the project and legitimized it in the view of the HGU Faculty Council and faculty. Surprisingly, we also received strong support from many professors who openly backed our project. In addition, the practical and largely non-judgmental work in the project, notably in the workshop spreadsheet exercises, made inequalities visible. Finally, our efforts to find and highlight constructive examples of gender equality were received positively by the project participants. This response made the possibility of follow-up work more likely.

Yet a positive outcome from 'Gender in Education' was the tangible tools we used. Seminars and workshops, supplemented by a reading list, can open up avenues of discussion and lead to an analysis of a variety of aspects of gender in education. Making and distributing transcriptions of such seminars and workshops add transparency to communication with participants. Spreadsheets for course and literature analysis can provide an overview of gender in the curriculum. Taken together, these tools are pragmatic methods that may illuminate both positive and negative aspects of gender in education.

It appears that 'Gender in Education' has had an influence at HGU since the work will continue in a new project. In Fall 2007 the gender equality ombudsperson received funding from the Faculty Council for a project that will begin in 2009. In order to include the new legal aspects of anti-discrimination actions, this new project will take an intersectionalist perspective (a recent research trend). The focus of the project is the inclusion of categories in education such as gender, ethnicity, class, religion, disability and age, among others. The project will also focus on how these categories affect each other, that is, how subjectivities are enacted in the simultaneous intersections of different categories. One expected result of the research is that it will illuminate the power relationships between teachers and students by focusing on these defining human categories. For example, an intersectional perspective in education may reveal new aspects of the power relationships between a middle class, Swedish homosexual teacher and an upper class, heterosexual foreign student studying in Sweden.

In our final report for 'Gender in Education', we discussed some startling impressions we had gained from the project (Eriksson-Zetterquist and Svensson, 2002). For example, we were amazed that some colleagues claimed the gender inequality problem was attributable to women themselves (for example, compared to men, women are less mathematically talented or have fewer analytical skills). This was a claim that we found not only out-of-date but also erroneous. Why would highly educated academics adopt these superficial explanations that are typically publicized by the media? However, as the workshops continued, the participants' reflections about gender equality became more sophisticated; they were willing to admit that unequal opportunities for women may be the result of insufficient knowledge about gender issues in education or of general male insensitivity. We interpreted this development as an example of how a discussion can become more nuanced when there is time and opportunity to reflect upon an issue.

While no fundamental changes in the HGU policies and programmes on gender in education have been reported so far, we have noted that some initial steps have been taken towards a more gender-inclusive approach. While we do not claim our project was faultless, its pioneering spirit is reflected by the current gender in education trend that has legitimized our work.

In working with gender-inclusive projects, the researcher has experiences that are a consequence of working with organizational change and of working with feminist issues. In a recent book Anna Wahl (2008), a well-known gender researcher in Sweden, and her co-authors discussed the resistance they found working with feminist issues at Swedish education organizations. This resistance may take many shapes, from being humiliated to being ignored. In the 'Gender in Education' project, I had concerns that I would encounter similar resistance. Looking back to the years of 1998–1999 when we led the project, it is clear that I feared people would not attend the seminars, that they would not listen to me since I was a doctoral student, and that the project would not result in positive change. With ten more years' experience in academic work, I now see those fears were groundless. It simply is hard to get people to attend seminars, whatever the agenda. Many senior faculty members are actually interested in what younger colleagues have to say, but major change is inevitably slow and difficult.

Finally, I raise the following question about gender equality in education. Why is it necessary to teach gender equality in education? By contrast, we do not find it necessary to teach the benefits of higher education accreditation or the basic scientific facts in environmental policymaking. In gender issues, we seem to start from square one; before we take steps to advance gender equality, we are required to study gender theory. It may be that learning fundamental gender theory thus obstructs the change process in organizations as attention is turned away from practical action.

NOTES

1. Prior to 2005, The School of Economics and Commercial Law.
2. In Swedish, *Handelshögskolan vid Göteborgs universitet*.
3. National Agency for Higher Education, Document 1998-06-05, reg. nr. 843-628-98.
4. In order to reveal the gender of the invited speakers (f) identifies females and (m) males.
5. The Swedish Research Council is a Government agency that supports and develops scientific research including medical research.
6. Our reading list is provided before the References that appear at the chapter end.
7. These questions relate to a more general scientific debate that Eva-Maria Svensson raised in the introduction to the brainstorming session ('objectivity as an ideal'). At the time of this project, positivism was a strong tradition at HGU and objectivity was the ideal. Today, positivism is still a strong ideal in some disciplines, but, in general, interpretative traditions and the insights from postmodernism are more well-known.
8. For example, an assignment might begin: 'Fifty per cent of men and fifty per cent of women drive cars.'

READING LIST

Alvesson, Mats and Yvonne Due Billing (1997), *Understanding Gender and Organizations*, London: Sage.
Cregård, Anna and Patrik Johansson (1997), *89 per cent män – Vem skriver kurslitteraturen*, Förvaltningshögskolans rapporter, No. 4, Gothenburg University, Sweden.
Dahlberg, Anita (1993), 'Androcentrin i juridisk utbildning, Vad skrivnings- och instuderingsfrågor förmedlar', in Peter Blume and Hanne Petersen (eds), *Retlig polycentri*, København: Akademisk Forlag.
Fogelberg, Paul, Jeff Hearn, Liisa Husu, Liisa and Teija Mankkinen (eds) (1999), *Hard Work in the Academy*, Helsinki University Press.
Gunnarsson, Britt-Louise (1997), Visst spelar könet roll! Kvinnliga doktorander i manlig seminariekultur, *Feministiskt perspektiv*, No. 4.
Lundgren, Britta and Eva Erson (1996), *Könsmedveten undervisning – två försök*, Undervisningscentrum Personalutveckling, Umeå University, Sweden.
Wahl, Anna (1996), Molnet – att föreläsa om feministisk forskning, *Kvinnovetenskaplig tidskrift*: 3–4.
Wennerås, Christine and Agnes Wold (1997), 'Nepotism and sexism in peer-review', *Nature*, **387** (22): 341–3.

REFERENCES

Bondestam, Fredrik (2005), *Könsmedveten pedagogik för universitetslärare – en introduktion och bibliografi*, Stockholm: Liber.
Eriksson-Zetterquist, Ulla and Eva-Maria Svensson (2002), *Genus i utbildningen*, GRI-rapport, Handelshögskolan vid Gothenburg University, Sweden.
Wahl, Anna, Maud Eduards, Charlotte Holgersson, Pia Höök, Sophie Linghag and Malin Rönnblom (2008), *Motstånd och fantasi. Historien om F*, Lund: Studentlitteratur.

8. Contributions of free-to-the-public web pages to liberatory education

David M. Boje

INTRODUCTION

I am a 'critical postmodernist' who makes web pages that I am told are used by academics globally. While developed initially for an academic audience, wider audiences are also using these web pages. Doing web pages is a highly important medium of communication in teaching, research, and public discourse. In particular, constructing web pages with an intellectual purpose strengthens civil society and education. I develop websites as a free-to-the-public pedagogy. A major contribution is to move beyond linear, sequential approaches to pedagogy into networked interconnectivity. This, for me, is inclusion.

I am a Professor of Management at the College of Business at New Mexico State University (NMSU) in Las Cruces. NMSU is a land grant university, chartered in 1862, and built against the jagged backdrop of the 9000-foot Organ Mountains, in the poverty-entrenched city, Las Cruces (2nd largest in the state) with a population estimated at 75 000. New Mexico is a minority majority state with a school population that is approximately 48 per cent Hispanic, 39 per cent Anglo, 10 per cent Native American, 2 per cent African American, and 1 per cent Asian. Ethnic diversity of Las Cruces is 51.73 per cent Hispanic or Latino, and a racial makeup that is 69.01 per cent White, 2.34 per cent African American, 1.74 per cent Native American, 1.16 per cent Asian, 0.07 per cent Pacific Islander, and 21.59 per cent from other races.[1] The university is located in a poor farm and ranch county of Doña Ana, with a 63.4 per cent Hispanic (or Latino) population.

My story of web-work begins in 1997, when my good friend Terence Krell visited my wife Grace Ann Rosile and me in our home in Las Cruces, New Mexico. He was a student of mine at UCLA in the early 1980s, and he had been developing web tools for students and faculty to use. Terence taught me how to use Netscape's free software to make web pages. We set up my first web page on the New Mexico State University server. With Terence's help I began to learn the basics of HTML code and became a frequent visitor to

JAVA Script online libraries. Soon after, I ordered Front Page, and a few years
ago, Dreamweaver. Now I have over 5000 web pages located on three servers.
Sadly, Terence passed away in 2004. Today, I searched for him on the web. His
'Free Resources for Creating Interactive Faculty Websites' is still online.[2]
Since Terence got me started, I moved some pages off the university servers
that were considered too activist, or threatened their fund raising interests.[3]

Education is transforming. Around the world, universities are becoming
virtualized. Cyberspace is playing an increasingly pervasive role in education.
The purpose of this chapter is to indicate to faculty and administrators positive
cyber-practices of a 'critical postmodernist' professor that can enhance inclusive academic practices. As a 'critical postmodernist' I try to combine Critical
Theory with Postmodern Theory. Thus, I have a focus on how education's
material practices are changing through the increased use of computers,
Internet, and cyberspace technologies. From a postmodern point of view, the
web pages I construct for education with ample hypertexts establishes virtual
communities that liberate pedagogy from linear typography. There are pros
and cons to this work.

CYBERSPACE AND EDUCATION: PROS AND CONS

Virtual communities can be defined as webs of social discourse relationships
that form in cyberspace (Falk 1999; Evans et al. 2001; Bieber et al. 2002;
Kardaras et al. 2003; Rosenberg 2004). Virtual communities contribute to
social openness (Walther 1996; Wellman and Gulia 1999). Cyber technology
can enhance education, making information more accessible, being able to be
in virtual contact with students who are in distant places thus preventing isolation. Virtual learning allows for collaborative projects in virtual teams
(Andrews, 2002; Uslaner 2004). Beyond education, virtual communities allow
another means of citizen participation in public discourse. Cyber connection
allows otherwise isolated users great freedom of speech, and (synchronous and
asynchronous) interaction with virtual classmates and instructors.

Cyber communities coalesce online, in niche virtual communities
(Wellman and Guilia 1999; Munir 2000), on a global scale (Hampton and
Wellman 2001; Garber 2004) around similar interests and worldviews resulting in positive emotional affect (Kuo 2003; Whitworth and De Moor 2003).
Cyber World allows for fluid identity, where online interlocutors develop new
personae for each interaction situation (Rheingold 2000). Cyber communities
are a form of social capital, allowing people to share knowledge, and more
democratic participation in public life (Schuler 1996; Blanchard and Horan
1998; Bakardjieva and Feenberg 2002; Flew 2005). Virtual communities, such
as Move-On encourage and supplement face-to-face interaction community

events (Haythornthwaite 2001; Wellman et al. 2001; Florida 2002, p. 166; Powazek 2002, p. 284). Cyberworld technologies are also changing the way universities are recruiting students. For example, New Mexico State University, where I work, has YouTube, FaceBook, MySpace, and Second Life web spaces.[4] I also have FaceBook, MySpace, and a Second Life avatar.[5]

However, there are also negative points to be considered. Not everything about cyberspace is liberatory pedagogy. Virtual communities can result in less time and inclination for face-to-face communities. Internet and virtual communities can be habit forming, even addictive to the neglect of face-to-face responsibilities (Rheingold 1993; Schuler 1996; Mitchell 2000). Also, access to the Internet varies across the world. Opinions vary concerning the exact extent of Internet use. Of the world's 6.6 billion people, only 365 million own a computer.[6] Estimates of how many people actually use the Internet worldwide vary from 694 million[7] to 1.5 billion.[8] The USA has the highest rates of computer ownership and Internet usage.

Further, some virtual communities are deviant subcultures, isolating themselves, and opposed to dominant views of society and to other subcultures with different worldviews (Newman and Newman 2001; Rimal and Real 2003). Some argue that virtual education and time on the Internet may actually degrade students' academic performance (Bugeja 2005). Kraut et al.'s (1998) empirical study of the effects of Internet use found a decrease in social engagement and in personal happiness. There are also some significant gender issues involved. Men use the Internet more frequently than women.[9] The Internet reduces time with family and friends, and increases time with people one has never met face-to-face. There are significant race issues as most users are white, and from fairly affluent nations.

Virtual communities may lead to a weakening of storytelling skills (Benjamin 1936), since the kinds of terse, mediated, written communication in virtual communication interaction truncates the range of quality face-to-face sensemaking time (something occurring since the advent of TV, that has increased with Internet technology). Walter Benjamin (1936) wrote a classic essay on 'Art in the age of mechanical reproduction'. Benjamin asserts that the printing press has changed art, making the copy more widely available than the original (painting, manuscript, sculpture, and so on). With the technology of the printing press, particularly lithography, sorting out authorship, and tracing edits to manuscripts has become more problematic, to the point that authenticity is difficult to assess.

We can extrapolate forward from Benjamin's concerns to what has happened to art in the age of cyber-reproduction. With copy machines and computers, then digital technologies of the Internet, and software such as Photoshop, Adobe, Moviemaker, and so on, there is more difficulty than ever with authenticity of authorship, and tracing changes to art as it passes from user to user on the World Wide Web. Here are some of the more important changes with regards to the art of storytelling.

BEYOND THE DUALITY

Haythornthwaite (2001) suggests that virtual and face-to-face communication can complement and strengthen one another. Matei and Ball-Rokeach (2001) did a qualitative study of the relation between online virtual and real life community and found people skilled at pursuing both. In what follows, I want to contribute six positive elements to cyberworld. Each of these has to do with creating web pages. To me, web page creation is a form of writing.

First, I write web pages that bring intellectual property to cyberworld that is freely available at no cost. Whereas journal article and book writing may reach a relatively small academic audience, the web writing, when it strikes a chord of interest, can be read by hundreds of thousands of people. That, to me, seems to fit the mission of my university: 'serving the educational needs of New Mexico's diverse population through comprehensive programs of education, research, extension education, and public service'. It is not referred, and not prestigious writing, yet it can reach a broad audience. Web writing can be timelier, without waiting for months or years of review. I am particularly interested in writing web pages that can reach the demographics of New Mexico, which is one of the poorest states in the US. According to the US Census Bureau, nearly one in four (24 per cent) New Mexico children under age 18 live in poverty.[10] Doña Ana County, where NMSU is situated, has median household income of $29 808, versus the State of New Mexico, $34 133. It has been estimated that around 72 per cent of the county's population lives at or below poverty level.[11]

If you use Google and look up a topic, you will find that over the past decade, publishing houses (and intermediaries) are requiring the public to pay for access to authors' articles and book chapters. The Internet is becoming increasingly commercial, less a place to exchange knowledge freely. This makes the knowledge less and less accessible to people without the means to pay. The vast majority of the world's poor has no computer and no Internet access.[12] There are class differences involved. What was once free access to Internet web pages, to scholarly knowledge in particular, now is increasingly only available to the most well off economic class. Those at the bottom of the economic ladder, in most need of free and equitable access to Internet knowledge, cannot afford the article fees.

Second, I want to help students interact with 'critical postmodern' ideas and theories. A critical postmodernist combines Critical Theory and Postmodern Theory. Critical Theory, for me, is situated in the pioneering work of the

Frankfurt School (Adorno, Horkheimer, Fromm, Marcuse, Benjamin, and so on) and those who continue the work (Habermas, Bakhtin), and the entire Critical Management Studies group (Willmott, Calás, Knights, Smircich, Clegg, Cunliffe, Oswick, Parker, and two hundred more).

This brings me to the theme of this chapter. For example, I maintain a 'What is critical postmodernism' website, as well as one that is a basic introduction to postmodern theory.[13] What is positive about 'critical postmodern'? Web links embedded in these pages, or in syllabi and study guides provide definitions, examples, and stories to make critical postmodern more accessible, more applicable. More important, they provide a space for nonlinear journeys. Students can create their own pathways through the intertextuality, via the hyperlinks.

Third, it is a positive thing to find out how political economies such as the US and Western Europe have transitioned from industrial production to 'spectacles' of consumption with outsourced production and globalization (Debord 1967).[14] For this reason I have developed websites tracing labor practices in the Nike sneaker and garment industry (Boje 1999a, b; 2000a, b),[15] and my websites on McDonalds and McDonaldization, for example, tracing the morphing of McDonald characters (Boje and Cai 2004, 2005; Boje, Cai and Thomas 2005; Boje, Driver and Cai 2005; Boje et al. 2005; Boje and Rhodes 2005a, b).[16] There are other corporate analyses, such as studies of the Enron financial debacle (Boje and Rosile 2002, 2003; Boje et al. 2004; Boje, Gardner and Smith 2006).[17] The positive aspect of these critical postmodern websites is to help students get a less managerialist (from view of management and corporate owners) counter-view in their education (for example Boje and Rosile 2008). Each of these web pages has links to other pages, and to other writers.

Fourth, I think a positive contribution of these 'critical postmodern' websites occurs in the area of ethics. My students are mostly sons and daughters of cowboys and ranchers who, for the most part, have never been exposed to critical or postmodern theory. I produce websites with a kind of critical postmodern tenor. I maintain a listing of articles and chapters (many of which have pre-press versions available).[18] One area of ethics, which I have been exploring is the idea of 'answerability' (Bakhtin 1990, 1993). When we hear a compellent story, are we answerable to identify our own complicity in the situation? There is something utilitarian and instrumental (means–ends logic) that a linear text, regimented, sequential classroom pedagogy, and bureaucratic university digital regimes imprint on the brain. To the extent that it is possible to implement nonlinear, networked, free exploratory journeys, we move to what I call Tamara. Tamara was a play, one where the audience fragmented, running or walking from room to room, networking their own enactment of experience. I think that sometimes web pages with their hyperlinks can simulate a Tamara networking, where no two students, in the same class, have the same journey.[19]

Fifth, I develop websites that allow students to take storytelling out of the 'once upon a time' backward-looking motif that stresses performance and entertainment rather than the way storytelling is part of the sensemaking of everyday life.[20] To me there is this important interplay between retrospective narrative, living story unfoldment (in the Now), and prospective antenarrating (bets on the future).[21] Sensemaking can be greatly changed by virtual communities in cyberspace. This is part of my exploration of the link between complexity and storytelling theories.[22] An important aspect of this storytelling is the ability to deconstruct one's own living stories, as well as grand (and small) narratives, and antenarratives (bets on the future).[23] Storytelling deconstruction involves finding the dualities, reversing their hierarchy, eliciting rebel voices, and so on, in order to generate a resituation of the particular hegemony.

Sixth, over the past 33 years, I have noticed a trend in university education in the US. What was freely available to the public now is being contained in courses, available only for enrolled students who have paid their tuition. For example, I used to be able to invite guests into the WebCT portions of courses I was teaching. Now, unless students pay their bill promptly, they are evicted from WebCT sections.

Our university is switching from WebCT to Blackboard. Blackboard recently acquired WebC and licensing costs for Blackboard have increased in some universities by 2000 per cent (Lassner 2006). There are open source solutions to 'learning management systems' such Moodle and Sakai, which my university did not choose. An open source project is where individual contributors add features to a central distribution everyone can use. My point here is that I view development of more of my websites outside of Blackboard (or WebCT), as a way to make my intellectual property freely available to the residents of New Mexico, and to the world of cyberspace. With Blackboard (and similar technologies), knowledge is cut off from students outside my course, from all other faculty, and from administrators (that one is OK by me, but I suspect they do surveillance without alerting me).

INCLUSION AND VOICE

I think the six positive aspects of 'critical postmodern' websites I construct help in two general areas: inclusion and voice. First, inclusion (and diversity) changes as university education enters cyberspace. There are two levels of inclusion this chapter deals with. The first one is the question of access, that is, how to give free access to materials for students and activists when there clearly is a trend to disregard open source solutions and to focus on buying and selling rather than free access. The second one is connected to deconstructing the power and hegemonic nature of the stories others and I are telling.

Second, websites can be used to work for 'voice' in at least two ways, giving voice to 'counterstories' and inclusion of the marginalized in a more dialogic (less linear, hierarchy) education experience. Affording people in remote locations access to teaching (and research) materials in websites is important. The State of New Mexico shares 53 miles of its border with Mexico, and has 37 of the state's 55 federally designated underdeveloped communities, called 'colonias'. These colonias are 97 per cent Hispanic, with residents living without safe, sanitary and affordable housing, drinkable water, sewers, or drainage systems, and with average annual income of $5000. In addition many of the tribes on reservations lack the broadband Internet access that allows more liberating educational technologies to be used. Geographic isolation can mean that virtual communities are one of the few means of scalability. Even where colonias or tribes have access to Blackboard (or WebCT), the isolation of the education materials (their confinement to enrolled students), reinforces separation.

Next, this chapter will focus on presenting two case examples (one course and one activist site) and look at them in more detail. I describe what each one delivers, how they deliver it, for whom they deliver, as well as what kind of stories are delivered, what has functioned well and what has not, and how the choices I made have enhanced inclusion.

COURSE WEBSITE EXAMPLE

In 1997, I began to understand that not all webpages are inclusive, non-linear, allowing for Tamara-like experiences (multiple journeys by students, each one unique). My university encourages us to put our entire course offering in the Blackboard. I try to have my own web pages, and use Blackboard just for the private chats, and to post grades. This way the material I write, such as study guides, learning modules, and information sites can be freely accessed by anyone on the Internet.[24] I frequently use SKYPE to include a guest speaker from another state or country, or to patch in distance students into a classroom discussion.

I will expand on one class. In the Small Business Consulting class, I use a combination of Blackboard and free-to-the-public websites. There are special projects I am doing such as the Arts Convention of Las Cruces and Mesilla Valley (Southern New Mexico along the Rio Grande River), where a site like http://talkingstick.org is quite helpful to post task force projects, photo slide shows, or gather comments on my blog, http://storytellingorganizations @blogspot.com. In the project in the fall of 2008, we conducted an Arts

Convention (three Monday evenings in September). There we developed eight task forces of students and artists to intervene in the small business (arts) community, to enhance coordination of some 127 arts service organizations. Some interventions involved cyberspace, such as creating integrated calendars, establishing an Arts Scene site that could be replicated or web-linked in other sites. Arts Scene: http://peaceaware.com/talkingstick/Las per cent20Cruces per cent20Arts per cent20Scene.htm; see Visitor's Bureau Arts Scene City-Site that came about http://www.lascrucescvb.org/html/las_cruces_galleries_and_artis.html as well as Las Cruces 360 (an entrepreneur's effort): http://lascruces360.com/. An innovation coming out of the Arts Convention was to work on marketing arts events beyond the local community, using Internet sites.[25]

ACTIVIST EXAMPLE

The http://peaceaware.com site I created was a boon to community organizing, to networking with other activists, announcing marches, vigils, and teach-ins. The website began when US President George W. Bush came to Las Cruces, New Mexico on August 24 2002. One hundred people held a protest across the street from the University campus. We then started meeting in peace vigils twice a week. I did the web work, posting calendars, templates for writing letters to officials, photos of events and so forth. At that time the local press, being quite conservative, refused to give any positive coverage of the peace movement events.

Eleven million people worldwide protested the probable Iraq invasion on February 15 2003. The invasion took place on March 20 2003. The day of the Iraq invasion all the PeaceAware.com web pages disappeared off line, and could not be found by the provider for several weeks. I switched server providers, from one in New Mexico to another in California. There is a case to be made that those web pages on non-university servers, by faculty, increases academic freedom of speech. Our university did not allow us to use university email, listserves, or faculty web pages for peace activities.

On April 12 2003, I was arrested by University police for failing to disband a peace vigil on University Avenue that divides the university from the community. I was handcuffed, taken in the police car to the University Police Station, where I was then leg-shackled and confined at New Mexico State Police Headquarters for over an hour without charge. I acted non-violent and peaceful, just choosing to meditate and not respond to the ridiculousness of my situation. After my release, several days later, the University officials apologized for arresting one of its own faculty, who was doing nothing more than exercising free speech rights on a public sidewalk. I have turned the

PeaceAware.com website into a living archive of the peace movement events leading up to and following the Iraq invasion. This includes writing articles about globalization and peace (Boje 2007).

DANGERS OF CYBERSPACE

Despite the many positive aspects of cyberspace for teaching and activism, there are some things to take care about. For me, Cyberworld can be addictive. When I started using email, I thought it was fantastic. Now, I spend too many hours a day staring at a screen, composing, sending, receiving and reading, sorting stuff I need from spam, and filing copies, some for legal purposes, others for research or nostalgia purposes. Once you open yourself to email, people you don't know send you stuff unsolicited, and people you know send you lots of stuff, too. I get such mass quantities of email each day (much of it spam; today 164 spam mails, about 2/3rds caught by spam filters), and despite the new versions of email software, spam-guard software, firewalls, and so on, there is more spam each year than the year before.

Am I an Internet addict? Here it is a Labor Day in the USA (September 1 2008) and I am slaving away writing an article about the positive uses of web pages for education. Shouldn't Labor Day be a time away from web pages, email, the Internet? Is it true? Do I suffer from what Wikipedia calls 'Internet addiction disorder' (IAD)?[26] What began as a hoax by Doctor Goldberg in 1995 is now being promoted as a real condition for as many as nine million Americans (mostly middle-aged women on home computers). South Koreans under age 19 are said to be at the highest risk for IAD. There are IAD subtypes such as gaming overuse, gambling, pornography (images and sexual conversations online), social networking (blogging), and Internet shopping.

Activities once done in person such as conversation are now done in chat rooms. Others are claiming that IAD is not a true addiction, just one more mental illness, a self-medication for depression, or a sort of obsessive compulsion. Self-proclaimed IAD sufferers are taking Internet companies and computer manufacturers to court. Soon addicts will be able to claim their IAD Internet addiction counseling to their insurance company. Virtual reality overuse on the Internet is said to induce dissociation, time distortion, and instant gratification addiction. The new IAD experts say it is not so much time spent on the Internet, but whether the Internet overconsumption affects marital relations, loss of job performance, increases depression, isolation, and anxiety. And with all these symptoms, you have IAD if you still can not cut back the number of hours spent on the computer, surfing the Internet, doing email, playing games, and so on. With IAD, it takes more and more hours of online time to get the same highness effects.

There are also dangers of cyberspace for storytelling. First, storytelling is more subject to being ripped out of its performative context (be it writing, orality, or dramaturgy), and redistributed without that context to other contexts, where not only is authorship erased, but the sensemaking currency of the storytelling is changed as it passes from site to site on the Internet with each site setting some fragments of storytelling into a new meaning milieu.

Second, storytelling is most apt to be fragmented, with some bits and pieces selectively attached (others ignored) and fitted to other such fragments, then put into some amalgam that distorts whatever contextualized meaning was present to co-participants in its construction, as well as along the pathways of its reconstruction, or decomposition, until there is precious little resemblance to the founding telling. Further, at some point, there is no way to sort out an originary telling, since fragments get arrayed, then passed along as an originary storytelling. This phenomenon was present in face-to-face communication, or the sharing of scriptorium texts, or in the passing along of performance rituals. However, it seems magnified, more pronounced, and commonplace in the cyber world.

Third, as for storytelling organizations, they have their ways and manners of storytelling greatly altered with digital technologies. In the days of land mail, face-to-face meetings, and times where people gathered in a common place, the sensemaking was a bit more multi-sensory (with touching, seeing, smelling, tasting, and hearing), not to mention some other types of sensemaking I cover recently (2008), such as chakras, horsesense (or if you will, seasense), a kind of body awareness of energy and motion. Communication, or sensemaking currency, is flattened, reduced to just seeing a screen, and hearing what comes out of speaker-device (or in some cases feeling the touch of a rumble-pack in a video-controller). There are also more disparities in time and space, where people are more detached from Being in the Now and Here. Storytelling organizations are a bit more impersonal, such as talking into a telephone receiver, to a robotic operator, who asks you to push a number or speak clearly, for this or that routing to some other robotic operator, who does it again, and maybe again, and again.

Fourth, with virtual communication technology, Storytelling organizations are providing more spaces for people to engage with avatars (for example, Second Life, Sim City, and so on). We are playing within virtual worlds in video games, in online cyber worlds that Disney, McDonald's, and others put together. There are more virtual meetings among authors in every type of academy disciplines. Classes and entire degrees are offered online. In some cases, administrators, given cuts to education funding by the State, oversee distance education in virtual classrooms, using more film clips of faculty no longer employed, and using lesser paid teaching assistants and instructors to manage list servers and chat rooms.

CONCLUSIONS

Proponents tell us that never before did humanity have such a powerful tool as the Internet to share knowledge. Or, that the Internet is creating a global economy. Or, anyone with access can find anything about anything. What a great knowledge revolution. The Internet claims to make life easier, give me free and open access to a worldwide library of information on web pages, blogs, film sites, and listservers. The Internet is supposed to facilitate distance education, so urban universities can reach people in the hinterland. Opponents say that it is overwhelming our senses, and that it is addictive. There are lots of sites, but most of them are dumb and dumber. The rest you have to pay for.

In my view there is a middle road, a less dualistic position. The web is closing its doors to free access to knowledge. Free-to-the-public faculty websites (especially with off-campus servers) provide a counter force to this development. As indicated in this chapter, I favor an open web, where knowledge is freely available. In my leadership and small business consulting classes, there is no charge to students for course materials. I write online books that are provided free of charge. There is also easy access to many of my chapters and journal articles.

Aristotle's ethics is to propose a middle way between extremes. On one extreme the cyber world is, for me, an addiction, and the overload of email tempts me into workaholism, and IAD. Like any other addiction it is an extreme behavior, but it is also one which is encouraged by an overly positive focus on educators and students, as well as universities, keeping up in the digital age. On the other hand, giving people in remote location access to education is an important consideration. At my own university, however, many of the distance courses are populated by students on the main campus, too lazy to walk away from their dorms, or perhaps from their computer screens, and head off to a building across campus.

To find the middle path between the extremes is a noble goal. For me, it means taking breaks, taking my dog Sparky for a walk in the desert (which he dearly loves), setting aside blocks of time each day when I don't work on web pages, don't do email, don't Skype, or web-surf. I like to take entire weeks in the summer, and weekends during the year and just unplug from the WWW. It is liberating, but when I return there are hundreds of emails. I have tried putting an attachment to my email, one that says I would like to do some premodern forms of communication, and just find a way to send old-fashioned letters, have a phone call or face-to-face visit instead of another email. I know its so much more efficient to be in touch with hundreds or thousands by email, but I feel I am cut off from my humanness, and from nature. I am preparing to write a book on Premodern Research Methods. To do this book, I will need to unplug, to spend more time in nature, in the old ways of note-booking and working with physical texts, instead of cyber texts. Still I realize that a middle path will be to balance my Being-in-the-World of Nature with Being-in-the-Cyber-World.

NOTES

1. Ethnic and population figures are from http://en.wikipedia.org/wiki/Las_Cruces,_New_Mexico.
2. 'Free Resources for Creating Interactive Faculty Websites' is still on the web. Accessed August 1997 and again August 18, 2008 at http://www.abc-xyz.com/faculty.shtml.
3. I went to one of Krell's 'Free Resources' and for the fun of it, created this web page http://www.webspawner.com/users/dboje/index.html. It sets up the basic page without any of the important codes that let search engines find the page. If I want something more from Web Spawner, it will cost me a monthly fee. I set up the same page with a few more bells and whistles on my server, using Dreamweaver: http://peaceaware.com/postmodern.
4. NMSU YouTube page http://de.youtube.com/newmexicostateu.
5. FaceBook http://www.facebook.com/profile.php?id=1128773846; MySpace http://www.myspace.com/davidboje.
6. World population estimate is 6 676 120 288.
7. '694 Million People Currently Use the Internet Worldwide According To ComScore Networks' (Comscore, 2004 press release) September 1 2008 http://www.comscore.com/press/release.asp?press=849.
8. 19.1 per cent of the world's population uses the Internet (1 463 632 361 people), according to a survey done by http://www.InternetWorldStats.com/stats.htm.
9. See slides of World Internet Project Media for these stats on male and female use http://www.authorstream.com/Presentation/Funtoon-34272-World-Internet-Project-Media-Percent-Users-Males-Females-Use-Information-Reliable-Accurate-Age-1-as-Entertainment-ppt-powerpoint/.
10. Poverty figure reported in *New Mexico Independent* 8/24/2008, http://nmindependent.mypublicsquare.com/view/todays-top-stories716.
11. For more on Doña Ana County, New Mexico demographic and poverty figures, consult http://www.donaanacounty.org/health/.
12. See online interactive world map of penetration rates, http://www.kwintessential.co.uk/map/internet-penetration.html.
13. Boje's What is Critical Postmodern website: http://business.nmsu.edu/~dboje/pages/what_is_critical_postmodern.htm and basic intro to postmodern theory http://www.horsesenseatwork.com/psl/pages/postmoderndefined.html.
14. Boje's Spectacle of Consumption website: http://peaceaware.com/special/1/pages/spectacle.htm.
15. See country-by-country summary of sweatshop factory locations: http://business.nmsu.edu/~dboje/nike/nikewithmap.html; monitoring practices by consultants and auditing firms: http://business.nmsu.edu/~dboje/AA/monitors.htm; and annotated listing of over 106 articles questioning sweatshop and monitoring practices of the sneaker and garment industries.
16. Boje's McDonald's characters genealogy http://peaceaware.com/McD.
17. Boje's Enron studies website: http://business.nmsu.edu/~dboje/enron/index.htm.
18. Boje's Ethics articles and chapters website: http://peaceaware.com/vita/ethics/.
19. See Boje (1995) 'Disney as Tamara-land', and Tamara Journal of Critical Organization Inquiry: http://tamarajournal.com.
20. Boje's storytelling gameboard website: http://business.nmsu.edu/~dboje/sto.html.
21. Boje's blog on storytelling organizations as interplay of narrative, living story, and antenarrative: http://storytellingorganizations.blogspot.com.
22. Boje's storytelling and complexity website: http://business.nmsu.edu/~dboje/655/index.htm.

23. Boje's Deconstruct This! website: http://business.nmsu.edu/~dboje/deconstruct.html.
24. Leadership, Storytelling, Consulting: http://business.nmsu.edu/~dboje/690, Leadership is Theatre: http://business.nmsu.edu/~dboje/388, Qualitative Methods: http://business.nmsu.edu/~dboje/qm, Small Business Consulting: http://business.nmsu.edu/~dboje/sbc, Systems/Complexity Theory: http://business.nmsu.edu/~dboje/655/index.htm, Organization Behavior from a critical perspective: http://business.nmsu.edu/~dboje/503. The leadership and storytelling consulting classes have their own books online (not hidden in Blackboard).
25. *How to Market your arts events:* City's Calendar of Events – press Register events for the Las Cruces' City Calendar, enter your organization and its Art and Culture at Las Cruces 360 site, then post events to Eventful E-mailed calendar of Dona Arts Council of Las Cruces, to El Paso Art Scene, and the New Mexico Department of Tourism Calendar. Join Dona Ana Arts Council's email list of current arts events & their Arts Calendar info. New Mexico Journey (AAA) can list events of Southwest NM if you give 4 months advance email to events@aaa-newmexico.com.
26. Wikipedia Internet Addiction Disorder: http://en.wikipedia.org/wiki/Internet_addiction_disorder.

REFERENCES

Andrews, D.C. (2002), 'Audience-specific Online Community Design', *Association for Computing Machinery: Communications of the ACM*, **45** (4), 64–8.
Bakardjieva, M. and Feenberg, A. (2002), 'Community technology and democratic rationalization', *Information Society*, **18** (3), 181–92.
Bakhtin, M.M. (1990), *Art and Answerability*, Edited by Michael Holquist and Vadim Liapunov; translation and notes by Vadim Liapunov; supplement translated by Kenneth Brostrom, Austin, TX: University of Texas Press. From Bakhtin's first published article and his early 1920s notebooks.
Bakhtin, M.M. (1993), *Toward a Philosophy of the Act*, Edited by Michael Holquist and Vadim Liapunov; translation and notes by Vadim Liapunov, Austin, TX: University of Texas Press. From Bakhtin's early 1920s notebooks. 1993 is the first English printing.
Benjamin, Walter (1936), 'The Storyteller: Reflections on the Works of Nikolai Leskov', in Hannah Arendt (ed.), *Illuminations*, translated by Harry Zohn, NY: Harcourt, Brace and World, Inc., pp. 883–110. Published in 1955 in German, and 1968 in English. 1936 was the original publication date of 'The Storyteller', Orient und Oksident.
Bieber, M., Engelbart, D., Furuta, R. and Hiltz, S.R. (2002), 'Toward virtual community knowledge evolution', *Journal of Management Information Systems*, **18** (4), 11–35.
Blanchard, A. and Horan, T. (1998), 'Virtual communities and social capital', *Social Science Computer Review*, **16** (3), 293–307.
Boje, D.M. (1995), 'Stories of the storytelling organization: A postmodern analysis of Disney as "Tamara-land"', *Academy of Management Journal*, **38** (4), 997–1035.
Boje, D.M. (1999a), 'Nike, Greek goddess of victory or cruelty? Women's stories of Asian factory life', *Journal of Organizational Change Management*, **11** (8), 461–80.
Boje, D.M. (1999b), 'Is Nike Roadrunner or Wile E. Coyote? A postmodern organization analysis of double logic', *Journal of Business and Entrepreneurship*, March, (II), 77–109.
Boje, D.M. (2000a), 'Nike is Out of Time', Introduction to Showcase Symposium for Academy of Management Meetings, August 2000, Toronto.

Boje, D.M. (2000b), 'Nike corporate writing of academic, business, and cultural Practices', *Management Communication Quarterly*, issue on Essays for the Popular Management Forum, **4** (3), 507–16.

Boje, D.M. (2007), 'Globalization Antenarratives', in Albert Mills, Jeannie C. Helms-Mills and Carolyn Forshaw (eds), *Organizational Behavior in a Global Context*, Toronto: Garamond Press, pp. 505–49.

Boje, D.M. (2008), *Storytelling Organizations*, London: Sage.

Boje, D.M. and Cai, Y. (2004), 'McDonald's: Grotesque method and the metamorphosis of the three spheres: McDonald's, McDonaldland, and McDonaldization', *Metamorphosis Journal*, **3** (1), 15–33.

Boje, D.M. and Cai, Y. (2005), 'A Laclau and Mouffe Discursive Critique of McJob', in Nico Carpentier (ed.), *Discourse Theory and Cultural Analysis*, Sage.

Boje, D.M. and Rhodes, C. (2005a), 'The Leadership of Ronald McDonald: Double narration and stylistic lines of transformation', *Leadership Quarterly Journal*, **17** (1), 94–103.

Boje, D.M. and Rhodes, C. (2005b), 'The virtual leader construct: The mass mediatization and simulation of transformational leadership', *Leadership Journal*, **4** (1), 407–28.

Boje, D.M. and Rosile, G.A. (2002), 'Enron whodunit?' *Ephemera*, **2** (4), 315–27.

Boje, D.M. and Rosile, G.A. (2003), 'Life imitates art: Enron's epic and tragic narration', *Management Communication Quarterly*, **17** (1), 85–125.

Boje, D.M. and Rosile, G.A. (2008), 'Specters of Wal-Mart: A critical discourse analysis of stories of Sam Walton's ghost', *Critical Discourse Studies Journal*, **5** (2), 153–79.

Boje, D.M., Cai, Y. and Thomas, E. (2005), 'Regenerating McDonaldland: A Play of Grotesque Humor', in Robert Westwood (ed.), *Humour, Organisation and Work*, University of Queensland Business School and Carl Rhodes University of Technology, Sydney.

Boje, D.M., Driver, M. and Cai, Y. (2005), 'Fiction and humor in transforming McDonald's narrative strategies', *Culture and Organization*, **11** (3), 195–208.

Boje, D.M., Gardner, C. and Smith, W.L. (2006), '(Mis)using numbers in the Enron story', *Organizational Research Methodologies Journal*, **9** (4), 456–74.

Boje, D.M., Enríquez, E., González, M.T. and Macías, E. (2005), 'Architectonics of McDonald's cohabitation with Wal-Mart: An exploratory study of ethnocentricity', *Critical Perspectives on International Business Journal*, 1.

Boje, D.M., Rosile, G.A., Durant, R.A. and Luhman, J.T. (2004), 'Enron spectacles: A critical dramaturgical analysis', *Organization Studies*, **25** (5), 751–74.

Bugeja, Michael (2005), *Interpersonal Divide: The Search for Community in a Technological Age*, NY: Oxford University Press.

Debord, Guy (1967), *Society of the Spectacle. La Société du Spectacle* was first published in 1967 by Editions, Buchet-Chastel (Paris); it was reprinted in 1971 by Champ Libre (Paris). The full text is available in English at http://www.nothingness.org/SI/debord/index.html.

Evans, M., Wedande, G., Ralston, L. and van't Hul, S. (2001), 'Consumer interaction in the virtual era: Some qualitative insights', *Qualitative Market Research*, **4** (3), 150–59.

Falk, D.S. (1999), 'The virtual community: Computer conferencing for teaching and learning social work practice', *Journal of Technology in Human Services*, **16** (2–3), 127–43.

Flew, T. (2005), *New Media: An Introduction*, 2nd edn, South Melbourne: Oxford University Press.

Florida, R. (2002), *The Rise of the Creative Class: And How It's Transforming Work, Leisure, Community and Everyday Life*, New York: Basic Books.

Garber, D. (2004),'Growing virtual communities', *International Review of Research in Open and Distance Learning*, 1–2.

Hampton, K. and Wellman, B. (2001), 'Long distance community in the network society: Contact and support beyond Netville', *American Behavioral Scientist*, **45** (3), 476–95.

Haythornthwaite, C. (2001), 'Exploring multiplexity: Social network structures in a computer-supported distance learning class', *The Information Society*, **17** (3), 211–26.

Kardaras, D., Karakostas, B. and Papathanassiou, E. (2003), 'The potential of virtual communities in the insurance industry in the UK and Greece', *International Journal of Information Management*, **23** (1), 41–53.

Kraut, R., Lundmark, V., Patterson, M., Kiesler, S., Mukopadhyay, T. and Scherlis, W. (1998), 'Internet paradox, A social technology that reduces social involvement and psychological well-being?', *American Psychologist*, **53** (9), 1017–31.

Kuo, Y.-F. (2003), 'A study on service quality of virtual community websites', *Total Quality Management*, **14** (4), 461–73.

Lassner, D. (2006), 'CIO's corner', *Info Bits*, **10** (1), online at http://www.hawaii.edu/infobits/s2006/.

Matei, S. and Ball-Rokeach, S.J. (2001), 'Real and virtual social ties: Connections in the everyday lives of seven ethnic neighborhoods', *American Behavioral Scientist*, **45** (3), 550–64.

Mitchell, P. (2000), 'Internet addiction: Genuine diagnosis or not?', *The Lancet*, **355** (9204), 632–5.

Munir, K. (2000), 'Net gain: Expanding markets through virtual communities', *Technology Analysis and Strategic Management*, **12** (2), 303–5.

Newman, B.M. and Newman, P.R. (2001), 'Group identity and alienation: Giving the we its due', *Journal of Youth and Adolescence*, **30** (5), 515–38.

Powazek, D.M. (2002), *Design for Community: The Art of Connecting Real People in Virtual Places*, Indianapolis: New Riders.

Rheingold, H. (1993), *The Virtual Community: Homesteading on the Electronic Frontier*, Reading, MA: Addison-Wesley.

Rheingold, H. (2000), *The Virtual Community: Homesteading on the Electronic Frontier*, http://www.rheingold.com/vc/book/, January 24, 2008.

Rimal, R.N and Real, K. (2003), 'Understanding the influence of perceived norms on behaviour', *Communication Theory*, **13** (2), 184–203.

Rosenberg, R.S. (2004), *The Social Impact of Computers*, 3rd edn, London: Elsevier Academic Press.

Schuler, D. (1996), *New Community Networks: Wired for Change*, New York: ACM Press.

Uslaner, E.M. (2004), 'Trust online, trust offline', *Communications of the ACM*, **47** (28).

Walther, J.B. (1996), 'Computer-mediated communication: impersonal, interpersonal and hyperpersonal interaction', *Communication Research*, **23** (1), 3–43.

Wellman, B. and Gulia, M. (1999), *Net-surfers Don't Ride Alone: Virtual Communities as Communities: Networks in the Global Village*, Boulder: Westview Press.

Wellman, B., Haase, A.Q., Witte, J. and Hampton, K. (2001), 'Does the Internet increase, decrease, or supplement social capital? Social networks, participation and community commitment', *American Behavioral Scientist*, **45**, 437–56.
Whitworth, B. and De Moor, A. (2003), 'Legitimate by design: Towards trusted socio-technical systems', *Behaviour and Information Technology*, **22** (1), 31–51.

PART III

Shifting academic identities and research strategies

9. Extending cross-ethnic research partnerships: researching with respect

Judith K. Pringle, Rachel Wolfgramm and Ella Henry

CONTEXTUAL SETTING

In this chapter, we consider how we might create productive equitable relationships across historically fractured ethnic lines. It considers a number of methodological styles, but is autobiographical and uses personal narratives. We aim to explore the struggle in dynamic research relationships as we seek authenticity in inquiry and representation cast within a macro context of unequal power.

The contextual foundations of our examination reside within experiences as Māori and Pākeha researchers from Aotearoa/New Zealand, a country founded on the ideal of a partnership relationship between the indigenous Māori and Pākeha (the colonizers). Although trade connections between Māori and the British Crown can be traced back to the 1790s, the formalization of a colonial relationship occurred in 1840, when the Treaty of Waitangi (Te Tiriti o Waitangi) was signed by 540 Māori chiefs and a representative of the British Crown, Governor Hobson (Orange, 2004).

As Māori chiefs became aware of the evolving powers of a colonial administration, they became increasingly agitated by the modus operandi of command, control and acquisition taken as the Crown, through its representative officials, and began to actively assert sovereign rule. This has resulted in a history littered with battles between Māori, the Crown and its representative governments (King, 2003; Orange, 2004). Whilst Māori continue to contest the dispossession of lands, rights and autonomous sovereignty, tribal claims and settlements are now being actively addressed by governments. This was facilitated by the establishment of the Waitangi Tribunal which, with a law change in 1985, enabled the Tribunal to look retrospectively to 1840 to hear and judge historical and contemporary grievances.

Over the past century, the struggle for Māori sovereignty (tino rangatiratanga) has led to active acknowledgements of biculturalism (Walker, 1991; Durie, 1998). However, these foundations are constantly shaken by contested power positions between Māori and Pākeha. Nevertheless a cultural and economic renaissance by Māori has gathered strength leading to a justifiable reluctance by the colonizers to speak for the colonized, as Māori intellectuals and activists have roundly criticized Pākeha for doing so.

For example, Seuffert (1997) offers a critique of 'traditional Eurocentric epistemology' which has 'claimed universal applicability across disciplines, cultures and historical periods' (ibid., p. 98) through a process of colonial imposition, or 'epistemic violence'. Further, there is recognition that research has been conducted by those who are not Māori in such a manner as to disempower, objectify and further alienate Māori from aspirations for self-determination. And, grassroots Māori educationalists have advocated for and created an alternative Māori educational system, operating alongside the mainstream. Added to this is the growing body of Pākeha intellectuals, politicians and community leaders who have walked alongside Māori through these endeavours and who are at the forefront of the movement for more respectful and mutually beneficial relationships between Māori and non-Māori.

INDIVIDUAL POLITICS OF LOCATION

It is within this macro context that we develop our discussion as Pākeha and Māori researchers working within a western academy. We now introduce ourselves and consider what cross-ethnic relations mean to us within our individual politics of location.

Ella Henry: I am a Māori woman who descends from three of the tribes of the Far North of the North Island, Ngati Kahu ki Whangaroa, Ngati Kuri, Te Rarawa. My whakapapa/genealogy is derived from both my parents, and I am not constrained by gender in my choice of which of these tribes takes preeminence in my identity. In fact, when I am in my different tribal areas, I may change the order of preference. That is my choice and my power. This gives me strength as a Māori woman, what we call our 'mana wahine'.[1] Being a Māori woman is the heart of my identity and the identity of my heart, so I seek like minds when I am engaged in knowledge production. When I find them I know them, not by the colour of the skin, or the shape of their genitals, but by the ahua (the face) they present and the wairua (spirit) they carry with them.

In the Far North of New Zealand are the tribes with the longest period of ongoing contact with Europeans, who were amongst the earliest to engage in extensive trade with the newcomers to our country from the late 18th century. As such, my people have been involved in cross-ethnic relationships which, for much of the period between 1769 and 1840 were mutually beneficial and rewarding. However, the relationship between Māori and Pākeha has been marred by mutual distrust and antipathy for much of the last one hundred years. This has been particularly true among women. For, as Pākeha women arrived in our country, they did not form the same types of political and commercial bonds as frequently as our menfolk.

Until very recently, those who 'inter-married' in Northland were often forced to align themselves exclusively with either Māori or Pākeha culture. However, in my experience, when relationships formed between Māori and Pākeha women, they were rich and rewarding if and when both parties acknowledged their power differentials, Pākeha being the dominant culture and Māori the minority one. These contexts have coloured my cross-ethnic research relationships in different ways over the last 20 years insofar as I have had extremely positive experiences of working on cross-ethnic research projects when I have worked with Pākeha women who were sensitive to our power dynamic and respectful of the knowledge and capabilities that I, as a Māori woman, brought to the relationship.

Rachel Wolfgramm: I am of Māori, Tongan and European descent and in this statement I signal several things. Firstly, as a Māori, I acknowledge that my ancestors never ceded sovereignty in signing a Treaty with the British Crown. Thus, when discussing power differentials in research, my frame of reference is institutional structures and cultures of exclusion in the western academy, not my own sense of tino rangatiratanga (sovereignty). Secondly, the bi-cultural nature of my heritage is reflected in my willingness to engage in cross-ethnic research partnerships that reflect the aspirations of nation building in Aotearoa/New Zealand. I acknowledge this in recognition of the fact that in 1859, when cross-ethnic relationships in New Zealand had yet to be challenged extensively by Māori, my ancestor Hineiahua Rangihaerepo (whose father Rangihaerepo was a signatory of Te Tiriti o Waitangi, on behalf of Ngai Tamahaua and Te Upokorehe of Whakatohea) married Lieutenant Colonel Balneavis, a member of the British military's 58th Regiment. Through the marriage of their daughter Georgina, I have connections to Northern tribes Te Aupouri and Ngai Takoto. Added to this, my father is of Tongan German descent and his ancestors were traders who settled and married in Vava'u, Kingdom of Tonga in the late 1800s. As a kingdom, Tonga's sovereign powers were ratified in a Treaty of Friendship with Germany (1876), followed by a Treaty of Friendship with Britain (1879) and a Treaty with the United States (1886). Although a British Protectorate (1900–1970), Tonga retained rights to control and determine its foreign policy thus always remaining a self-governing kingdom.

Whilst I was born, raised and educated in a metropolitan city (Auckland Tamaki Makaurau), I consider it advantageous to have a diverse and rich heritage, one that enables me to move across and within a range of cultural and social contexts with relative ease. Reflecting on my ancestral heritage allows me to elucidate both the tensions and the opportunities that exist when building and sustaining cross-ethnic research partnerships. In the context of the academy, the recognition of power differentials provides the impetus for ensuring cross-ethnic research relationships move forward in positive and progressive ways that facilitate the expression of diversity and the growth of new knowledge.

Sustaining me in my research endeavours are my ancestors Hineiahua (spirit of woman) and Waimirirangi (sweet waters from heaven), my whanau (family) and my tamariki (children) who simultaneously represent the past, present and future. My approach to research reflects this along with aspirations of a broader collective community. Those that collaborate with me in research partnerships simply accept all of the above.

Judith Pringle: I am Pākeha, and in that statement I signal to you that I am a descendent of the colonizers, originating mainly from Scotland coming to the South Island in the late 1860s. I grew up in the rural South Island far removed from Māori people, brought up to believe that we were 'one people' in New Zealand. My awareness of identity politics of difference began through the feminist movement and was expanded through the 1981 anti-apartheid protests in New Zealand. My consciousness of the politics of difference was further extended when I relocated in 1990 to an academic position in the multi-cultural city of Auckland. It was there, through my Māori and Pacific Island students, I began to learn of a different worldview and its importance.

As a member of the dominant Pākeha or European group my research relationships are imbued with institutional and societal power. A challenge to me was how could I ameliorate the distinctions? I passionately believe that we need to extend our knowledge base beyond white men; as a feminist researcher and as someone involved in research and teaching of workplace diversity. How can research be carried out sensitively so as not to silence the voices; without guilt, patronizing, or being paralysed by political correctness?

CROSS-CULTURAL RESEARCH RELATIONSHIPS

Cross-ethnic research relationships create multiple challenges. Difficulties arise in access to the communities of interest, miscommunication in the protocols and content of the interviews, challenges in the interpretation of the resulting data (cultural stories) exacerbated by the macro institutional frames within which the relationship is built. Even well-intentioned individual players enact the relationship within a wider context of historical and deep-rooted societal power differences. For instance, Lugones and Spelman have clearly inferred, get out of the way white girl: 'Out of obligation you should stay out of our way, respect us and our distance, and forgo the use of whatever power you have over us' (1983, p. 581). In other words members of the dominant white culture should step back, and let the 'others' take their own time and space to theorize their own experiences.

It is in response to this bold challenge that we write. How can we research with non-dominant cultures without violation, at something approaching authenticity? Is it even possible? Old wrongs may not be righted but new travesties can be avoided. Whatever approach is used, Spoonley (2003) notes that cross-cultural research in Aotearoa/New Zealand has been fraught because of a history of abuses due to the power differences between the two peoples; Pākeha – the colonizers – and the Māori indigenous people.

Researching across ethnic groups becomes problematic when a power gap is recognized for it raises ethical struggles (Narayan, 1995). Much research has reproduced the colonizing discourse of the 'other' (Fine et al., 2000) for differences are quickly constructed and differently valued; which differences are contentious and change according to various local geographical and cultural contexts. Indigenous peoples such as Māori have been both over-scrutinized and yet under-researched (Bishop, 2005; T. Smith, 2005). There is a lack of public knowledge from indigenous perspectives yet there exist many accounts of these 'others' from western anthropologists, sociologists and now organizational theorists. For some years our colleagues in other disciplines such as education have discussed the pedagogical traps and teaching practice involved in bi-cultural relations (Jones, 2001), but within areas such as organization studies has been an absence of research in spite of recent growth in Māori organizations. Our business curriculums are in urgent need of research-based knowledge relevant to Māori students.

This chapter does not report on research findings or the nature of participants, but will apply some of the discussions of insider–outsider and the power relations of 'one' and 'other' to the researchers themselves. Specifically we examine the power relations in research practice and specifically in cross-ethnic research partnerships by considering what makes the partnerships work. Firstly we distinguish between two influential epistemological strands to our work – kaupapa Māori and feminist epistemology. We then describe a number of illustrative research approaches where we sought to address the power inequalities enacted through Māori–Pākeha research partnerships. Finally we reflect on lessons learned.

LOCATING COMMON EPISTEMOLOGICAL TERRAIN

In setting the theoretical context we draw from kaupapa Māori and feminist methodologies. Additionally, the power dynamics within the relationships between the researchers are informed by a localized post/neocolonial setting. We advocate the need for a multi-cultural sensitivity to consider how we might reach across the divide. We ask: 'Who can or should reach across the divide of diverse identity groupings to conduct research?'

Post-colonial or more appropriately neocolonial theory in Aotearoa/New Zealand (Johnston and Pihama, 2005) is contextualized locally within a strong bipartite frame. The dominant discourse is signified within bicultural relations between Māori and Pākeha. The contemporary and shifting relationship of the modern players is derived from an historical macro context emphasizing the rhetoric of a bicultural partnership. As research partners originating from opposing colonial positions we are creating new links and understandings arising out of this shared historical and socio-political space. Together we aimed to displace domains of difference between colonizer and indigenous, and to create new domains of inclusion and difference.

As we were negotiating our inter-cultural relationship at a micro level there were important academic developments within Māori scholarship. In parallel with the growing call for Māori sovereignty and self-determination, there emerged an indigenous approach to knowledge creation termed Kaupapa Māori (G. Smith, 1996). '[The] meanings are embedded in Māori culture. It literally means the Māori way or agenda ... encapsulated in a Māori worldview or cosmology' (Henry and Pene, 2001, p. 236). The founding principles of the Kaupapa Māori discourse can be articulated as: that which is done for, with and by Māori; that which validates and legitimises Māori language and culture; that which empowers Māori, as whanau, hapu and iwi[2] (T. Smith, 1999; Wolfgramm, 2007).

Further, Henry and Pene have argued that Kaupapa Māori is both a set of philosophical beliefs, and a set of social practices (tikanga) combining the interconnection between mind, body and spirit. Tika means 'that which is right/correct', and tikanga means 'doing the right thing'. Values/ethics such as recognizing a continued connection to the ancestors, the importance of tribal identity and respect for others are manifest in tikanga such as whanaungatanga (kinship), wairuatanga (spirituality) and manaakitanga (caring for and hosting others) (Knox and Henry, 2008). Taken together, these ethics inform traditional Māori ontology and assumptions about human nature (Henare, 2003). These traditional Māori ethics and philosophy also drive Māori epistemology.

> The contemporary use of kaupapa Māori continues to be imbued with these values and beliefs ... Over the past two decades the Māori Renaissance, has engendered an environment in which Māori intellectuals have begun to challenge Western models of knowing and knowledge-construction. (Henry and Pene, 2001, p. 242)

Kaupapa Māori methodology emerged because of the colonization of indigenous people and situates the emancipatory goals of critical theory firmly into a 'local' historical, political and social context (T. Smith, 1999). The core values within Kaupapa Māori framework are described by common Māori proverbs (T. Smith, 1999, p.120) that provide a code of conduct for research. Loosely translated they are: exhibit a respect for Māori people, do not diminish their mana;[3] conduct the research face-to-face; observe and listen carefully; be cautious; do not flaunt one's knowledge; share with and host people. In practice, this has resulted in tensions when research funds were sought. For example, Kaupapa Māori research includes koha (donating to community) and kai (feeding and hosting participants). It is only in recent years in Aotearoa/ New Zealand that funders have changed their policies after much lobbying from concerned researchers.

Whilst some Kaupapa Māori researchers are adamant that only insiders can participate, others are more moderate and encourage outsiders to engage with Māori through working to understand the 'other' and develop 'an intercultural discourse' (Ritchie, 1992, p. 109). Working on Kaupapa Māori research projects with Māori and non- Māori researchers, Henry and Pene found,

> These researchers reflect the kaupapa Māori ontology, with its emphasis on connection, interdependence, spirituality and guardianship. Their ethnicity, their Māoritanga or ' Māori-ness', is not as significant as their identification with the kaupapa, the objectives and processes of the research, and the ways that they enact and practice research as a set of ethics and values as well as methodological practices. (2001, p. 240)

It is this position on Kaupapa Māori research that we adopted to guide our research partnerships. An example of this is ensuring that when we research in Māori communities, we begin with the powhiri: welcome protocol, ensure karakia (ritualistic prayers) are performed and all hui (gatherings) are consummated by the sharing of food. Irrespective of the approach taken, self-awareness, reflexivity of process and a cultural sensitivity are paramount considerations, all of which can be subsumed under the broad label of bicultural or partnership research (T. Smith, 1999, p. 178). The development of the principles and practices of Kaupapa Māori research have provided a welcome framework for research with indigenous peoples internationally as well as immigrant groups in Aotearoa.

We also owe a debt to feminist critiques of methodology and to feminist scholars (such as Oakley, 1981; Harding, 1987; Reinharz, 1992; Stanley and Wise, 1993) who connected feminism with the research enterprise. Feminist critiques have played a key role in shattering the myth of research outcomes as scientific truths, firstly by asking questions of representation. Does the science reflect women's experiences? Whose voices are known and whose are silenced? Where and how has the knowledge been obtained 'and by whom, from whom and for what purposes?' (Olesen, 2005, p. 238). These questions directly echo the concerns of indigenous researchers.

Significantly, feminist researchers queried the apparent objectivity of the researcher and have highlighted the power gap between researcher and subject, exposing issues of exploitation of the research subject (Ramazanoğlu and Holland, 2002). Feminist theory has evolved from a notion of a universalized essentialized woman to ideas of a situated woman, understanding that 'multiple identities and subjectivities are constructed in particular historical social contexts' (Olesen, 2005, p. 241). As part of the feminist research process we are encouraged to make explicit our own social location and moral position which is a guide for this chapter. Being exposed to feminist epistemologies has helped some Māori women researchers to develop the understanding of, and commitment to, the evolution of the Kaupapa Māori paradigm (Henry, 1995; Johnston and Pihama, 1995).

As contemporary awareness has grown around the politics of location there has evolved a concomitant crisis in representation (Lal, 1999; Visweswaran, 1994). Dilemmas in adequate representation were pondered in constructing this chapter as we shared the writing process. An initiating voice comes from a Pākeha, but three experiences are voiced, with each writer reflecting on her ethnic identity and on her personal experience in the cross-ethnic research partnerships.

Another dilemma arising in cross-ethnic partnerships is the insider–outsider tension, where a member of the ethnic group conducting the research is educated in another culture. This tension affects not only white researchers but also indigenous researchers. It is when research crosses cultures that insider and outsider tensions are highlighted. These insider–outsider roles are not oppositional, but are ambiguous states. Even indigenous researchers can be outsiders to their community. There has been lively discussion of insider–outsider tensions in feminist ethnography (Hesse-Biber et al., 1999), and women and development. These researchers may originate from the so-called 'developing world', but are often educated in the west before returning to their own country to engage in field work and to give back to their communities through their research (for example Lal to India, 1999; Steyn to South Africa, 2001).

In various ways feminist critiques have been integrated and extended in contemporary methodological developments. Traces of these feminist ontological and epistemological positions are recognizable in indigenous Kaupapa Māori research. Kaupapa Māori research calls upon the researchers to conduct their research for the purpose of Māori (regardless of their ethnicity); when this occurs, Māori and Pākeha relationships are enhanced by the shared purpose.

RESEARCHING TOGETHER

Within this section we discuss our experiences as research collaborators, where consciousness of our ethnicity and power positioning played a central part of the process. Rachel and Ella, initially postgraduate students supervised by Judith, became research partners in two different but related research projects aimed at better understanding Māori (Henry and Pringle, 1996) and Pacific Island women-run organizations (Pringle and Wolfgramm, 2005).

Judith: Over the past decade I have initiated multiple strategies in an attempt to foster research about Māori and Pacific Island organizations. As the initiator of the research I am researching the experiences of ethnic groups who are recognized as having lesser societal power. I am open to criticisms of 'do-gooder' or colonizer. Yet I will not be paralysed into inaction as we call for capacity building within Māori and Pacific Island groups. Although observers may question my actions I have been encouraged and supported by my students and co-researchers to continue in this enterprise. My bosses and my universities have not been actively supportive. Rather there has been a benign acceptance of cross-ethnic research and supervisory efforts as a contributor to the grand and broad mission of the university to increase the numbers of Māori and Pacific Island students. The research has not been hampered by the institution, but equally it has not been lauded. Nevertheless as part of a feminist ontology and my own principles, I wished to bring a critical awareness to taken-for-granted power embedded in research, and within the supervision–student relationship.

As a white researcher I have had a number of formative research experiences outside of the specific partnerships with Ella and Rachel. In institutional terms as a supervisor within the university, I am clearly the designated leader of the supervisory process; furthermore this inequality of power is unproblematic in institutional terms and even viewed as necessary to the learning process. I am expected to initiate, direct and add additional resources all within a standard frame. As supervisors we have acknowledged research experience, technical skills and presumed process proficiency to manage and utilize everyone's expertise. We all participate in this power-imbued relationship as part of our scholarly work affirming and sustaining students from a variety of ethnicities, enabling them to become proficient and to add to the canon through blending the extant (white, western) literature with their 'other' perspectives. However, this assimilation model of knowledge creation does not protect the integrity of knowledge from diverse social identity groups (Prasad et al., 2006).

I wanted to move beyond the power-differentiated roles of supervisor and student to develop a programme of research that somehow provided amplification for the voices of particularly Māori and Pacific Island[4] women. I was concerned not to perpetuate research on the 'other', but to be aware of the dynamic power relations between us. For example, in moving into a Māori cultural milieu I am the undoubted novice and need mentoring and shepherding by my colleagues, who are experts in this setting even if they are my graduate students and 'junior' in a western university context. My aim is to develop flexible power-sharing and knowledge-sharing strategies.

Previously I had been involved in a 'cross-cultural' research project which occurred before the cross-cultural dyadic partnerships discussed in this chapter. It was conceptualized and subsequently labelled as a transcultural methodology (Pringle and Park, 1993). This research project involved a multi-ethnic team where a leader was difficult to distinguish. It resulted from a larger project aiming to replicate a US survey in New Zealand. It drew on a feminist epistemology and as a result participants collaborated to modify the original survey to produce questions more appropriate to the diverse ethnicities involved. Research participants had valuable dual roles as participants in and critics of the research. Participants met in ethnically similar groups, matched as far as possible with an ethnically similar researcher. Central research questions were replicated in all sample groups although multiple methods were used across different ethnic groups. For example, the Pākeha women filled in the questionnaire alone and then debriefed in groups afterwards. Groups of Māori women met in separate groups in the evening as they were not so available at the weekends because of community responsibilities. They answered the questions by discussing each as they went. In keeping with a women-friendly culture, food and drink was supplied to all participants as part of the research process. Researchers from US, Pākeha NZ, Māori, Pacific Island and Japanese ethnicities acted as facilitators assisting each group. Power was actively shared amongst all participants but there were still asymmetries of power, and the white researchers led the process with 'input' from the 'others'.

In another cross-ethnic research situation I adopted a more removed, supervisory role in the research providing resources and acting as office anchor to two field workers[5] (one Māori and one Samoan) as they carried out research with their own people on the nature of women-run enterprises. I wished not to impose my views or power directly on the project. My active role took place in the office as a source of resources, supporter and mentor. This 'hands off' approach disadvantaged the analytical phase of the research. We successfully created summaries of the research for participants, but the bridge to the western academic community proved to be more challenging for I did not experience the field work and my researchers were not yet disciplined in the production of academic writing. I was too far removed from the cultural experiences of the interview to hear and see their world and I lacked the specific cultural knowledge for interpretation. I was relying on the 'others' to do the work of integration to educate me.

The two research partnerships that follow are described by all the researchers. We offer these as different styles of managing unequal power relations; the micro interpersonal relations serve to mitigate the macro power inequalities in ways that aim to maintain the integrity of the research.

BICULTURAL PARTNERSHIP: ELLA AND JUDITH

Judith: As we describe the project we highlight that we were interdependent researchers, working towards the same research objectives although we had different but equivalent roles. It was a bicultural research partnership, where we were equal collaborators combining reflections from separate projects on Māori women-run organizations and feminist organizations. We researched those like us – matching the ethnicities of the researcher and researched (Bell and Nkomo, 2001). Although we had common questions on organizational functioning, we conducted and summarized our studies separately. We drew and reflected on each of our experiences, encouraging each other to move forward confidently. In this situation we were two persons reaching across the void, both building the bridge – not leaving the 'other' to do the work of integration.

We conducted the research independently although we had a linked agenda to learn more about Māori and Pākeha women-run organizations. Ella studied women-run Māori organizations, both business and non-profit organizations that varied in their tikanga and their cultural awareness. I studied white women-run organisations that varied in the explicitness and implementation of their feminist ideology. We summarized our studies separately but also engaged in many conversations together; drawing and reflecting from each of our experiences – mirroring and matching (Henry and Pringle, 1996). Each of us encouraged the other to move forward confidently between the Māori and Pākeha worlds, thus the research process itself became a bicultural model.

Ella: Frequently wariness is felt by Māori women when they work with Pākeha women. So often white women's lack of acknowledgement of their own power means that they do not know when they abuse it. Successful research partnerships need a commitment from both partners; it goes both ways. Pākeha women researchers can be negatively perceived by Māori and it can be a harsh exchange. It is important that a white woman brings her assets – access to knowledge, institutional power and resources – and presents them as resources for empowerment rather than as a blunt instrument.

As I carried out my own postgraduate research I felt denuded as I read about what had been written about myself and my people. It was not only the writings of Pākeha but also some Māori men scholars as well. *Mana* is an important part of the research process and the koru of ethics (Henare, 2003) or the web of Māori beliefs that shape behaviour. Relationships were central to our research and to some extent it is encapsulated by the Māori tuakana–teina relationship; the elder/senior with the younger/junior. Who is the tuakana and who is the teina shifts with the settings. In Māori situations I am the tuakana and Judith is the teina; in the university setting I was the teina and Judith the tuakana. So self-reflexivity and adaptability play key roles. As I have written earlier, 'biculturalism is not about white people sharing power with "nice" Māori; it is about working toward structural change, toward a time when power sharing and mutual respect are the norm for Māori and Pākeha' (Pringle and Henry, 1993, p. 202). It is about authenticity, openness, honesty; and respect is central to this research relationship.

SHIFTING DYNAMICS: RACHEL AND JUDITH

Judith: In the most recent extensions of this bicultural research work I have deliberately played more of a background role. In this research I became more involved in all aspects of the process. In the interviews I took a background role as technician for the recording equipment and as a listener. I felt the warmth and engaged in the laughter. My education continued back in the office as I strove to understand some of the 'others'' worldview as outsider while my 'insider' co-researcher interpreted and explained the cultural meanings embedded in the narratives. I was able to reflect the social meaning against my memories and the audio and transcribed materials. My co-researcher, Rachel now picks up the narrative.

Rachel: My approach to research has been influenced by my early experiences in the university system. Upon entering the western academy, an identity construct was immediately imposed upon me as the institution branded me a 'double minority'. This was extremely uncomfortable and I experienced a degree of social and cultural distance previously unfamiliar to me even though I had entered the university system with extensive work experience, a cosmopolitan lifestyle and upbringing that included international travel, and a culturally diverse but connected family. Fortunately, leaders that had preceded me, both Māori and Pākeha, had established institutional facilities that eased these feelings of alienation.

However, these initial experiences left residual feelings of distance, unease and distrust in institutional processes. I became increasingly aware that I had entered a sphere of practice that was constructed outside of Māori or Pacific knowledge growth and learning paradigms. From the outset I decided that if I was to engage in any research and knowledge development in this institution it would be on my own terms or at least in situations wherein I would feel a sense of measured control over my own destiny. I also considered the research process itself as important as the outcome as I did not wish to reinforce the sense of distance and alienation that I had felt in the academy into the research endeavour. As a process, I believed research should be enjoyable, relaxed and engaged.

When Judith, as a senior academic, requested my participation as a co-researcher, I felt privileged as I was made to feel that my contributions and perspectives were important. I recognized the value that my own insights as an 'insider' bought in terms of qualification and representation of data but was equally careful not to take this for granted. This required constant reflection of my own assumptions and biases. This is an important facet of conscientization as a self-conscious and continuous process of reflexive learning. I was also aware of the need to respect the women and their respective communities whilst also according respect to my Pākeha co-researcher. In some instances there was an inversion of power relations with Judith relying on me to mediate relationships between her and co-participants. As a Pākeha researcher, she may not have been conscious of cultural nuances in social engagement and practices that occur which means that I would have to interpret and moderate situations and circumstances in a proactive manner. The relationship that developed in this research activity led to positive feelings of mutual trust and Judith became a primary supervisor for my doctoral thesis (Wolfgramm, 2007).

LESSONS LEARNED

The relationships between researcher and the researched are important in both feminist and Kaupapa Māori methodologies but this discussion re-oriented the lens to the research team. When seeking to create new knowledge, we believe that the research process itself must be considered. The research team itself should include diverse social identity groups that reflect different ontological positions. We argue that the nature of the relationship between researchers is a central concern in the development and execution of 'authentic' research – bridging indigenous knowing to western knowledge. The core of this research relationship is epitomized by the phrase 'researching with respect' (Bishop, 2005, p. 110), or maintaining the mana of all the people involved. When engaging across difference it is important to bring our whole selves to the research experiences and that may include our whakakapa (genealogical heritage) as well as our present abilities.

The experiences of cross-ethnic research partnership in Aotearoa/New Zealand discussed here demonstrate the flexibility of roles that are needed; in particular we have drawn attention to the shifting roles of insider–outsider and expert–novice across the research settings inside and outside of the university. The interpretation of 'findings', in this case the stories of organizational life by Māori and Pacific Island women, needed the involvement of individuals who understood the nuanced cultural knowledge and in most cases that understanding will come from members of that cultural community. The process of cross-cultural research conducted in shared bicultural partnerships brings conscientization; a continuous process of reflexive learning of power relations inflicted by the past. A consciousness-raising process that signals not just an increase in knowledge, but changes in hearts as well as minds to provide new understanding.

We have only just begun to develop research partnerships across what was a colonial divide, but the potential benefits are extensive. Clearly, both partners in these bicultural relations benefit. As we have shared our experiences of researching together with different audiences within academe, overall we have received positive and supportive responses. Critical management scholars have encouraged us to spread our story. Māori and Pacific Island postgraduate research students have been particularly excited by the open discussion of the research relationship; for many of them are still likely to be supervised by a Pākeha supervisor. Research relationships are usually shrouded in the cloak of academic rigour and institutional protocols. Scholars familiar with and involved in Kaupapa Māori research have been our most scrutinizing audience; constructively questioning our assumptions and urging us to go deeper.

Our hope is that this discussion may serve as a prompt for other colleagues deliberating similar issues. As researchers we can assume an active facilitative role, allowing multiple voices to be heard. Researchers do not act independently but we are all involved in a group process; a process whereby the researchers become whanau and together become part of the wider research community.

We have a more glorious goal of greater understanding, fewer disagreements and greater understanding between the cultures in Aotearoa/New Zealand. Working from our personal relationships, talking, writing and demonstrating them in educative and community settings, we are working towards emanicipatory goals for no less than the creation of a more inclusive country, *Ka Whawhai Tonu Matou – Struggle Without End* (Walker, 1990).

NOTES

1. Wahine is woman/women.
2. Whanau, hapu and iwi are groupings foundational to the organization of Māori society and may be loosely translated as extended family, sub-tribe and tribe (Wolfgramm, 2007).
3. Status, power.

4. Peoples from the Pacific Islands of the south west Pacific are a major immigrant group to Aotearoa/New Zealand. They come from islands such as Samoa, Cook Islands, Tonga, Niue and Tokalau.
5. Neither of these women are authors in this chapter.

REFERENCES

Bell, E. and S. Nkomo (2001), *Our Separate Ways: Black and White Women and the Struggle for Professional Identity*, Boston, MA: Harvard Business School Press.

Bishop, R. (2005), 'Freeing ourselves from neocolonial domination in research: A Kaupapa Māori approach to creating knowledge', in N. Denzin and Y. Lincoln (eds), *Handbook of Qualitative Research*, 3rd edition, Thousand Oaks, CA: Sage, pp. 109–38.

Durie, M (1998), *Te Mana, Te Kawanatanga: The Politics of Māori Self-determination*, Oxford University Press, Auckland.

Fine, M., L. Weis, S. Weseen and L. Wong (2000), 'For Whom? Qualitative research, representations and social responsibilities', in N. Denzin and Y. Lincoln (eds), *Handbook of Qualitative Research*, 2nd edition, London: Sage, pp. 107–31.

Harding, S. (1987), *Feminism and Methodology: Social Science Issues*, Bloomington: Indiana University Press.

Henare, M. (2003), 'The Changing Images of Nineteenth Century Māori Society, from Tribes to Nations', unpublished PhD, Victoria University of Wellington.

Henry, E. (1995), 'Rangatira wahine: Māori women and leadership', unpublished M. Phil thesis, University of Auckland.

Henry, E. and H. Pene (2001), 'Kaupapa Māori: Locating indigenous ontology, epistemology and methodology in the academy', *Organization*, **8** (2), 234–42.

Henry, E. and J.K. Pringle (1996), 'Making voices, being heard in Aotearoa/New Zealand', *Organization*, **3** (4), 534–40.

Hesse-Biber, S., C. Gilmartin and R. Lydenberg (eds) (1999), *Feminist Approaches to Theory and Methodology*, New York: Oxford University Press.

Johnston, P. and L. Pihama (1995), 'What counts as difference and what differences count: Gender, race and the politics of difference', in K. Irwin and I. Ramsden (eds), *Toi Wahine: Worlds of Māori Women*, Auckland: Penguin Books, pp. 75–86.

Jones, A. (2001), 'Cross-cultural pedagogy and the passion for ignorance', *Feminism and Psychology*, **11** (3), 279–92.

King, M. (2003), *Penguin History of New Zealand*, Auckland: Penguin Books.

Knox, C. and E. Henry (2008), 'Indigenisation of the MBA', poster presentation, Australian and New Zealand Academy of Management conference, University of Auckland, December.

Lal, J. (1999), 'Situating locations: The politics of self, identity and "other" in living and writing the text', in S. Hesse-Biber, C. Gilmartin and R. Lydenberg (eds), *Feminist Approaches to Theory and Methodology*, New York: Oxford University Press, pp. 100–137.

Lugones, M.C. and E. Spelman (1983), 'Have we got theory for you! Feminist theory, cultural imperialism and the demand or women's voice', *Women's Studies International Forum*, **6** (6), 573–81.

Narayan, U. (1995), 'Colonialism and its others: Considerations on rights and care discourses', *Hypatia*, **10** (2), 133–40.

Oakley, A. (1981), 'Interviewing women: A contradiction in terms', in H. Roberts (ed.), *Doing Feminist Research*, London: Routledge and Kegan Paul, pp. 30–61.

Olesen, V. (2005), 'Early millennial feminist qualitative research: Challenges and contours', in N. Denzin and Y. Lincoln (ed.), *Handbook of Qualitative Research*, 3rd edition, London: Sage, pp. 235–78.

Orange, C. (2004), *An Illustrated History of the Treaty of Waitangi*, Wellington: New Zealand: Bridget Williams Books.

Prasad, P., A.M. Konrad, and J.K. Pringle, (2006), 'Examining workplace diversity', in A.M. Konrad, P. Prasad and J.K. Pringle (eds), *Handbook of Workplace Diversity*, London: Sage, pp. 1–22.

Pringle, J.K. and E. Henry (1993), 'Diversity in women's organisations: Māori and Pākeha', Women's Studies Association Conference Proceedings, pp. 200–204.

Pringle, J.K and J. Park (1993), 'Transnational crosscultural research and feminist social science', in M. Cresswell (ed.), *Celebrating Women in Science*, Wellington: NZ Association for Women in Science, pp. 189–92.

Pringle, J.K. and R. Wolfgramm (2005), 'Ethnicity and gender in women's businesses in New Zealand', in S. Fielden and M. Davidson (eds), *International Handbook of Women and Small Business Entrepreneurship*, Cheltenham, UK and Northampton, MA, USA: Edward Elgar, pp. 133–47.

Ramazanoğlu, C. and J. Holland, (2002), *Feminist Methodology: Challenges and Choices*, London: Sage.

Reinharz, S. (1992), *Feminist Methods in Social Science*, New York: Oxford University Press.

Ritchie, J. (1992), *Becoming Bicultural*, Wellington: Huia Publishers and Daphne Braswell Associates.

Seuffert, N. (1997), 'Circumscribing knowledge in Aotearoa/New Zealand: Just epistemology', *Yearbook of New Zealand Jurisprudence*, (1), 97–125.

Smith, G. (1996), 'Kaupapa Māori as Theory and Praxis', unpublished doctoral thesis, University of Auckland.

Smith T.L. (1999), *Decolonizing Methodologies: Research and Indigenous People*, Dunedin: Otago University Press; New York: Zed Books.

Smith, T.L. (2005), 'On tricky ground: Researching the native in the age of uncertainty', in N. Denzin and Y. Lincoln (eds), *Handbook of Qualitative Research*, 3rd edition, Thousand Oaks, CA: Sage, pp. 85–107.

Spoonley, P. (2003), 'The challenge of cross-cultural research', in C. Davidson and M. Tolich (eds), *Social Science in New Zealand*, Auckland: Pearson Education.

Stanley, L and S. Wise (1993), *Breaking Out Again: Feminist Ontology and Epistemology*, London: Routledge.

Steyn, M. (2001), *Whiteness Just Isn't What It Used to Be: White Identity in a Changing South Africa*, Albany, NY: State University of New York Press.

Visweswaran, K. (1994), *Fictions of Feminist Ethnography*, Minneapolis: University of Minneapolis Press.

Walker, R. (1990), *Ka Whawhai Tonu Matau: Struggle Without End*, Auckland: Penguin.

Wolfgramm, R.M. (2007), 'Continuity and vitality of worldview(s) in organisational culture: Towards a Māori perspective', unpublished doctoral thesis, University of Auckland.

10. Making sense of gender: self reflections on the creation of plausible accounts

Albert J. Mills and Jean Helms Mills

INTRODUCTION: MAKING RETROSPECTIVE SENSE OF GENDER RESEARCH

In this chapter we reflect on twenty years of collaborative work in gender and organization studies. As we shall explain below, our research journey began with a more structuralist feminist focus and gradually shifted to a feminist post-structuralist lens, but one that is explored through our growing interest in sensemaking.

Our most recent journey began very much at the turn of the century when we turned our attention to Karl Weick's (1995) notion of organizational sensemaking as a potential heuristic for studying gender. In the process, we developed something we call critical sensemaking that allows us to focus on the power relations between sensemakers, and the contexts in which they are performed. However, in keeping with the sensemaking approach, we have also been drawn to the role of identity construction in the process of engaging in gender research. In this chapter we look back on the development of our various research projects, the turn towards sensemaking, and the role of identity construction. We conclude that critical sensemaking is a valuable heuristic for examining gender discrimination because it focuses on the situated nature of knowledge in a practical and positive way.

A VIEW FROM THE MIDDLE

To begin at the end or, more plausibly, the middle, we recently worked with Kathy Sanderson and Donna Boone Parsons, two of our PhD students, to complete a paper on Stewardesses for Women's Rights (SFWR), a short-lived, highly successful but troubled organization that operated in the mid-1970s. The organization was established by a small group of female flight attendants to fight for a range of women's rights in the United States commercial aviation industry. In the four short years of its existence it gained a lot of attention and support from leading feminists and effected a number of changes in the industry before collapsing in ignominy and in-fighting. Our interest in studying this organization was to find out what factors facilitate and what mitigate against all-female controlled organizations. For Donna this was part of a journey of feminist discovery, learning what she can about gender inequities and how to redress them. For Kathy, the manager of a women's drug and rehabilitation centre, this was the start of a more directly personal quest to improve the organizational processes and outcomes for the women she is involved with. For Jean and Albert this was another important piece in a life-time research strategy to find ways of dealing with discrimination at work. Four feminists, including a male 'aspirational feminist' (Mills, 1989), setting out to develop strategies for dealing with gender inequities.

The SFWR paper arose out of a government-funded grant to study the way that organizations become gendered over time. It was our third grant to be funded by the Social Sciences and Humanities Research Council of Canada (SSHRC). The first looked at the development of British Airways (Mills, 1995, 1996, 1998) over time, the second at Air Canada (Helms Mills, 2002; Mills and Helms Mills, 2004, 2006), and the third at Pan American Airways and commercial aviation in the United States (Mills, 2006).

These airline studies have formed the core of our collaboration on gender and organizations over the past fifteen years and have been informed by a developing methodological approach that we call critical sensemaking. Critical sensemaking arose out of a fusion of our post-structural (Albert) and sensemaking (Jean) approaches to gender and change. What constitutes critical sensemaking and how we use it to make sense of gender discrimination and our own selves in the process is the subject of the rest of this chapter.

CRITICAL SENSEMAKING AND AN ONGOING SENSE OF GENDERING

Critical sensemaking is a research strategy for understanding gender at work. It essentially draws on Weick's notion of organizational sensemaking (Weick, 1995, 2001), Mills' theory of organizational rules (Mills, 1988; Mills and Murgatroyd, 1991), and Foucault's concept of discourse (Foucault, 1979, 1980). It is an approach that developed out of our original collaboration as we sought to ground sensemaking in (post)structural arrangements (particularly organizational rules) to account for power and gendered relations. In the process we also found a way to explain the development, maintenance and changing of organizational rules through the tracing of socio-psychological (namely sensemaking) processes.

Simply put, Weick (1995, 2001) suggests that sensemaking is the outcome of seven socio-psychological properties – social sensemaking (that is, reflecting on an embedded sense located in shared social groups), retrospective sensemaking (that is, dealing with a sense of something after it has occurred), enactment (that is, translating a sense of something into action), plausibility (that is, weighing the comfort level or plausibility of an enacted sense), cues (that is, being influenced by selected cues) and identity construction (that is, the relationship between a sense of self and how something is made sense of). While sensemaking has a great potential for exploring agency in the social construction of events what, for us, was missing, was power (for example, are all sensemakers equal?), knowledge (for example, do all sensemakers invent/reinvent sense?), structure/context (for example, is sensemaking devoid of processes of structuration? (Giddens, 1976)), and, specifically for our own research interests, gender (for example, is the sensemaking process gender neutral?). To deal with power, knowledge, structure and gender we use sensemaking as a heuristic alongside critical discourse analysis (van Dijk, 1993).

However, it is not our purpose here to expand at length on critical sensemaking but rather to provide the basic outline of a method we shall use to position our own selves (and others) in the process of developing analyses of the gendering of organization. Those who are interested in the approach can follow its development through several iterations (Helms Mills and Mills, 2000, 2009; Helms Mills, 2003, 2004; O'Connell and Mills, 2003; Helms Mills and Weatherbee, 2006; Mullen et al., 2006; Mills, 2008; Thurlow, 2010).

ENACTING GENDER: FRAGMENTS IN TIME

Retrospective Sensemaking

In this section of the chapter we use critical sensemaking to explore the influence of what we call sensemaking communities on selected events and theoretical developments that we have been involved in. The chapter, thus, is itself a self-consciously retrospective sense of the development of ideas and strategies over time. To the extent we are successful (that is, read plausible) we will end up enacting our given sense of the events described.

What does this mean and how does it help us 'better' to understand the problematic of gendering and gender discrimination?[1] Retrospective sensemaking is a socio-psychological process whereby we act first and then make sense of our action. This is usually an iterative process but can be the outcome of dramatic changes that force us to rethink the sense of a situation. For example, in 1965 Albert witnessed an incident at a branch meeting of his union (National Union of Railwaymen). Attending his first meeting he noticed that a sole female member sat outside the door of the meeting room, waiting to be called. On entering the room she asked for specific union help, then left the room while the issue was being debated. It was only after Albert enquired as to why the woman had been asked to sit outside the room that an enacted sense was made of the situation. He was told that women do not usually like to attend and only come when they need specific help. Whatever the actual reasons for the relative non-attendance of female members, a sense of female union behaviour was enacted after the fact. However, within a relatively short period of time the widespread action and publicity of the women's liberation movement encouraged people to re-evaluate the sense they had been making of innumerable mundane and not so mundane (gendered) acts.

What we have come to learn from this is that the act of retrospection is an important process through which gendered practices are reproduced but also changed. In making sense of actions we may actually change the way they are viewed. However, as we shall show below, whether something is reproduced or changed will very much depend on a range of socio-psychological sense-making processes and their embedment in structured contexts.

We did not always take this view. At the start of our working and academic careers we subscribed to more structuralist and essentialist notions of gendered practices. Jean had spent seventeen years working as a customer agent in the Canadian airline industry before embarking on an academic career in 1993. She came from an industry marked by formal discriminatory practices (Kane, 1974; Newby, 1986) that were accompanied by a range of informal (hetero)sexualized behaviours (for example, employee parties and trips built around heavy drinking and sexual liaisons). For Jean the informal references to biology and heterosexual attraction served to normalize notions of men and women as essentially different, while the formal references to abilities linked to those essential differences jarred with her experience. There was a plausibility gap. She left the industry feeling that while men and women were essentially different, the company wrongly misused the supposed differences to discriminate against women. Thus, for Jean the challenge of sexual discrimination was not about the way that gender is socially constructed so much as about (sexist) attitudes and structural arrangements – what Canada's Royal Commission on inequities at work would call 'systemic discrimination' (Abella, 1984).

In a similar vein, Albert entered London Transport as an underground railway guard in the mid-1960s in an employment system that was rigidly gendered, with male-only train crews and female employees confined to a narrow range of jobs. A Marxist at the time, Albert viewed his discriminatory workplace as an outcome of capitalist ideology, which encouraged the view of women as sources of cheapened labour (either as cheap labour or as domestic labour – see Kuhn and Wolpe, 1978). While accepting that women were somehow (essentially) different from men, Albert believed that discrimination distorted the differences between the sexes for socio-economic gain.

For both of us there were underlying but unclear truths that – like feminist consciousness raising (Segal, 1996) – when revealed could expose gender discrimination at its roots. But those truths along with essentialism were eroded over time as we moved through different junctures.[2] However, as we move through our retrospective account of our changing approach to understanding gender discrimination it is important to be reminded that it is just that, a retrospective account. In other words, our story is constructed from selected events or cues, which are influenced by our current location within sensemaking communities. We shall return to this point at the end of the chapter.

Ongoing Sensemaking

Ongoing sensemaking can be thought of as a dominant flow of a sense of things, whose influence is felt through a series of interrelationships in which we are involved. In some ways it is like common sense, a shared sense of people and/or events that is accepted as normal and in common usage; so much so that failure to adopt a particular sense of a situation can be faulted for 'not showing common sense'. Albert encountered a powerful example of this when he first began teaching at Bradford and Ilkley College in West Yorkshire, England. This was the mid-1970s but there was still a strong ongoing sense that business was a man's world. It was not difficult to see how this ongoing sense was perpetuated. Much of the imagery of the business world was of male leaders, managers, professionals, skilled and unskilled employees – in annual reports (Tinker and Neimark, 1987; Benschop and Meihuizen, 2002), advertisements (Shields and Heinecken, 2002), television and film (Creedon, 1989), business magazines and other corporate materials (Mills, 1996). Worst still, much of the same imagery was embedded in many, if not most of the leading management textbooks and journal articles (Hearn and Parkin, 1983; Mills and Helms Hatfield, 1998). On the other hand, the women who constituted the majority in Albert's classes in 1978 had not got the message, or were prepared to ignore it. It was this disjuncture (gendered imagery and research versus a majority of female students) that spurred Albert's research into gender and organizations. The initial idea was to populate course materials with feminist studies – imported from sociology and women's studies – of work and organization.

During this initial phase it became apparent that while there were numerous feminist studies of work there was little or nothing from that perspective on organization. Feminists had more or less left the field of management and organizational studies to the malestream (O'Brien, 1981) managerialists who, in turn, had left gender out of account. Such was the field in the late 1970s that

Acker and van Houten's (1974) article in the *Administrative Sciences Quarterly* was almost completely unnoticed – it was not, for example, cited in business textbooks until the end of the 1990s (Mills, 2004). Kanter's (1977a) *Men and Women of the Corporation*, on the other hand, was almost instantly popular as much for the uniqueness of its contribution as its well written narrative. The fact that it faulted organizational structure rather than capitalism and patriarchy did not hurt. Nonetheless, even Kanter's work on gender was also hugely neglected by the management textbook (Mills, 2004).

It was as a reaction to this apparent lacunae of gender studies of organization that 'Organization, gender and culture' (Mills, 1988) came to be written, by which time excellent studies by Jeff Hearn and Wendy Parkin (Hearn and Parkin, 1987; Hearn et al. 1989), Gibson Burrell (1984), Barbara Gutek (1985), David Collinson (1988), and others were beginning to appear. The makings of a new sensemaking community were beginning to emerge.

At one level, these articles began to provide the basis for an alternative sense of gender. At another level they all grappled with the root cause of the existing dominant ongoing sense of gendered reality. 'Organization, gender and culture', for example, made the case for a 'materialist feminist' analyses of the complex of organizational rules that constitute the cultures of organizations, that is, the structural contexts in which sense of gender is made.

It would take several more years before anti-discriminatory views constituted an alternative ongoing sense within which multitudes of retrospective accounts were/could be developed. This has meant that an important element of the struggle to convince people of the need for employment equity is addressed through an important (alternative) ongoing sense of gender at work. While it was possible in the early 1980s to list the number of scholars and scholarly works dealing with gender at work by the mid-1990s it was impossible due to the proliferation of feminist and gender studies within the field of management and organization. That is not to say that current generations of students are necessarily confronted with research on gender at work; far from it. Gender research is an important alternative ongoing sense but, as we describe below, there are still far too many business schools where it is completely missing from the curriculum. As we were to discover, much of the process of translating a given ongoing sense of gender might well depend on involvement in sensemaking communities that serve as important conduits of sensemaking.

Social Sensemaking

As generations of feminist scholars have observed, social forces shape gendered outcomes, whether those outcomes are negative (for example, attitudes to female abilities – Spender and Sarah, 1980) or supportive (for example, 'consciousness raising' – Skevington and Baker, 1989). In the latter case, feminists have fostered the idea of support groups and organizations to counterbalance those social forces that negatively influence women's perceptions of self. The Stewardesses for Women's Rights, for example, was one such group that both fought for changes in women's working conditions while offering an ongoing support group to build the confidence of women in the commercial aviation industry. Within feminist organizational analysis Kanter (1977a) and Gutek (1985) have both spoken of the importance of having a critical mass of women at work in order to build on shared experiences that can make employment equity more plausible, while Ferguson (1984) has called on feminists to develop workplace support groups to develop alternative discourses at work. The message is as important for those researching gender inequities as the disadvantaged women they are writing about. The existence of supportive sensemaking communities can be vital for sustaining gender research and making it plausible to increasing audiences of people.

One thing that was broadly lacking within management and organization studies in the late 1970s and early 1980s was the existence of feminist sensemaking communities. Nowhere was this more evident than in the scholarly associations. A 1973 Academy of Management (AoM) report on the 'Participation of Women', for example, stated that 'women currently play a relatively minor role' in the association (Bartol et al. 1973, p. 1). By the end of the decade there was an AoM 'Status of Women Interest Group' and it was not until well into the 1980s that a Women in Management Division was established. It was to be some years later before similar 'interest' groups were established in equivalent Canadian (the Administrative Sciences Association of Canada) and UK (British Academy of Management) associations. The initial absence of such communities made it difficult to sustain a sense of morale or to make a plausible case against systemic discrimination. This was especially the case in the face of an ongoing sense of women's place in business that was dominated by 'malestream' points of view.

By the late 1980s things were beginning to change and those of us teaching business (specifically management and organization theory) were able to renew our optimism periodically by attending WIM sessions at the Academy of Management and similar caucuses in academia. Inevitably feminist organizational scholars sought each other out. Albert, for example, invited Gibson Burrell, Jeff Hearn and Wendy Parkin to address his Bradford students. The following year he took over part of Jeff Hearn's teaching while he was on sabbatical leave. Some time later, having moved to Canada, Albert was able to gain university funding to explore feminist analyses of organizational culture and, in the process, meet up with Peta Tancred and Linda Smircich. These meetings were followed by two important initiatives that Albert became involved in. The first was in the fall of 1988 when Linda Smircich and Marta

Calas brought together a group of 32 feminists and organizational scholars, in Snowbird, Utah, to encourage mutual interest in feminism and organizational analysis. The group included Silvia Gherardi, Mark Meier, Ella Bell, Kathy Ferguson, Stella Nkomo, Gareth Morgan, Jane Flax, Roy Jacques, Sandra Harding, Karl Weick, and several other prominent scholars in their respective fields. Although a planned book from the conference never materialized, the event had a profound influence on the participants, and contributed to the emergence of a feminist poststructuralist presence in gender studies of management and organization. The second contribution to an emerging sense-making community of feminist organizational scholars came out of the meeting with Peta and was in the form of an edited book – *Gendering Organizational Analysis* (Mills and Tancred, 1992). The book was as much designed to pay homage to that feminist community as to reflect on the gender research of its authors: in addition to Albert, the book included four of the participants of the Snowbird conference – Linda Smircich, Marta Calas, Ella Bell and Stella Nkomo.

About the time that *Gendering Organizational Analysis* was being pulled together Jean had entered a PhD programme in the UK, with a dissertation focused on two 'hot' topics of the day – organizational culture and change. In a department consisting of a combination of organizational sociologists and social psychologists she developed a theoretical model combining insights from organizational rules theory (Mills and Murgatroyd, 1991) and activity theory (Blackler, 1992, 1993). While convinced that 'rules' served as important heuristics in guiding and constraining activity Jean was nonetheless dissatisfied with the inability of either rules or activity theory to explain agency in the micro processes that linked rules with activity. In her search for a solution she came, quite serendipitously, upon the work of Karl Weick. She had wanted 'to make sense' of her data – based on a longitudinal study of a Canadian utility company undergoing a series of changes – so was cued to Weick's (1995) book that promised *Sensemaking in Organizations*.

In the process of fusing together sensemaking and organizational rules Jean began to wonder about the potentially gendered character of organizational change. Did gender, for example, influence the way sense was made of change? Did change influence a sense of gender? But she did not get very far with this line of questioning. She was discouraged from focusing on gender. She was confronted with 'a sense of reality' that arose from a direct sense-making environment that lacked feminist, gender scholars and female academics, and a group of academics that ignored gender studies because they felt that it was unimportant and/or that it would be detrimental to a PhD student's academic career. Lacking power and the support of a feminist community Jean heeded the advice to leave gender out of account but she did manage to include a critique of the gender neutrality of Weick's sensemaking, and an outline of further research on gender, culture and organizational change in the concluding chapter of her thesis. Some time later, now as part of a community of feminist organizational scholars, Jean was able to develop a gender analysis of her data (Helms Mills, 2005).

Identity

Identity work is a crucial part of the struggle to address inequities at work. It ranges from women struggling to be taken seriously as organizational members (Ferguson, 1984), men fighting to maintain a sense of masculinity in the changing workplace (Livingstone and Luxton, 1989), people of colour dealing with the double jeopardy of race and gender (Bell et al., 2001), a multiple of people coping with their sexual identities at work (Schneider, 1982), and researchers who attempt to juggle their own identities as they study the lives of others.

Jean's attempt to include gender in her PhD work, for example, was, in part, influenced by the identity work of the various actors involved. To begin with, one of her advisors conveyed a sense that gender studies were marginal within management and organization studies. This was made plausible by the fact that the overwhelming majority of the literature on organizational culture and change completly ignored gender (Mills, 1988a). There was a sense that involvement in gender studies could be problematic for academic identity, including the stereotyping of female researchers as self-interested and methodologically weak, a questioning of male researchers' masculinity, and doubts about the scientific rigour of the studies produced. Jean was encouraged to embrace this sense of academic identity and build a career around identification with organizational change, organizational culture and sensemaking.

Interestingly enough, while Jean, a Canadian, was receiving this advice in her British university, Albert, a British-born scholar, was receiving similar advice from a senior administrator at his Canadian university. In this case, because of his developing track record in gender studies, Albert was advised to make his résumé seem 'less like that of a woman's' if he wanted to progress further in academia.

Our own identity work has not all been negative, far from it. Much of it has been complex rather than simply good, bad or indifferent. As a 'man in feminism', for example, Albert periodically has to face questions about his identity that speak to his motives, competence and sexuality. This can range from the close (male) friend who refrained from telling sexually explicit jokes around Albert for fear that it would offend him. Or students who take a long time to respond to Albert's jokes because they are not sure how far they are allowed to see gender as humorous. This speaks to expectations of a display of identity that is consistent with the observer's sense of what a man doing feminist research should be like. Not too 'masculine', but more gender-neutral (and neutered) in terms of displays of sexuality and behaviour. It can and has led to expectations of overperformance where administrators and colleagues signal that numbers of publications may compensate for their gender focus. Both Jean and Albert have experienced that kind of problem, with Jean being told at a promotion hearing at a previous university that she 'published too much with the same publisher'. She was turned down for the promotion despite being in the university's top 5 per cent of those doing research of any kind.

The issue of identity crops up in various other ways. This is often the case when publications require some kind of biography. There you get the opportunity to craft a sense of self. It would be an interesting study to examine the different ways that researchers present themselves to different audiences. The most common we suspect is to reference as many publications as possible to present as a legitimate scholar. In two cases Albert was asked to present an identity that was to be common to all male contributors in a book. In the first case, the male scholars were to identify themselves with the label 'feminist supporter'. Feeling that 'supporter' sounded too removed Albert opted for 'aspirational feminist' to capture the notion that (a) as a man he could only aspire to be a feminist and (b) that feminism should be seen as something to be constantly strived for rather than a fixed end in itself. In the second case, the requirement was a referencing to Connell's (1995) notion of 'hegemonic masculinity' as part of a broader identity project. For various reasons, not least of which was a resistance to a perceived notion of the editor's hegemonic masculinity, Albert withdrew from the project.

Probably the more constant identity work comes from our own relationship as a married couple that undertakes joint research projects: we even work in the same university department. It is a constant process to avoid gendered perceptions of our separate roles in the process of research. Nonetheless, we have managed to be seen as a dual personality at times and two separate researchers on other occasions, even to the extent of our election as the first co-chairs of an Academy of Management Division (Critical Management Studies), where, although standing as 'one', Jean managed to receive more votes!

Plausible Accounts and Enacted Realities

In a personal and a practical way we have come to learn that if we want to have our sense of reality taken seriously, that is, enacted, it has to be plausible but it also has to be responsible. This simple point is much more complex than we may have once thought. Weick (1995) contends that we accept a sense of something not so much because it is accurate but that it is plausible. However, plausibility, as we have discovered, is something of a moving target. It may well depend, among other things, on powerful discourses that prevail through-out a particular community, and the passage of time. For example, women were rarely hired by the UK railway companies or the Post Office in the nine-teenth century but by the first half of the twentieth century while the railways continued to hire few women the Post Office employed large numbers, and the emergent commercial aviation business hired a sizeable minority of women (Mills, 2006). While it was plausible to hire women in one industry it was implausible in another.

The same is true about enactment of ideas about discrimination, that is, conference presentations and publications. While the employment of women had flourished in North America during World War II the Cold War era saw reversals of many of the advances in attitudes to women's abilities (Friedan, 1963). Management theory in the United States, which largely developed in the Cold War era, barely referenced women, female employees, gender, or sexual discrimination (Mills and Helms Hatfield, 1998; Runte and Mills, 2006) – a situation that continued throughout much of the 1960s and 1970s despite the advent of the women's liberation movement.

In the 1980s the field of feminist organizational analysis and gender stud-ies began to take off as two different communities of feminists began to make an impact. On the one hand, there were a disparate group of feminists from outside the management field – usually sociology – who were arguing for challenges to capitalism and patriarchy. Many of this group came from the Marxist and socialist left, including Janet Wolff (1977) , Joan Acker (1988) and Rosabeth Moss Kanter (1977b). The other group, including many within the Women in Management Division of the Academy of Management, were arguing for changes in the professional and managerial ranks of the system. All were united in arguing for women's rights but beyond that they constituted very different sub-groups within those associated with feminist organizational analysis. There were two (and clearly more) discourses, each with different cues of plausibilities. 'Organization, gender and culture' (Mills, 1988) was very much written with the left feminist discourses in mind.

However, by the early 1990s the collapse of communism had created new sensemaking possibilities for many on the left, with a number of formerly Marxist scholars, including feminists, turning towards poststructuralist accounts of management and organization theory. One related outcome was a renaming of the Women in Management Division of the Academy of Management the Gender and Diversity in Organizations Division (GDO), with more of a focus on the socially constructed character of race and gender and away from its strongly essentialist and managerialist biases. The influence of poststructuralism and feminist poststructuralism in new journals (for example, *Organization*; *Gender, Work and Organization*; *Culture and Organization*) and conferences (for example, Critical Management Studies; Gender, Work and

Organization) has influenced the way gender studies in management have developed and the cues of plausibility, that is, the ways that accounts are structured and argued. That is not to say that feminist poststructuralist accounts are the dominant force in feminist accounts of management and organization but rather that it is an important influence and one we have been drawn to. Indeed, mainstream journals and conferences in the field continue to ignore gender for the most part and privilege functionalist liberal feminist accounts (Calas and Smircich, 2005) when they do pay attention. Interestingly enough the GDO Division of the Academy of Management has returned to a more liberal feminist dominance.

This means that the battle over ongoing sensemaking still has a long way to go but should be seen as a constant process of change, which now includes more space for different alternative views of reality. With this realization there goes the responsibility of knowing that enactment of a given sense of reality has the power to influence someone else's understanding (or sense). To that end, we have a duty to warn them that this is our perspective that, while based to the best of our ability to attempt to construct a sense of equity, is only ever partial and changing.

TOWARDS THE END OF THE MIDDLE

In reflecting on some of our own journeys and the lessons learned we return to our opening comments about the nature of retrospective sensemaking. We firmly believe that critical sensemaking can help us in the struggle for greater equity. If we can understand the socio-psychological processes by which discriminatory acts and rules occur we are better able to address them but we also need to situate and understand our own role in the process. Retrospection is an area for change if we can develop strategies of plausibility. Undermining the plausibility of gendered, discriminatory rules and practices can open space for alternative senses. Building alliances and support groups, we contend, goes beyond simply strength in numbers, rather it provides an all important sensemaking community from which to build plausible alternatives. In all this we need to reflect on the influences on our own sensemaking accounts, particularly our identity work. We also need to understand the changing character of plausibility and how our own understanding and strategies need to change in the process.

In this way a powerful lesson to be learned is the situated nature of knowledge. This directs our own (research) role in the process and how we contribute to a given sense of a situation through our translation (or enacted sense). To that extent we need to reflect on the influence of our own enactments and the potential power relations involved. It also directs our attention to the fact that sensemaking, as ongoing, changes from setting to setting and over time and thus gendered practices need to be dealt with not through some universal strategy but through examination of local practices. It tells us that strategies of change are always ongoing, as a sense of a situation always relies on the maintenance of plausibility. And finally it tells us that some changes, although seemingly small, may disturb the plausibility of a situation and open up the possibilities of change.

NOTES

1. For us gendering refers to the outcome of processes that associate ways of thinking and behaviours with the sexual identity of a person. Gender discrimination refers to those situations where gendering results in the privileging of one embodiment (usually male) over another. Thus, for example, symbols on toilet doors encourage gendered thoughts but are not necessarily discriminatory in their outcomes.
2. Defined as 'a concurrence of events in time in which a series of images, impressions and experiences come together, giving the appearance of a coherent whole that influences how an [era] is understood' (Mills (2010).

REFERENCES

Abella, R.S. (1984), *Equity in Employment. A Royal Commission Report*, Ottawa: Ministry of Supply and Services Canada.

Acker, J. (1988), 'Class, gender and the relations of distribution', *Signs* (13), 473–97.

Acker, J. and van Houten, D.R. (1974), 'Differential recruitment and control: the sex structuring of organizations', *Administrative Science Quarterly* (9), 152–63.

Bartol, K.M., Pledger, R., Steade, B.A., Higginson, M.V., Filley, A.C. and Hellriegel, D. (1973), 'Participation of Women in the Activities of the Academy of Management. A Preliminary Report', *Academy of Management Archives*, Ithica, NY: in the Kheel Center for Labor–Management Documentation and Archives, Martin P. Catherwood Library, Cornell University.

Bell, E.L., Edmonson, J.E. and Nkomo, S.M. (2001), *Our Separate Ways: Black and White Women and the Struggle for Professional Identity*, Boston: Harvard Business School Press.

Benschop, Y. and Meihuizen, H.E. (2002), 'Reporting Gender: Representations of Gender in Financial and Annual Reports', in I. Aaltio and A.J. Mills (eds), *Gender, Identity and the Culture of Organizations*, London: Routledge, pp. 160–84.

Blackler, F. (1992), 'Formative Contexts and Activity Systems: Postmodern Approaches to the Management of Change', in M. Reed and M. Hughes (eds), *Rethinking Organization*, London: Sage, pp. 273–94.

Blackler, F. (1993), 'Knowledge and the theory of organisations: organisations as activity systems and the reframing of management', *Journal of Management Studies* (30), 863–84.

Burrell, G. (1984), 'Sex and organizational analysis', *Organization Studies* (5), 97–118.

Calas, M. and Smircich, L. (2005), 'From the "Woman's Point of View" Ten Years

Later: Towards a Feminist Organization Studies', in S. Clegg, C. Hardy, T. Lawrence and W. Nord (eds), *The Sage Handbook of Organization Studies*, London: Sage.

Collinson, D.L. (1988), 'Engineering humour: masculinity, joking and conflict in shopfloor relations', *Organization Studies* (9), 181–99.

Connell, R.W. (1995), *Masculinities*, Berkeley, CA: University of California Press.

Creedon, P.J. (ed.) (1989), *Women in Mass Communication: Challenging Gender Values*, Newbury Park: Sage Publications.

Ferguson, K.E. (1984), *The Feminist Case Against Bureaucracy*, Philadelphia, PA: Temple University Press.

Foucault, M. (1979), *Discipline and Punish: The Birth of the Prison*, New York: Vintage Books.

Foucault, M. (1980), *Power/Knowledge*, New York: Pantheon.

Friedan, B. (1963), *The Feminist Mystique*, New York: Dell.

Giddens, A. (1976), *New Rules of Sociological Method: A Positive Critique of Interpretative Sociologies*, London: Hutchinson.

Gutek, B.A. (1985), *Sex and the Workplace*, San Francisco: Jossey-Bass.

Hearn, J. and Parkin, P.W. (1983), 'Gender and organizations: a selective review and a critique of a neglected area', *Organization Studies* (4), 219–42.

Hearn, J. and Parkin, P.W. (1987), *'Sex' at 'Work' – The Power and Paradox of Organizational Sexuality*, Brighton: Wheatsheaf.

Hearn, J., Sheppard, D.L., Tancred-Sheriff, P. and Burrell, G. (eds) (1989), *The Sexuality of Organization*, London, Newbury Park: Sage.

Helms Mills, J. (2002), 'Employment practices and the gendering of Air Canada's culture during its Trans Canada Airlines days', *Culture and Organization* (8), 117–28.

Helms Mills, J. (2003), *Making Sense of Organizational Change*, London: Routledge.

Helms Mills, J. (2004), 'Sensemaking Perspective', in C. Vibert, *Theories of Macro Organizational Behaviour*, Armonk, NY: M.E. Sharpe, pp. 134–9.

Helms Mills, J. (2005), 'Representations of diversity and organizational change in a North American utility company', *Gender, Work and Organization* (12), 242–69.

Helms Mills, J. and Mills, A.J. (2000), 'Rules, Sensemaking, Formative Contexts and Discourse in the Gendering of Organizational Culture', in N.M. Ashkanasy, C.P.M. Wilderom and M.F. Peterson (eds), *Handbook of Organizational Culture and Climate*, Thousand Oaks, CA: Sage, pp. 55–70.

Helms Mills, J. and Mills, A.J. (2009), 'Critical Sensemaking and Workplace inequities', in M. Ozbilgin, *Theory and Scholarship in Equality, Diversity and Inclusion at Work: a Research Companion*, Cheltenham, UK and Northampton, MA, USA: Edward Elgar, pp. 171–8.

Helms Mills, J. and Weatherbee, T. (2006), 'Hurricanes hardly happen: sensemaking as a framework for understanding organizational disasters', *Culture and Organization* (12), 265–79.

Kane, P. (1974), *Sex Objects in the Sky*, Chicago, IL: Follett.

Kanter, R.M. (1977a), *Men and Women of the Corporation*, New York: Basic Books.

Kanter, R.M. (1977b), *Work and Family in the United States: A Critical Review and Agenda for Research and Policy*, New York: Russell Sage Foundation.

Kuhn, A. and Wolpe, A. (1978), *Feminism and Materialism: Women and Modes of Production*, London: Routledge & Kegan Paul Ltd.

Livingstone, D.W, and Luxton, M. (1989), 'Gender consciousness at work: modifications of the male breadwinner norm among steelworkers and their spouses', *The Canadian Review of Sociology and Anthropology* (26), 240–75.

Mills, A.J. (1988), 'Organization, gender and culture', *Organization Studies* (9), 351–69.

Mills, A.J. (1989), 'Gender, sexuality and organization theory', in J. Hearn, D.L. Sheppard, P. Tancred-Sheriff and G. Burrell, *The Sexuality of Organization*, London: Sage, pp. 29–44.

Mills, A.J. (1995), 'Man/aging subjectivity, silencing diversity: organizational imagery in the airline industry – the case of British Airways', *Organization* (2), 243–69.

Mills, A.J. (1996), 'Corporate Image, Gendered Subjects and the Company Newsletter – The Changing Faces of British Airways', in G. Palmer and S. Clegg (eds), *Constituting Management: Markets, Meanings And Identities*, Berlin: de Gruyter, pp. 191–211.

Mills, A.J. (1998), 'Cockpits, hangars, boys and galleys: corporate masculinities and the development of British Airways', *Gender, Work and Organization* (5), 172–88.

Mills, A.J. (2004), 'Feminist Organizational Analysis and the Business Textbook', in D.E. Hodgson and C. Carter (eds), *Management Knowledge and the New Employee*, London: Ashgate, pp. 30–48.

Mills, A.J. (2006), *Sex, Strategy and the Stratosphere: The Gendering of Airline Cultures*, London: Palgrave Macmillan.

Mills, A.J. (2008), 'Getting Critical About Sensemaking', in D. Barry and H. Hansen (eds), *The Sage Handbook of New Approaches to Organization Studies*, London: Sage.

Mills, A.J. (2010), 'Juncture', in A.J. Mills, G. Durepos and E. Weibe, *Sage Encylopedia of Case Study Research*, Thousands Oaks, CA: Sage, pp. 509–11.

Mills, A.J. and Helms Hatfield, J. (1998), 'From Imperialism to Globalization: internationalization and the Management Text', in S.R. Clegg, E. Ibarra and L. Bueno (eds), *Theories of the Management Process: Making Sense Through Difference*, Thousand Oaks, CA: Sage, pp. 37–67.

Mills, A.J. and Helms Mills, J.C. (2004), 'When Plausibility Fails: Towards a Critical Sensemaking Approach to Resistance', in R. Thomas, A.J. Mills, and J.C. Helms Mills (eds), *Identity Politics at Work: Resisting Gender and Gendered Resistance*, London: Routledge, pp. 141–59.

Mills, A.J. and Helms Mills, J. (2006), 'Masculinity and the making of Trans-Canada Air Lines, 1937–1940: a feminist poststructuralist account', *Canadian Journal of Administrative Sciences* (23), 34–44.

Mills, A.J. and Murgatroyd, S.J. (1991), *Organizational Rules: A Framework for Understanding Organizations*, Milton Keynes: Open University Press.

Mills, A.J. and Tancred, P. (eds) (1992), *Gendering Organizational Analysis*, Newbury Park, CA: Sage.

Mullen, J., Vladi, N. and Mills, A.J. (2006), 'Making sense of the Walkerton crisis', *Culture and Organization* (12), 207–20.

Newby, N.J. (1986), *The Sky's The Limit*, Vancouver, BC: Mitchell Press Ltd.

O'Brien, M. (1981), *The Politics of Reproduction*, London: Routledge and Kegan Paul.

O'Connell, C.J. and Mills, A.J. (2003), 'Making sense of bad news: the media, sensemaking and organizational crisis', *Canadian Journal of Communication* (28), 323–39.

Runte, M. and Mills, A.J. (2006), 'Cold War, chilly climate: exploring the roots of gendered discourse in organization and management theory', *Human Relations* (59), 695–720.

Schneider, B.E. (1982), 'Consciousness about sexual harassment among heterosexual and lesbian women workers', *Journal of Social Issues* (38), 75–98.

Segal, A. (1996), 'Flowering feminism: consciousness raising at work', *Journal of Change Management* (9), 75–90.

Shields, V.R. and Heinecken, D. (2002), *Measuring Up: How Advertising Images Shape Gender Identity*, Philadelphia: University of Pennsylvania Press.

Skevington, S. and Baker, D. (eds) (1989), *The Social Identity of Women*, London: Sage.

Spender, D. and Sarah, E. (eds) (1980), *Learning to Lose: Sexism and Education*, London: The Women's Press.

Thurlow, A. (2010), 'Critical Sensemaking', in A.J. Mills, G. Durepos and E. Weibe (eds), *Sage Encyclopedia of Case Study Research, vol. I*, Thousand Oaks, CA: Sage, pp. 257–60.

Tinker, T. and Neimark, M. (1987), 'The role of annual reports in gender and class contradictions at General Motors: 1917–76', *Accounting, Organizations and Society* (12), 71–88.

van Dijk, T.A. (1993), 'Principles of critical discourse analysis', *Discourse and Society* (4), 249–83.

Weick, K.E. (1995), *Sensemaking in Organizations*, London: Sage.

Weick, K.E. (2001), *Making Sense of the Organization*, Oxford: Blackwell.

Wolff, J. (1977), 'Women in Organizations', in S. Clegg and D. Dunkerley, *Critical Issues in Organizations*, London: Routledge and Kegan Paul, pp. 7–20.

11. Carving a niche for a feminist scholar: shifting academic identities in UK universities

Beverly Dawn Metcalfe

INTRODUCTION

The growth of business and management studies programmes at both the undergraduate and postgraduate level throughout the 1990s in the UK saw the development of traditional business areas in organization behaviour, marketing, strategy, finance and operations. In the mid 1990s a number of university departments began to include human resource management (HRM) and international management as part of their curriculum structure. Organizational behaviour (OB) was a core business and management subject, and yet the vast majority of organizational behaviour texts did not include gender or diversity as topics of study. The publication of Fiona Wilson's *Organization Behaviour and Gender* in 1995 filled a complete void in the literature and provided valuable source material for studies of gender and diversity in organizations. However, where gender, diversity and organization studies have been a component of programmes they have been so as an option, not as a core subject.

Today, gender and diversity subject is slowly being written out of new business curriculums (Metcalfe, 2008). Globalization and competitive education markets have further reinforced gendered organizational cultures, and in respect of business curriculums have resulted in equality and diversity being withdrawn from option module lists. Equality and inclusion issues are now likely to be included only as a one week session in an HRM/OB module (Metcalfe, 2008). This development is reflected in the downturn of women's studies programmes in the UK and in the integration of specialist gender centres into broad interdisciplinary sociology departments (Riley et al., 2006; Oxford, 2008). The current state of teaching gender and diversity in the UK is thus characterized by dynamic educational policy developments, together with ongoing debate about the nature and value of diversity research and scholarship.

Given this context, in this chapter I would like to offer positive reflections of my academic identity management over 13 years in higher education while teaching a range of undergraduate and postgraduate equality and diversity courses, in three UK institutions. This feminist identity management is characterized by an appreciation of the formation and reformation of diverse identities and power relations in learning environments that I have experienced (Alvesson and Wilmott, 2002). This ongoing process of identity formation shows how identity management is 'played out', and how individuals are empowered, or not, to subvert, resist or remake their identities (Collinson, 2003: 257). This social constructionist perspective acknowledges the disciplinary discourses that shape individual identities, but also that identity is negotiated through discursive agency by navigating cultural repertoires. I argue that feminist identity management in higher education is difficult terrain to navigate, and moulded and shaped by a myriad of 'hidden transcripts' (Morley, 1999, 2006) that help frame gender relations. These gendering processes do not take place visibly but are subtly embedded in the organization and social daily practices that are part of teaching (Deem and Morely, 2006; Martin, 2007). This academic navigation involves an awareness of, and constant assertion against, deeply entrenched institutional conventions and hegemonic practices which hinder personal, political or critical engagement (Stanley and Wise, 2006). In navigating my personal academic terrain I reveal the opportunities and obstacles to do identity work 'differently' (Halford and Leonard, 1999).

To illustrate identity management processes I draw on the work of Yuval-Davies (2006) who asserts that the politics of belonging can help assist feminist academics achieve emancipatory aims for social development (see also Hughes, 2002). Yuval-Davies describes the politics of belonging as being concerned with identity management, and in forming secure attachments allowing one to feel part of a community. Belonging involves acknowledging identities and identifications, and critiquing individual and collective narratives of self and other. Belonging is also about the differential ways in which people articulate belonging to organizations as well as appreciating the social and political effects of displacement, and disconnections/marginalizations from those communities. Yuval-Davies states: 'Belonging is where the sociology of emotions interfaces with the sociology of power, where identification and participation collude' (2006: 197). These observations are central to understanding oneself as a critical feminist practitioner, and in this case, in university institutions.

I will sketch my academic career of 'doing' and 'teaching' diversity in three institutions and show how I was fully integrated in the academic communities, or even displaced, working the margins/borders. In the first teaching role in a post 92 university[1] I show how my academic identity was positioned on the 'margins' of organization and management theory, yet I resisted this discursive positioning by 'standing up' for feminist organization analysis. In the second role, in a pre 92 Russell group university, in a social science faculty I reveal how both gender subjects and identity were 'mainstreamed' and central to the ethos of an international development department. In the third role, although in a pre 92 and traditional university I outline how my academic identity shifted to the marginal position in organization studies once again. In tracing these experiences through three institutions I aim to provide a reflexive review and draw out the interplay of social and organizing processes that help constitute how I engage/enact gender and diversity teaching and research. I also show how I resist this positioning in different social, cultural and political contexts (Hughes, 2002; Collinson, 2003).

FEMINIST, GENDER AND DIVERSITY STUDIES IN THE UK ACADEMY

There is a great deal of literature that has emerged in the UK management Academy that is concerned with the gendered dynamics that shape understandings of management curriculums (Deem and Morley, 2006); the learners' experiences and also the teacher's identity position (Barry et al., 2006; Metcalfe, 2008). Universities have been described by feminist and other radical scholars as major centres of white middle class privilege and power, harbouring the Western values of male dominated hierarchies (usually white) where existing power relations get reproduced through competitiveness and through myths of objectivity and meritocracy (Hughes, 2002; Jackson, 2002; (Deem and Morley, 2006). As highlighted at the beginning of this chapter, this perhaps reflects the lack of interest in business faculties in gender and diversity subjects, its displaced position and illustrates the difficult climate that academics have to navigate. That is, not only are feminist academic identities seen out of place in the malestream culture in business schools, but the subject domain of gender and diversity itself is afforded lesser than status. Marketization, semesterization and increasing quality surveillance regimes reinforce masculinist management education curriculums (Simpson, 2006). The limited coverage of gender and diversity issues in key organization and management journals has also positioned gender and diversity researchers, and the subject, in another place/community (Ozgilbin, 2009).

NAVIGATING FEMINIST ACADEMIC IDENTITIES

It is important to note from the start that I have consciously navigated my academic career with two complementary/interwoven identities, a management academic and a feminist academic researching management. Perhaps like Collinson (2003) suggests I engaged in 'survival' strategies within disciplinary regimes to 'secure' my sense of self in physical, economic and symbolic realms. My PhD which was in the feminist sociology of organizations would have ideally placed me in a women's studies or sociology department. As there are very few job openings in these areas I was advised by my PhD supervisor to develop general HR expertise, an HR identity if you like, as this was more marketable. Organizational scholars note that researchers who focus on gender and diversity have tended to be seen as different, on the margins, and outside of 'malestream' organization research/interests (Katila and Merilainen, 2002; Sinclair, 2002, 2007).

STARTING FROM THE MARGINS: STANDING UP FOR FEMINIST THEORY AND ORGANIZATION ANALYSIS

I will begin my journey at Staffordshire University Business School where I was appointed as a lecturer grade at age 29 in 1995 and was one of the youngest in a predominantly male (65), white department numbering 105. The student population was primarily from the UK. It is also of note that a large number of faculty staff were over 50 (approximately 75 per cent). There were only two male professors and the majority of the female faculty at lecturer grade. The institution was primarily teaching focused with ambitions to develop research capability hence my appointment. Despite having two Masters and consultancy experience my role was largely confined to UG teaching. I was given responsibility to establish from scratch three subject areas related to my Masters work: gender and diversity in organizations, human resource development and International HRM. In addition to curriculum design I was given administrative responsibility for all UG dissertations, pastoral support for international students as well as being research co-ordinator.

The socio-cultural and political context of Staffordshire University was markedly different to other UK institutions. In 1995 Staffordshire was one of only two universities in the UK that was led by a recently appointed female Vice Chancellor, Professor Christine King. Professor King was committed to promoting women in academic roles and had just published a practice-oriented text entitled *Through the Glass Ceiling: Effective Senior Management Development for Women.* She had been Head of and actively involved in the formation of a government body promoting women in senior public administration. Hence, within the UK university community Staffordshire was perceived as a leading proponent in supporting diversity and equality agendas in society. However, while the 'sole' senior female may support greater inclusion and diversity in terms of academic representations and in terms of curricula, this did not necessarily follow that support for gender agendas was widespread in university departments. The structural and cultural organizing arrangements reproduced gender hierarchies, with male academics in senior decision-making roles as Directors and Subject Heads, and female academics predominantly engaged in administration. In addition, a large number of older male faculty had been recruited from local organizations and this sub-group, with expertise in areas such as finance and operations, with local connections and networks, as well as managerial authority, helped create a cultural environment that supported masculinist behaviours. These organizational arrangements reflected the development of 'new managerialism' in UK universities (Deem and Brahoney, 2005) which emphasized the importance of private sector practices such as increasing measures for performance monitoring and control, as well as managerial structures that represented local business interests. The academic culture thus provided a dynamic organizational space that both supported and contested feminist agendas.

At Staffordshire I led an UG module in 'Gender and Diversity in Organizations' and had significant freedom in the curriculum design. The module contained developments in feminist theorizing, critical race studies, gender and organization studies including critical men's studies as well as more general policy-oriented aspects of equality and HR planning. One colleague critically commented 'You teach feminisms?' both aghast and impressed that it was included in the BA Business Studies curriculum, since it did not fit with the traditional operations management, strategy and finance portfolio. Another questioned whether feminist theory was relevant to diversity and human resource policies. While I have experienced that most students do not initially want to hear about the gendered pay gap and male dominance in management, and the general belief that diversity and equality is not relevant for *their* generation, in 'keeping it real' and grounding diversity issues relevant to everyday lives of students I was able to make feminist consciousness-raising efforts to engage students via popular film and media representations (such as *Ally McBeal* and *Prime Suspect* TV programmes). Despite attempts to streamline curriculums and drop the option, the course's popularity and high student rankings, however, allowed me to 'save' the module.

As one of the youngest faculty I was risky and daring, in purposely articulating my feminist concerns, as well as integrating feminist ideas in learning interventions and faculty meetings. In terms of securing a sense of professional self I felt I had to manage my discursive positioning in this way. I was resisting articulations of patriarchal notions of professional identity that made me feel uncomfortable, a place I did not belong . As a young female lecturer my voice had little influence on strategic development decisions of the business school. I was not on key resource or decision-making committees. Diversity subjects were not valued as modes of study. This was demonstrated when I was excluded from a PhD workshop the faculty organized to assist research development. The Research Director communicated to me that gender was not an important area of study for the business school. This was reaffirmed several times publicly at research and teaching faculty meetings as a way of displacing me, and the gender subject, from the mainstream academic community.

I resisted this displacement by further forging space for feminist teaching and voice. I actively identified myself as a feminist in departmental meetings and promoted gender issues through the Professional Women's Development Network (PWDN), a regional women's networking organization that provided support to women in business and was supported by the Vice Chancellor. In addition, together with the Vice Chancellor I undertook consultancy activities for local government which focused on development strategies required to meet the obligations of the Opportunity 2000 initiative launched by the government in 1991.[2] The 'riskiness' of this academic positioning however, was mediated through a strategic organizational and leadership lens that was female (Professor Christine King). The cultural environment allowed me to 'play' this risky identity. The support of the Vice Chancellor enabled one to be more 'empowered' as a feminist academic.

Naming yourself as a feminist teaching and research scholar however, can also unveil power relationships and make identity work fraught with anxiety and tension. Scholars have shown that doing management education in the wrong body can cause anxiety and tension (Swan, 2005; Sinclair, 2006), since bodies are inscribed surfaces of events and are interpreted in gendered ways. Being the only gender and diversity researcher (and one of only a few young female academics) this clearly positioned me as 'different from' other business academics. In discursively positioning me as 'other', the questioning of gender research acted as a surveillance device, probing my academic and body competence and worth (Morley, 2006). Working in this gendered organization culture where managerial practices undermined who I was, what I did, and what I stood for undoubtedly affected my confidence, and raised emotional dilemmas for feeling safe, secure and valued.

To summarize, there was a moving interplay of opportunities and constraints for me to play with my identity and discursively move in the academic space at Staffordshire. While a senior female leader supported my gender and diversity work, the politics at department level, and the general negative cultural labels of teaching gender associated with biases about what feminism is and can do, along with the 'riskiness' of being labelled a feminist academic, meant that I was positioned on the margins of the business faculty. However, my commitment to standing up for feminist theory and organization analysis meant that I carved a space for a professional self (Collinson, 2003). In the next stage of my academic journey I reveal how being re-positioned in a different subject environment offers a female academic further opportunities to carve a niche and play with identity.

SHIFTING TO THE MAINSTREAM: FROM FEMINIST ORGANIZATION THEORY TO GENDER AND DEVELOPMENT

In 2000 I moved to Manchester University to the Management, Governance and Development research centre, a part of the Institute for Development Policy and Management (IDPM) which has existed since 1953. The institute provides only PG teaching, as well as research and consultancy services. It is regarded as one of the leading international development centres globally both in terms of teaching, research and policy development. The student population is primarily from developing or transition countries and the faculty, although predominantly male (75 per cent), is culturally diverse, representing many ethnicities and nationalities. In contrast to Staffordshire organization and managerial structures are premised on a traditional collegiate system with academic leadership and administrative roles shared and routinely rotated. Within an international development community comprising political scientists, sociologists, economists and management scholars, gender and diversity research concerns are seen as a 'central' and 'key' category of social analysis.

Importantly, IDPM as an international development centre has played a role in 'shaping' global discourses of gender and development and provides a transnational location in which feminist and women's issues in developing countries can be taught and researched. The cultural and political environment thus nurtures an academic space that unites those 'marginalized' and 'disconnected' sections of organizations, communities and societies. Consequently, as a feminist scholar I was positioned as being at the centre of academic debates. This academic 'legitimacy' provided a belonging space (Yuval-Davies, 2006) that felt comfortable and safe and allowed me to pursue feminist-oriented teaching and research, and carve a feminist professional identity.

Within this supportive environment I developed a curriculum that focused on comparative and international diversity management and examined how the socio-cultural and economic environments in different geographic spaces shaped dominant/salient diversity and gender themes (Metcalfe, 2008). Since these were knowledge terrains that were 'new' and 'unfolding' I was encouraged by the department to focus on women's empowerment issues in developing countries and address specifically the organization and managerial dimensions of inequality that inhibit women's advance in the political and public sphere. I was also afforded the opportunity to work overseas on consultancy assignments and it was at this time that I first began working in the Middle East for women's NGO organizations, providing training workshops and advice on women's employment rights and leadership development.

In terms of my own career I subsequently developed research expertise on gender, identity and development in Eastern Europe and more recently in the Middle East. The integration of these literatures uncovers how feminist movements have evolved very differently and that gender work regimes have subtle and nuanced differences and fluid social organizing arrangements (World Bank, 2003; Acker, 2005).

My experiences at Manchester reveal that a feminist academic identity can shift to the centre and be positioned as 'mainstream' in development discourses/departments. Importantly this academic environment empowered me to forge an academic identity and allowed me as a gender practioner to feel comfortable in my body doing feminist education (Sinclair, 2006). This re-examination of situated self and organizational practices (Yuval-Davies, 2006) helped me question dominant theorizings of gender, identity and space, better understand the complex process of academic identity formation, and invigorated my own intellectual journey in trying to explore transnational feminist movements and the implications this had for work and organization.

SHIFTING TO THE MARGINS AGAIN: INTERNATIONALIZING DIVERSITY AND EQUALITY CURRICULUMS

A promotion to Hull University in 2004 saw my research and teaching status as a gender expert 'shift' to being on the margins again in a business faculty (Barry et al., 2006). The faculty was predominantly male (70 per cent) including fifteen professors, only one of which was female. The socio-cultural political environment was similar to Staffordshire University. Hull has gendered organization structures and management processes. It currently runs MBA programmes in Oman and Bahrain and my management expertise in the Middle East was one of the key reasons that I was employed. However, teaching allocation and departmental administration and management was not based on subject expertise or knowledge. Workloads and teaching assignments were largely premised on time served status, the majority being white males in their 50s. The political organization of teaching meant that all overseas work (which was paid extra) was allocated to a small number of white men and one white woman, all of whom had long service histories and were not research-active. The gendered organization of work had thus become culturally embedded in management decision-making processes and structures over many years. This meant that new recruits, who were predominantly research-active, were more likely to be positioned as 'outsiders' primarily in terms of their research status with limited possibilities to do overseas work. Similar to Staffordshire University, gender and diversity research was positioned on the 'margins' of 'malestream' organization research.

However, I resisted this 'marginal' and remedial status in essence through two positioning strategies. Firstly, the 'internationalizing' of the management curriculum in UK business schools. This involves incorporating global dimensions in management curriculums. Consequently I began to 'remake' (Collinson, 2003) my academic identity by stressing the international oriented aspect of my work and highlighted my cross-cultural teaching experience. Secondly, I refocused the practitioner orientation inherent in academic work and built on my women's management training experience gleaned in public institutions in the UK and women's organizations in the Middle East. In 'remaking' this international identity I have carved a niche in terms of my research and teaching in the Eastern Europe and Middle East and feel that I am making a difference.

The carving of this academic niche was intense and emotionally challenging (Alvesson and Wilmott, 2002). I 'subverted' (Collinson, 2003) the gender organizing arrangements in Hull by sidestepping subject line authority. I outlined my 'international credentials' to the Dean and I was immediately assigned overseas work in Bahrain and Oman. While undertaking MBA work there I was able to gain access to women's NGOs and get involved in women's leadership training and development. In the following I briefly outline how doing gender and doing gender research in the Middle East is empowering in respect of academic identity.

The subject of women's management education and development in the Middle East make for a fascinating case study on account of gender and globalization debates and the role that Islam plays in forming gender roles and identities in the home and work sphere (Badran, 2005). Globalization has transformed women's private and public roles in complex ways in Middle East states (Acker, 2005). The Middle East region has the lowest levels of female labour participation in the world, yet paradoxically many of the regions universities women outnumber men (Metcalfe, 2007).

There are cultural differences in terms of the way in which women only training is viewed. In the UK and Western developed economies, women only skills training has been strongly criticized as reinforcing the different qualities of women, as well as serving as a mechanism to marginalize women and gender issues. Moreover, where these programmes do exist they rarely focus on philosophical debates of inequality and difference, nor on feminist and race theory, but skills and competency development. In contrast, in the Middle East women only programmes are seen as necessary in countering the inequalities and injustices that women have faced. An equal but different philosophy puts a premium on the value of sex differences, acknowledging that men and women may require different policy frameworks to enable equal participation in the public sphere. An appreciation of feminist theory and equal rights in education curriculums is seen as important in understanding the struggles women have to manage in less egalitarian societies.

In the Middle East there is generally great support for all scholars and female academics who are engaged in encouraging women's skills development. Unlike the UK where it is often felt that feminism and equality in business education is something that does not belong to this generation, as it has been 'done' and 'achieved'; in the Middle East, the discourses of feminism and women's empowerment are seen as an important process of economic and social development. The social and cultural frames position me as knowledgeable, and in having an important political role to play in developing women's skills to further their advance in the public sphere. My academic identity is thus empowered to articulate feminist organization principles. This academic identity work is fascinating terrain to navigate as it highlights how social and organizational discourses that abound about gender relations and feminist work are culturally and historically constituted. Right here, right now, in the Middle East feminist identity work can be empowering, and make a political difference. Feminist political rhetoric is seen as socially relevant and necessary to ongoing debates about human rights and individual freedoms. This is not the case in universities, and within dominant societal culture in the UK. Right here, right now, in UK education contexts feminist identity work is tremendously risky, since feminist ideas and activism are seen as passé. Equal opportunities it is assumed have been achieved. The global landscape of doing gender and teaching gender is thus characterized by fluidity and risky terrain to navigate and requires us to 'craft' and 'remake' identities to both fit in and reminds us that gender relations and gender identities is on ongoing social process (Gherardi, 1995).

CONCLUSION: REFLECTING ON SHIFTING ACADEMIC IDENTITIES: CONSCIOUSNESS RAISING, COMMUNICATION AND FEMINIST ACTION

This chapter has explored shifting academic identities in UK universities. I have shown through sharing my experiences of working in three UK universities and in Middle East women's associations that academic identity work is not stable or fixed, but involves exploring the various ways identity work is 'played out' and how individuals are empowered, or not, to subvert, resist or remake their identities (Collinson, 2003: 527). As I suggested at the beginning of this chapter I have navigated this terrain and played my part in accordance with the opportunities and constraints provided. This reveals that we are able to simultaneously occupy many subject positions, identities and allegiances at work, as part of managerial and organizational processes that require us to sustain identity work. I explored how my identity shifted from the borders of the academy, to the centre and back to the borders again. Characterized also by Alvesson and Wilmott's (2002) 'intensive' remedial identity work I stressed that the challenge for me throughout this journey was to hold on to my sense of professional competence. Navigating these different academic identities creates ambiguities and intensifies identity work.

Organization commentators note that competing discourses are constantly at play and intersecting that help shape organizational subjectivities and experiences. As Yuval-Davies (2006) highlights, identity work involves exploring where one belongs, is connected or disconnected. Gender relations in organizations and communities, and the subject of gender as an academic field of study need to be considered within the many interweaving landscapes that help constitute identity positions: the local, ethnic, national and state equality and diversity regulatory frameworks, as well as the institutional and informal everyday practices that govern communication between individuals in organizations and societies. I suggest that these multilayered dimensions can be seen to operate on three levels. At the societal level there is a need to assess the extent to which a particular societal culture is responsive or not to specific diversity agendas. This incorporates how the structural, cultural and political ideologies in nation states help shape gender and inequality regimes, and ultimately how this influences the formation in broader educational policy developments. The second level relates to the organizational culture and how the social norms and organizing processes create and produce gendered hierarchies and gendered meanings and effects. This also incorporates whether the subject of gender and diversity itself is considered worthy of inclusion in the subject terrain in specific institutions. The final level of analysis is at the individual academic level. Here, identity plays are made up through navigating the myriad of societal and organizational frames/discourses that help position who one is.

At the societal level there are undoubtedly equality and diversity agendas that make salient, or conversely silence/marginalize diversity issues within specific cultural spaces. In UK university institutions gender and equality curriculums are incorporated in HRM syllabuses and largely marginalized. In contrast, the Middle East (which has arguably many challenges in terms of gender equality) has acknowledged the significance of improving gender disparities. This is perhaps best illustrated by differing spatial and geographic concerns as evidenced in the descriptions of doing and teaching gender. In the Middle East, dominant societal discourses of empowering women legitimize and support gender talk and gender development issues. One can actively articulate a feminist identity in the public sphere and feel comfortable and safe. In contrast, to articulate feminist identities in both the UK and Eastern Europe is risky. Women's subject positions are disciplined by anti-feminist discourses.

Secondly, academic cultures have a significant influence on how much, and what, gender, diversity and teaching is included and counted, and the opportunities and obstacles that they provide for 'doing gender' and 'doing gender and diversity research'. Business schools on the whole, and this seems true in other western cultures such as Finland and Sweden, rarely see gender and diversity as significant and central to management curriculums. The masculinist cultures predominant in UK academia also serve to marginalize the academic identity work of gender researchers. The subject is kept alive by those scholars who have dual researcher identities, and can offer other knowledge expertise in additional management areas.

However, there are academic spaces where gender and diversity agendas are valued, and where the feminist label is an accepted part of that identity. Academics can discursively play the feminist role confidently. As my own experience at Manchester University suggests, gender scholarship united together with international management and business studies, in particular in the Middle East, is a relatively new subject domain and offers academics the opportunity to fashion 'internationalized' identities. I have carved this niche and made a difference both theoretically and in terms of practical interventions for empowering women. I have made these advances by 'positioning' my academic identity and locating it within feminist spaces that are interested in the same debates and theoretical issues that I am interested in, such as the gender and development (GAD) group and Gender in Management Special Interest Group (GIMSIG). Moreover, these academic groups bring together those marginalized/disconnected, create unity of purpose and sustain commitment to social and political action.

However, while I have highlighted the largely positive experiences of my academic journey, I would still suggest that feminist academic identity management is still difficult terrain to navigate (Metcalfe, 2008). Having experienced marginalized status in business schools, being aware of the dominant discourses that abound about academic authority and academic expertise means identity work has to be in constant play, remade and reconfigured (Hughes, 2002; Katila and Merilainen; 2002). As highlighted at the beginning of this chapter organizational surveillance schemes require ongoing efforts to secure professional competence and status (Collinson, 2003). Female professors find it difficult to sustain an authoritative position in organization structures and cultures that are gendered.

The forgoing suggests that learning to do gender and diversity in UK universities is an interactive and embodied process that requires intellectual connection between students and educators (McNay, 2000; Sinclair, 2006). What I hopefully revealed is that while my identity work was ambiguous and fragile, this was not necessarily attempting to fashion an appropriate professional identity required in business schools, but skirt the borders (Alvesson and Wilmott, 2002). That is, I resisted disciplinary professionalizing effects. As both Collinson (2003) and Yuval-Davies (2006) argue, this fluid approach suggests that men and women are active agents in their body/learning/education positioning, they can play with, and resist, gender identity positions. Discursive agency provides a space for how women knowledgeably, competently and flexibly draw upon, interpret and reinterpret cultural discourses (Metcalfe, 2008). And importantly, in writing about my academic experiences of teaching gender, diversity and inclusion I have created a further space for articulating resistance to dominant discourses of management and organization (Halford and Leonard, 1999). I hope that through my embodied, contexualized and critical accounts I have opened up opportunities for scholars to feel again that the personal is political, and that feminist theorizing is important in contributing to management education and curriculums (see Simpson, 2006; Sinclair, 2006, 2007). Being aware of the politics of belonging is thus an important academic tool and armour to carve a confident academic subject position. While I definitely see myself as a feminist sociologist, rather than 'belonging' to women's studies and organization studies, I am happy to be associated with all three, for they have coexisted within my professional life. My career has been as both an 'other' and as an organization and international management theorist. Thinking about academic identities in a way which positions such hybridic interests as 'other' to some supposed core does not reflect the intellectual complexities which in fact continue to characterize the careers of many professional organization scholars. Management and organization should remain an open intellectual space in to which develop hybridic intellectual and political/ethical combinations, but which form a unity in diversity. Working the borders in business schools, however, is an emotionally challenging process, calling for reaffirmations of credibility and legitimacy that is inherent in identity work in academe. Sustaining an academic identity that is professionally valued and is comfortable for oneself is 'really hard work' (see Collinson, 2003; Sinclair, 2006).

NOTES

1. In the UK a pre 92 university is a traditional university usually with a long heritage, has always held the status of university, has an academic bias and is often conceived of as elite institution. A small number of pre 92 universities have formed an alliance called the Russell Group (inter alia: Manchester, Durham, Oxford) which represents the collective interests to the

government of the leading universities in the UK. Post 92 universities were originally poly-technics and given university status in 1992 and have historically had a vocational orienta-tion, although recently many have established active research cultures.

2. Opportunity 2000 now renamed Opportunity Now was a government initiative to try and raise the profile of gender and diversity issues in HR planning. The initiative was intended to provide organizations with a 'quality' label if they had shown that in their HR policy devel-opment and training they could show good practice in respect of diversity and inclusion in workforce management. This has not been realized.

REFERENCES

Acker, J. (2005), 'Gender, capitalism and globalization', *Critical Sociology*, **30**(1), 17–41.

Alvesson, M. and Wilmott, H. (2002), 'Identity regulation as organizational control: Producing the appropriate individual', *Journal of Management Studies*, **39**(5), 619–44.

Badran, M. (2005), 'Between secular and Islamic feminism/s: Reflections on the Middle East and beyond', *Journal of Middle East Women's Studies*, **1**(1) Winter, 6–29.

Barry, J., Berg, E. and Chandler, J. (2006), 'Academic shape shifting: Gender, manage-ment and identities in Sweden and England', *Organization*, **13**(2), 275–98.

Collinson, D.C. (2003), 'Identities and securities: Selves at work', *Organization*, **10**(3), 527–47.

Deem, R. and Brahoney, K.J. (2005), 'New managerialism in higher education', *Oxford Review of Education*, **31**(2), 217–35.

Deem, R. and Morley, L. (2006), 'Diversity in the Academy? Staff perceptions of equality policies in six contemporary higher education institutions', *Policy Futures in Education*, **4**(2), 185–202.

Gherardi, S. (1995), *Gender, Symbolism and Organizational Cultures*, London: Sage.

Halford, S. and Leonard, P. (1999), 'New identities, professionalism, managerialism and the construction of the self', in M. Exworthy and S. Halford (eds), *Professionals and New Managerialism in the Public Sector*, Buckingham, Oxford University Press.

Hughes, C. (2002), 'Pedagogies of and for resistance', in G. Howie and A. Tauchert (eds), *Gender, Teaching and Research in Higher Education: Challenges for the 21st Century*, Aldershot, Ashgate.

Jackson, S. (2002), 'Transcending boundaries: Women, research and teaching in the Academy', in G. Howie and A. Tauchert (eds), *Gender, Teaching and Research in Higher Education: Challenges for the 21st Century*, Aldershot, Ashgate.

Katila, S. and Merilainen, S. (2002), 'Metamorphis: From nice girls to nice bitches: resisting patriarchal articulations of professional identity', *Gender Work and Organization*, 3, 335–54.

King, C.F. (1993), *Through the Glass Ceiling: Effective Senior Management Development for Women*, London: Hodder and Stoughton.

McNay, L. (2000), *Gender and Agency: Reconfiguring the Subject in Feminist and Social Theory*, Cambridge, Polity.

Martin, P.Y. (2007), 'Seeing and doing gender at work', in J. Lorber (ed.), *Gender Inequality: Feminist Theories and Politics*, Oxford, Oxford University Press.

Metcalfe, B.D. (2007), 'Gender and HRM in the Middle East', *International Journal of Human Resource Management*, **18** (1), 54–75.

Metcalfe, B.D. (2008), 'A feminist poststructuralist analysis of HRD: Why bodies, power and reflexivity matter', *Human Resource Development International*, **11**(5), 445–65.

Morley, L. (1999), *Organising Feminisms: Micropolitics of the Academy*, London: Palgrave Macmillan.

Morley, L. (2006), 'Hidden transcripts: The micropolitics of gender in Commonwealth Universities', *Women's Studies International Forum*, **29**(6), 543–51.

Oxford, E. (2008), 'Still second among equals', *Times Higher Education Supplement*, March, 30–35.

Ozgilbin, M. (2009), 'From journal rankings to making sense of the world', *Academy of Management Learning and Education*, **8**(1), 113–21.

Riley, S., Frith, H., Archer, L. and Veseley, L. (2006), 'Institutional sexism in academia', *The Psychologist*, **19**, 94–7.

Simpson, R. (2006), 'Feminising the MBA', *Academy of Management Learning and Education*, **5**(2), 182–94.

Sinclair, A. (2002), 'Teaching managers about masculinities: Are you kidding?', *Management Learning*, **31**(1), 89–104.

Sinclair, A. (2006), 'Body and management pedagogy', *Gender, Work and Organization*, **12**(1), 89–104.

Sinclair, A. (2007), 'Teaching leadership critically to MBAs', *Management Learning*, **38**(4), 461–75.

Stanley, L. and Wise, S. (2006), 'Having it all: A future for feminist research', in Kathy Davis, K. Evans and J. Lorber (eds), *Handbook of Gender and Women's Studies*, London, Sage Publications, pp. 430–70.

Swan, E. (2005), 'On bodies' rhinestones and pleasures: Women teaching managers', *Management Learning*, **36** (3), 317–33.

Wilson, F. (1995), *Organization Behaviour and Gender* (revised edition 2003), London: Ashgate.

World Bank (2003), *Gender and Development in the Middle East and North Africa; Women in the Public Sphere*, Washington, World Bank.

Yuval-Davies N. (2006), 'Intersectionality and feminist politics', *European Journal of Women's Studies*, **13**(3), 193–210.

12. Carrying on the collaborative effort: becoming academics in the wake of a feminist intervention project

Elina Henttonen and Kirsi LaPointe

INTRODUCTION

We represent a new generation of gender scholars in our academic work community; the unit of Organization and Management at Helsinki School of Economics, Finland. The purpose of this chapter is to discuss the construction of our professional identities as academics in the wake of a feminist intervention project undertaken by two former colleagues, Saija Katila and Susan Meriläinen, who also serve as the editors of this book (for published details of the projects see Katila and Meriläinen 1999, 2002). Our perspective in this chapter is that of female doctoral students who are in the process of learning what it means to be an academic. We both have a Master's degree in Organization and Management from our unit and began our doctoral studies in 2002 – some time after the most active debate concerning Saija's and Susan's participatory interventions had subsided.

Saija and Susan's feminist interventions date back to their five-year research project which started in 1996. The aim of their participative, action-oriented project was to make visible and change practices that were constraining the construction of women's professional identities in our unit, and to open up discussion about gender discrimination and unequal power relations in academia (Katila and Meriläinen 1999, p. 164). As part of their project, Saija and Susan used their own experiences and incidents from the unit to analyse and write about the apparent gender-neutrality of organizational discourses. Moreover, they openly challenged these practices by sharing and discussing their results with colleagues as well as with the wider community in the university.

Reflecting on the impact of their project (Meriläinen 2001), Susan points out two achievements. Firstly, women have become more visible in the unit and sensitivity towards the problematic nature of gendered discourses has increased. She offers two possible explanations for this: one, that members of the community have become more politically correct; or two, they may have become more aware of underlying assumptions of the gendered discourses and their effects. Secondly, and perhaps as the most visible expression of these interventions, has been the changing status of gender studies in the unit. Unlike previously, it is now considered a legitimate research area and included as a (small) part of the teaching curriculum. Moreover, the collaboration with feminist researchers in other units of the university has increased (Meriläinen et al. 2009).

Our purpose here is not to evaluate the impact of their project or the efforts of the work community per se, but offer our experiences for comparison. Although entry into the unit and the positions we have occupied differ, both of us have been engaged in research, teaching and daily organizational life. Our shared experience has been marked by a contradictory sense of a tolerant and supportive work community on one hand, and a disturbing awareness of, and exposure to, various practices of inclusion and exclusion on the other. To make sense of these experiences, and in relation to the work of our former colleagues, we will use as our theoretical resources the perspectives of professional identity construction (for example Davies and Thomas 2002), doing gender (for example West and Zimmerman 1987; Gherardi 1994; Katila and Meriläinen 1999) and practices of exclusion/inclusion in academia (for example Martin 1994; Elg and Jonnergård 2003). In particular, we will reflect on our differences and similarities as women doctoral candidates and gender researchers in terms of the practices of exclusion and inclusion in our socialization and identity development as academics. We illustrate our experiences by focusing on the specific themes of gaining membership in the community, establishing supportive collegial relationships, pursuing openly feminist (research) agendas and finding our academic voices and identities.

We have structured our reflections in the form of a dialogue to reflect the results of the exchange of ideas and the new insights we gained during the writing process. Moreover, this format allows us to make sense of the contradictory experience of our work community both as a special and supportive environment in which to work and as a contested arena of covert organizational politics and exclusionary power relations. Finally, we will conclude by summarizing with what we consider to be the main consequences and benefits of the intervention project and by discussing the challenges that remain now and those that might be expected in the future.

TEN YEARS AFTER: A DIALOGUE

The dialogue that follows represents our experiences as female doctoral students constructing professional identities as academics several years after

the most active phase of Saija's and Susan's interventions. As a research
community our unit has a long history of continuous development and an open
and supportive culture that encourages diversity and novel approaches. As a
result, several members of the community have been actively engaged in
developing alternative ways of doing research, teaching and being an academic. Also doctoral students are expected to choose their own research topics
independently, rather than working on professors' projects, and are allowed a
relatively flexible time frame to complete their doctorates (Meriläinen et al.
2009). Whereas Elina has been a full-time researcher on a gender research
project at the department and been exposed to the unit's practices from the
start, for the first two years Kirsi received separate grant funding and her
participation in the unit was sporadic until she took up teaching responsibilities and was therefore given a workspace. It was only after taking parental
leave and getting a full-time employment contract in 2007 that she became
fully engaged in the everyday formal and informal life of the unit.

Gaining Membership in the Community

K: How did you end up becoming a doctoral student at this unit?

E: While I was studying for my Master's degree it bothered me that I had not
found any special topic or theme during my studies that I would feel particularly enthusiastic about. I was feeling confused about what to focus on in my
Master's thesis, let alone in my life after graduation. I wanted to do something
meaningful with my life but the obvious career choice of business students,
that is, working in the business world, did not attract me.

 Then, I found out about a doctoral course on 'Feminist approaches to organizational studies' that was taught by Saija and Susan. This course represents a
genuine turning point in my studies. Even though I had been exposed to gender
issues before – by reading some feminist classics from my mother's bookshelf,
for example – I could not imagine how I could work or build a career with these
issues with my business degree. However, the course opened up a novel
perspective to my studies as it showed a vast terrain of issues in areas of organization and management calling for gender analysis. Even more important was
that I became acquainted with gender researchers and saw that people do have
these kinds of interest in academia and they are able to work on them.

 Then, just before my graduation, Susan recommended me for a gender-
related research project at our unit (which she was also personally involved in)
led by Päivi Eriksson (who has since left the unit and been appointed as a
professor at another university). After joining the project, I applied to the
doctoral programme and began my doctoral studies. Thanks to Päivi and
Susan, I got an excellent (and probably exceptional) start to my research

career: to work as a salaried employee in a gender research project supervised by two competent feminist researchers. After three years in this project, I was chosen for a three-year junior researcher position in our unit and just recently was re-nominated for this position for another three years. How about you?

K: My decision to begin doctoral studies was a result of years of intense reflection and searching. During my undergraduate studies, I felt as you did – no great enthusiastic feeling about any of the topics. It just took me a bit longer to figure it out what would be meaningful work for me. I do remember two courses from my studies that I found engaging: a course on gender in philosophy and another on research methods. However, they only helped me to see that something was missing but back then I didn't know how to fill in the void. To make the long story short, about ten years later the small start-up company I had worked for went under and I found myself writing a research plan on a topic I had been interested in for a while.

Actually, I hesitated about going back to a business school, for many reasons, but the years have proven to me it was a good choice. I feel that our unit has offered me a safe space and encouragement to grow as a researcher and develop my academic voice. Also, there seems to be a genuine openness towards alternative approaches and topics outside mainstream management and business research. Early on in my studies, I experienced a sense of finding a community where issues close to my heart, such as meaningful work/careers, identity construction and gender issues, were considered not only legitimate but important and worthy of dedication. After years of feeling a bit dislocated, this gradually growing sense of belongingness has been very rewarding and comforting. In my previous jobs in corporate education and HR consulting, gendered practices were one significant source of these feelings of not-fitting-in. However, this kind of understanding has only come after learning in my doctoral studies about research on the gendered practices in management and organizations.

Everyday Interaction and Gendered Practices

K: Now that I have reread Saija's and Susan's articles they have had, once again, a powerful impact on me. I was shocked, appalled, disgusted. In some ways I found the vivid examples of particular incidents very extreme, yet completely believable and familiar. While I admired the courage of their participatory project and their resistance and felt empowered by their act of making the female experiences visible, I also realized another impact of their work: in our unit, something has changed. Thinking back on my experiences, I do not remember one single event where I would have felt being openly discriminated against or not taken seriously due to my gender.

E: The everyday practices have certainly changed. The process seems to have taught the members of our unit sensitivity regarding how social and discursive gendering practices are sustained and reproduced, and how they can be done differently. It is a delight, and this happens often, to notice how someone says something very gendered and suddenly realizes how he or she might or should have phrased the issue differently. For example, I have been apologized to for being referred to as 'a girl' in a professional context. These are important achievements, because often the less visible and less overt discrimination, such as unequal discursive positioning, is the most difficult form of discrimination to grasp and account for.

K: Finnish people tend to think that we are a very equal country, and business students in particular seem to be reluctant to admit that gender would play a role in working life and its practices. In our unit the myth of gender neutrality has been identified which has resulted in sensitivity to gender issues. At the individual level, there are of course differences. However it has been quite amazing to hear gender-sensitive comments and understanding of the process of gendering among people whose research work has nothing to do with gender; or they think it doesn't – in my reading most topics in organization and management are gendered in one way or another.

E: This is indeed something that I personally find one of the most important contributions of Saija's and Susan's work: awareness, how we all, including myself, are part of the discursive production of gender inequalities, both at work and other spheres of life, such as bringing up my daughter. Nowadays I pay more attention to my own discursive practices – including how I profile my research and describe my academic success – and how I use both verbal and physical space in interactive situations, such as seminars and personnel meetings. What's more, this awareness has helped me to resist gendered categorizations in academic situations. When I have been told that 'Oh, you have such a nice and special perspective' (gender studies) I have publicly pointed out the contradictory nature of the term 'nice' and 'special'. When I have received comments on my looks, I have been able to respond by 'Why don't you ask about my research, it's more interesting'.

K: I have also become more aware of how I do gender although it can be very difficult to identify the role of gender in various situations one is involved with. Another challenge is the continuous struggle to avoid certain gendered practices that only contribute to my disadvantage. Modesty is a good example: I have become habituated in displaying it but as a gendered practice, it certainly works against my best interests in academia. The fact that I need to pay attention to the ways I reproduce gender and possibly my own devaluation makes me angry as it turns gender into a personal problem. In other words, whether I am considered a nice girl or a nice bitch (Katila and Meriläinen 2002) it is always a problem with my self, and something I need to do something about.

E: Sometimes I also face situations where I cannot put into words whether what I experience has something to do with gender or not, and what it means if it does. For instance, when we have been discussing the division of teaching work in our unit I have suggested several (male) doctoral students for certain teaching duties. The response has repeatedly been 'he cannot take that much teaching, he needs time to focus on his doctoral thesis'. Even though I have had much heavier teaching loads and my doctoral research is in a more advanced stage, I have never heard anyone suggesting that my teaching load should be reduced for me to complete my thesis – so I have taken the issue up myself. Certainly this has to do with the junior researcher position that I am in – compared to doctoral students on external funding – personal characteristics and work experience, and so on. Still, I cannot help wondering if my doctoral thesis is, for some reason, considered as less important than that of some others.

K: One important formal site in which to consider gendered practices is our research seminar. It functions as the key medium for doctoral students to participate in the research community, to learn about its research practices and values as well as to construct one's professional identity. In their research, Saija and Susan paid attention to the asymmetrical nature of the conversations in the seminar (Katila and Meriläinen 1999); male participants tend to dominate and define the discussion whereas women remained silent or, even when making comments, tend to be almost apologetic and hesitant. In this respect, I feel that there has certainly been some improvement. Generally women take part in the conversations and their views are acknowledged but the dynamics of the seminar vary. Finding your academic voice and the right to speak requires time and learning for everyone but it may have got easier due to the interventions that have questioned 'the silence of the lambs'.

Legitimization of Gender Studies in Research and Teaching

E: In finding my academic voice, an important contribution of Saija's and Susan's work has been the legitimization of gender studies as a research area and part of the curriculum. As a result, I do not have to justify my choices for making feminist-oriented research to people in our department – in some other instances I do – and I am able to find like-minded people to discuss my research.

K: What has been good to see is that gender issues are not only a legitimate but also valued area of research and interest for those not doing research explicitly on gender. For example, gender-related topics in our research seminar attract diverse audiences and lively discussions.

E: Still, we have only one study module in our curriculum solely dedicated to gender issues: an optional essay-writing course on gender, organization and management, for which I am responsible. I certainly think that gender issues should be made a more visible (and to some extent compulsory) part of our curriculum. In this respect, the situation looks promising, though, because a new course on gender issues in organizations and management is now scheduled for next year. Isn't it interesting though how such a course is becoming a reality now that we have a male professor promoting it?

Collegial Relationships, Role Models and Support

E: One issue Saija and Susan bring up in their research articles is the desperate need many female academics have for suitable role models. I have been lucky to have senior female academics willing and capable to supervise my doctoral thesis from a gender studies perspective, and to arrange funding for it. Also, as a junior researcher, I have found it important to have a group of feminist-oriented researchers, both our peers and the more senior colleagues, as mentors and friends. Discussions with them have given me the resources to consider how I construct my own professional identity as a young female gender researcher. However as with any other organizational groups feminist researchers can also be hierarchical and maintain exclusionary practices. In an informal study group on feminist philosophy, for example, we have had discussions on whether we accept male members in our meetings or not. Our own practices have to be questioned as well: Do we welcome everybody? What are our own practices of inclusion and exclusion? Does adhering to this group rule out some other possibilities?

K: Your close collaboration with feminist mentors has certainly been ideal. My situation has been different as I have worked in a rather marginal position, particularly at first when I received grant funding and was not a full member of the unit. I feel I have experienced a variety of exclusionary and inclusionary practices – to the point that it sometimes seems that's what life in academia is all about! I have been fortunate to be included in teaching early on but as my doctoral research is an individual project I have not been exposed to similar (feminist) collaboration and mentoring as you have. However, the senior feminist researchers in our unit have been important for me too, serving as positive role models from the start. It was only until relatively recently, thanks to our joint research initiative with two other colleagues in our unit, that I have got the opportunity to actively and collaboratively pursue my interests in gender issues.

I think that the most evident sign of gender inequality in our unit still continues to be the low number of women as permanent professors.[1] In this respect, the significance of having female professors is not only in showing the career possibilities available to women but also their power to redefine the boundaries of what counts as important and interesting research. However, not all female professors are interested in gender studies. Therefore, from the perspective of gender research, it is important to have inspiring role models who can legitimize different ways of knowing, doing research and being an academic – whether they are male or female. After all, becoming an academic is not only about learning the skills and knowledge of the trade but essentially about constructing professional identity.

E: In this regard, it is very regrettable that Saija, Susan and some others have had to leave this unit and seek permanent positions elsewhere. In terms of the visibility of gender issues and studies, it has certainly been damaging. Luckily, there are a couple of professors actively engaged with gender studies who include gender issues in their courses and encourage their students to write gender-oriented Master's theses. After all, the senior-level scholars have more power to keep gender on the agenda.

Having women and gender researchers in higher academic positions is particularly important to facilitating our inclusion in various academic activities. Teaching is a good example of a core activity of many academics where the mechanisms of inclusion and exclusion are at play. It certainly matters who is included in teaching and on which courses. My earlier example on the allocation of teaching responsibilities in our unit can also be interpreted from this angle. Even though the teaching responsibilities sometimes feel like an extra burden, taking valuable time away from doing research, they are also an important part of academic socialization and professional career development. At the start of my career, it was Päivi, my supervisor, who encouraged and offered me possibilities to participate in teaching with her. Also, other gender researchers included me in their courses which helped me gain confidence to independently design and teach my own courses today.

K: It is definitely very important to have someone who will speak out for you and support you in the organizational politics, because we have only limited authority and resources as junior researchers. The career practices seem far from transparent which makes it all the more difficult to see whether gender is at play in certain decisions. This is an issue that we need to deal with even before finishing our doctorates. There are not enough positions in our unit for post-doctoral researchers which means that we have to take responsibility for arranging our own research funding from external sources. Therefore, we have to speak for ourselves and come up with post-doctoral research projects that include our own research interests. However, we could not do this without senior academics that are influential enough supporting us.

E: Altogether, it has been somewhat disappointing to notice that the visibility of gender issues is always threatened. It requires continuous work to keep gender issues on the agenda. However, thanks to Saija's and Susan's work, what we do have now is awareness, vocabulary and strategies to tackle this 'lifetime project', as they themselves label it.

K: A lifetime project it surely is. At the same time, the organization of academic work is changing. The masculine values of the business world that I tried to flee from have been entering academia in the form of growing control of academic work, intensifying competition, and instrumentalism. Academic work is becoming a very masculine game that is problematic not only for women but also for many men. Although we have already felt these pressures intensifying as doctoral students, they will become more problematic once we graduate with our doctorates and need to enter the race for postgraduate funding and positions.

In the attempts to explain the low number of women in corporate management, women themselves are sometimes accused of not pursuing the opportunities. Considering my own career perspectives and family situation with three small children, I can easily see how the process evolves when one's values do not match with the values and practices of work organizations. And this does not mean that I wouldn't be ambitious, achievement-oriented or work-focused. However, it easily becomes my personal career problem instead of a problem at the level of work and career practices.

E: I have thought about this too and I certainly think that having supervisors and senior colleagues that understand one's situation as a mother or father of small children is important. This is also a major gender issue as long as women use the majority of the available parental and family leaves[2] to take care of the children. Luckily, I have had colleagues around me who realize that the fact that I am a mother and might take some time out of work to take care of my children when they are small, does not mean that I would become somehow less intelligent or handicapped as an academic, or lose interest in research work. Role models are also important in this respect: even though it might not always have been easy, I have witnessed several of my colleagues raising children in parallel to having productive academic careers.

K: It is so valuable to have such colleagues who share our research interests and ways of being and working as an academic, both in our unit as well as through our networks elsewhere. These relationships enable us to maintain hope and inspiration and keep this work meaningful and worthwhile.

E: Actually, I have now realized how Saija's and Susan's close collaboration with each other and with junior colleagues such as myself has prepared me to engage in collaborative research work with colleagues with shared interests – an example is the research collaboration with you. Learning to work collaboratively in various combinations is so important in facilitating academic learning and careers.

K: As I work on my dissertation alone, our collaboration in gender studies outside our doctoral research projects has been truly inspiring and rewarding. Although collaboration is certainly essential in terms of professional development, its most significant value for me is the way it enriches my life in academia. Also, only this kind of collaboration manages to keep gender actively on the agenda in our unit and at the university at large.

CONCLUSIONS

In this chapter, we have reflected on the gendered practices of our own academic work unit from the perspective of our experiences as two female doctoral students who are in the process of becoming academics. The main result of Saija's and Susan's project (Katila and Meriläinen 1999, 2002) was first, gender issues became a legitimate part of teaching and research and second, the acknowledgement of the problematic nature of the daily gendered practices in the unit. Now, more than ten years since the start of Saija's and Susan's project, we can appreciate the contribution of their courageous interventions, and the collaborative efforts of other members of the unit (Meriläinen et al. 2009), towards a more tolerant and equal workplace.

Reflecting on our experiences and the legacy of Saija's and Susan's work more specifically, we have identified here several changes that have contributed positively to the development of our professional identities. Firstly, although at different points of our career, we were able to take a course on gender studies and find a meaningful connection to our studies on organization and management. Without this exposure to the gendered nature of organizing we might have opted out of the field altogether or remained with the constant feeling of not quite fitting in. Secondly, particularly in the case of Elina who has had the opportunity to collaborate with feminist researchers from the very beginning, having close mentors has been an essential support in professional identity construction. Their importance is not only in serving as examples of what one might become but, most importantly, in supporting our research, including us in various initiatives and having the power to define legitimate and relevant research. The example of feminist women has also been crucial in how we both, although to a different degree of exposure, have learned to reflect on our own role in doing gender and make efforts to manage the double-bind – doing gender without reproducing inequality (Gherardi 1994).

Thirdly, as a result of increasing sensitivity towards gendered practices, we have not had to experience anything as openly discriminatory in our unit as did Saija and Susan. The discursive practices in more formal events, such as the research seminar, and in more informal interactions have become more gender sensitive. This kind of environment has been a prerequisite for us to be able to construct positive identities as women academics and feminist researchers in our unit. Overall, as academics in the making, we both feel that our research community has provided a supportive environment that encourages us to find our distinctive academic voices.

Yet, we have our reservations. In changing gendered practices, the local accomplishments are always in danger of dissolving over time due to the pervasiveness of gendering. If gender researchers are forced to leave our unit, and the new people coming in are not aware of gendering processes, the practices can easily resort back to the old order. In other words, enduring change is possible only if the change efforts are constantly reproduced. Therefore, we need to ask ourselves how we, in turn, can keep on making gender visible, challenging gendered practices and creating forms of inclusion that support academics in the making. The research collaboration in gender research was the first initiative we personally initiated. It is a good example of an act of inclusion through collaboration; something Elina had learned from her feminist mentors. Writing this chapter and discussing it with members of our work unit is another step in the process of keeping gender on the agenda. It is our way of signalling the importance of continuous efforts and the need for the whole community to continue to question gendered practices in the future. Encouraging students to consider gender issues and participating in the development and teaching of a new Master's level course on gender and organizing are also examples of our actions in this process. Furthermore, by engaging with our own gender-related research pursuits and actively promoting collaboration with our colleagues who share similar interests, we also attempt to strengthen research on gender issues in the long run.

In addition to the continuous struggle to keep gender on the agenda, another enduring problem concerns the career prospects of women academics, and feminist researchers in particular. As Bagilhole and Goode (2001) have argued, the patriarchal support system naturally (mostly) promotes men academics at the exclusion of women. As a result, women academics need to promote themselves more consciously and actively and build networks in order to advance their careers, or simply to secure employment in academia. This calls attention to the gendered practices of career making and 'the importance of being asked' (Benschop and Dooreward 1998) to include women and thus support them in developing their skills. Towards the end of our doctoral studies, we have become keenly aware of the necessity to build our own support systems in order to be included. Seeing the low number of women in the highest academic positions and realizing the fragile position of gender research and teaching, we have no illusions about the struggle ahead of us in our future careers.

Although our own unit can be perceived as gender sensitive, we need to be aware of the deeply entrenched and pervasive nature of gendering. There are concealed organizational processes and practices that are problematically gendered. For example, organizational politics maintain and construct organizational power relations and thus, are linked to gendered forms of inclusion and exclusion in academic work (for example Mackenzie Davey 2008). Also, the current changes in academic work have gendering effects. This is because the increased managerialism and new performance culture in universities have resulted in the intensification of academic work and promotion of masculine practices (Thomas and Davies 2002), such as competitiveness and careerism (Collinson and Hearn 1994). The characteristics of the seemingly gender-neutral 'ideal worker' (Acker 1990), such as goal-orientation, instrumentality and authority, appear to become increasingly prevalent in defining academic identities and careers.

In our personal work context, the merger of Helsinki School of Economics, Helsinki University of Technology and the University of Art and Design Helsinki into the cross-disciplinary Aalto University this year (2009), presents yet another initiative that has the potential to reinforce gender inequalities. Coming with the major governance reform from a public institution to a private foundation and the introduction of a board of directors with industry representatives, we might expect managerialist discourses to intensify and a strengthening of gendered practices. The next major challenge, therefore, is to find ways to deal with the new forms of exclusion and inclusion emerging from the increasingly competitive and managerially controlled academic environment. The efforts to change these practices of exclusion in order to develop more just communities of work concerns not only gender but also ethnicity, class, age and sexuality. This struggle can take the form of resistance at the level of individual strategies and identity, but most importantly, as in doing good academic research, it should be a collaborative effort.

NOTES

1. At present (11 March 2009), the unit has approximately 35 full-time employees in research and teaching positions. There are four permanent male professors and one female professor in a donation funded professorial position of five years. In addition there are three temporary professor positions, two temporary associate professor positions, two lecturer positions and two temporary junior researcher positions with an approximately equal representation of gender. The remainder of the research staff receives external funding.
2. In Finland, the following compensated parental leaves are available: maternity leave up to four months before and after the birth; paternity leave three to seven weeks; and parental leave (for mother/father, or used in turns), six months. In 2007, according to the Statistic Bulletin of the Social Insurance Institution in Finland (26 May 2008), 70 per cent of fathers used their right to paternity leave. Altogether, mothers used 94 per cent of the parental leave.

REFERENCES

Acker, J. (1990), 'Hierarchies, jobs, bodies: a theory of gendered organizations', *Gender and Society*, **4** (2), 139–58.

Bagilhole, B. and J. Goode (2001), 'The contradiction of the myth of individual merit, and the reality of a patriarchal support system in academic careers', *The European Journal of Women's Studies*, **8** (2), 161–80.

Benschop, Y. and H. Doorewaard (1998), 'Covered by equality: the gender subtext of organizations', *Organization Studies*, **19** (5), 787–805.

Collinson, D. and J. Hearn (1994), 'Naming men as men: implications for work, organization and management', *Gender, Work and Organization*, **1** (1), 2–22.

Davies, A. and R. Thomas (2002), 'Gendering and gender in public service organizations: changing professional identities under new public management', *Public Management Review*, **4** (4), 461–84.

Elg, U. and K. Jonnergård (2003), 'The inclusion of female PhD students in academia: a case study of a Swedish university department', *Gender, Work and Organization*, **10** (2), 154–75.

Gherardi, S. (1994), 'The gender we think, the gender we do in our everyday organizational lives', *Human Relations*, **47** (6), 591–610.

Katila, S. and S. Meriläinen (1999), 'A serious researcher or just another nice girl?: doing gender in a male-dominated scientific community', *Gender, Work and Organization*, **6** (3), 163–73.

Katila, S. and S. Meriläinen (2002), 'Metamorphosis: from "nice girls" to "nice bitches": resisting patriarchal articulations of professional identity', *Gender, Work and Organization*, **9** (3), 336–54.

Mackenzie Davey, K. (2008), 'Women's accounts of organizational politics as a gendering process', *Gender, Work and Organization*, **16** (6), 650–71.

Martin, J. (1994), 'The organization of exclusion: institutionalization of sex inequality, gendered faculty jobs and gendered knowledge in organizational theory and research', *Organization*, **1** (2), 401–31.

Meriläinen, Susan (2001), *Changing Gendered Practices: A PAR Project within an Academic Work Community*, Helsinki School of Economics and Business Administration, A-192.

Meriläinen, Susan, Keijo Räsänen and Saija Katila (2009), 'Autonomous renewal of gendered practices: interventions and their pre-conditions at an academic workplace', in S. Andresen, M. Koreuber and D. Lüdke (eds), *Gender und Diversity. Albtraum oder Traumpaar? Interdisziplinärer Dialog zur 'Modernisierung' von Geschlechter- und Gleichstellungspolitik*, VS Verlag für Sozialwissenschaften,Wiesbaden, Germany, pp. 209–30.

Thomas, R. and A. Davies (2002), 'Gender and new public management: reconstituting academic subjectivities', *Gender, Work and Organization*, **9** (4), 372–97.

West, C. and D. Zimmerman (1987), 'Doing gender', *Gender and Society*, **1** (2), 125–51.

PART IV

Conclusions

13. Practising inclusion: diversity matters!

Silvia Gherardi

INTRODUCTION

This is a book which discusses academic practice without directly naming it and yet doing so from a point of view shared by all the authors. This shared point of view – this positioning that gives unitariness to a polyphonic account – consists in the standpoint of diversity. In other words, this book proposes a semantic shift from academic practice to academic practices. It shows that it is possible to be and to do different things in academe and in the higher education system in general. My intention in this concluding chapter is to conduct a cross-wise reading which brings out the plurality and the transformative dynamics of academic practices as they result from the personal experiences of its practitioners.

Let us start from the fact that academe has founded its legitimacy as an organization on the ideal (and the ideology) of universality. As the locus of the production and transmission of knowledge, the university can only furnish valid and legitimate knowledge if it fulfils the criteria of truth, disinterest and universality. Founded on this ideal is a vision of knowledge 'in the singular', as indivisible and universally valid. It is this sole ownership/production of knowledge that underpinned the image of the university as an ivory tower and as an institution independent from society when it first arose in medieval Europe.

Against this background, what is the place for an image of knowledge 'in the plural', that is, situated and rooted in a plurality of experiences and visions of the world? The answer is obviously 'none' because on the one side stands the mode of production of 'legitimate' knowledge, and on the other the 'minor' knowledge that cannot aspire to the level of theory (this too in the singular) and therefore remains confined to practice and to the theory/practice dichotomy that systematically devalues the latter. We may therefore ask what might be an image that corresponds to a university in the plural and is able to encompass knowledges in the plural.

The alternative between university and multiversities has an illustrious historical precedent. In 1966 Clark Kerr, when discussing the system of higher education in America, argued that universities should be called 'multiversities' because they were responsible for a 'dizzying variety of programs and activities'. As early as the 1960s Kerr's book enquired as to where the university was heading and whether its project for diversification was driven and regulated by the market. The book went into five editions (the last was published in 2001), and as Kerr subsequently returned to its principal topic over four decades, his views on American higher education grew increasingly sombre. And the theme of multiversities had yet to be treated in relation to the politics of university policy and governance!

The subsequent literature dealt with the managerialization and the reform of universities (Parker and Jary, 1995; Chandler et al., 2002; Barnett, 2005) and was even more pessimistic. Practitioners increasingly pressed for 'meaningful academic work' (Räsänen, 2008), that is, autonomous, inherently rewarding and socially significant, while they shared the experience of losing control over their work. This is a debate which is now extremely topical, especially in Europe with its student mobilization, yet it forms only an unfocused backdrop to the contributions in the book, which show slight awareness of it, when not deliberately ignoring it. In fact the authors more forcefully resume Kerr's theme – the relationship between university and society – against the background of governance.

In focusing on the relationship between university and society, this book concentrates on ethical problems concerning the profession's practice and social responsibilities. When considering the multiversities, on the one hand it shows the ideological aspect of the social representation of academic practice as a body of knowledge and activities shared by the entire profession. On the other hand, it shows how the apparently monolithic nature of practice and its isomorphic force (we all do the same activities in the same way) allows and safeguards the allomorphism of practices (we all do different things, asserting the legitimacy of a practice as unique) and experimenting with different ways of doing.

FROM ACADEMIC PRACTICE TO ACADEMIC PRACTICES

As a profession, academics form the 'invisible college' (Crane, 1972) which forges individual and professional identity around the image of sharing an academic practice in the singular, and which divides among three macro-practices: research, teaching and administration.

We therefore need the expression 'practice in the singular' in order to ground the idea of the profession and its self-governance. At the same time, if we observe the discursive practices of academics, for instance at international conferences, we can easily notice the extent to which their discursive practices, in public and private meetings, rotate around comparison of how the same things are done in different ways. The discussion of practice among practitioners is not a mundane, folkloric, activity of little importance. Nor is it solely description and sensemaking that turns the plurality of situated practices into the monolithicity of practice. On the contrary, the discursive practices of practitioners are constitutive of that epistemic object – the practice – which is discursively built in the singular.

When discussing practice, practitioners set in motion the process itself of change in practice by making plural practices accountable and confirming and/or contesting what is considered to be a good or a bad practice. The dynamic of endogenous change in practice resides in the normative accountability of practices according to ethical and aesthetic judgements (Gherardi, 2009). Practitioners engaged in 'private' discourse – that is, discourse within the community and addressed to those considered to be legitimate participants – discuss and dispute as they collectively construct the knowledge object defined as academic practice. In so doing, they historicize the practice, locating it in historical time and in a socio-political context. Knorr-Cetina (2001: 184) defines epistemic objects in the following terms:

> Objects of knowledge seem to have the capacity of unfolding indefinitely and in this they lie at the opposite end from the tools and the commercial goods which are ready-to-be-used or traded. These tools and goods have the character of closed boxes. Objects of knowledge are always in the process of being materially defined, they continually acquire new properties and change the ones they have.

The dynamics that bring about change through successive redefinitions of the epistemic object ensure that the practice is constantly emergent and situated in the interactions among those practising it.

This process is common to all the professions and all the communities of practitioners that collectively build a memory of the community and the object of practice amid the multiplicity of situated practices. This is nothing new, but the question that interests me here is this: in what way have the practitioners participating in this collective construction of a book on practice performed a representation of their practices through writing?

BEING CRITICAL AND POSITIVE

These two adjectives – critical and positive – constitute, I believe, the two organizing principles of this book. They can be seen and read diachronically as a criticism on which an alternative experience is based, or synchronically as a neologism, as a single critical-positive term. The neologism emphasises the utopian dimension intrinsic to every critical movement when critical thought implicitly delineates a term in respect of which an alternative is constructed. However, I prefer to begin by keeping the two movements – that of the criticism and that of positive experience – separate, although I am mindful that the editors of this book have endeavoured to unify them.

All the contributions to the book are critical of academic practice in the singular, but their authors perform their critical work in a personal manner. They are critical not so much in what they say as in the effect produced by what they say. Their discourse is performative of the criticism against practice in the singular also and especially because they speak of the alternatives to it. In representing their positive experiences, they also implicitly enact the 'other' practices co-present in academe.

After reading all the contributions, what most struck me emotionally and occupied my night-time thoughts was disgust with the inequality that reigns in academe. Yet, paradoxically, the authors describe their work for inclusion, and they testify through their personal experiences and biographies that it is possible to make academic practice more inclusive and attentive to the society in which universities operate. The performative effect of their writing is twofold, as in ambiguous figures. When delineating an object and distinguishing it from the background, one simultaneously describes the object and its background. In this way the context of practice 'in the singular' becomes legible while a practice alternative to it is being described. In other words, if legitimating the singularity of academic practice within the universality of the profession pays the price of obscuring and silencing the context, the enactment of practices evidences their situatedness in time and space, that is, their embeddedness in the socio-political context. The relationship between university and society thus becomes legible because it constitutes the background to the object fore-grounded.

Contextualized and situated academic practices convey an image of an academe all the more ruthless in that the authors simply describe it as a 'given'. Without explicitly critical language being used, the university in the background is a strongly classist, racist and gendered university which denies all diversities besides. By way of explicit reference, consider the articles by Zanoni and Siebers, or by Danowitz and Tuit, or again by Pringle, Wolfgramm and Henry, and think about which students are 'inside' higher education and which are 'outside' it. We can see a process of inclusion (the figure) and one of exclusion (background). Analogously, when reading Eriksson-Zetterquist's project to make universities more gender-aware, I was astonished by the sexism expressed by people that I consider my 'colleagues': highly educated people who by their profession produce 'knowledge'. Ironically, Sweden is considered one of the most egalitarian European countries in terms of gender relationships because of greater participation by women in the labour market or politics. But this seems to have no effect on the reproduction of sexist stereotypes. Another example, on a different level, is provided by Boje's chapter, which, in opposing a restrictive policy on internet access, describes a background in which universities are actively engaged in producing the digital divide and making anti-democratic technological choices.

All the articles make this twofold figure/background reading possible. And their criticism of academic practice is all the more effective because it is not couched in critical terms. It is not necessary to conclude that the university constitutes a system of domination and power – a conclusion for that matter generally accepted – to offer a contribution to critical knowledge. Simply locating academic practices in their context, making them plural and situated, is to criticize the ideological operation of de-contextualizing and de-politicizing academic practice.

As the editors of the book aptly put it in the first lines of the introduction, 'it is possible to challenge the mainstream and live to tell the tale!'. This sentence encapsulates one of strongest meanings of the book and illustrates the epistemological and methodological criterion that has organized contributions by practitioners describing their experiences to the community of practitioners. The challenge against the mainstream is not made explicitly; rather, it is the by-product of a rhetorical and methodological strategy imbued with the concept of 'positive experience'.

I shall illustrate my understanding of the concept of positive experience as an epistemological choice by recounting an illuminating example that I came across many years ago in Barker's (1985) book *Using Metaphors in Psychotherapy*, and which since then has entered my preferred repertoire of examples. Barker describes how a group of men at the University of Wisconsin started a writers' club which they called 'The Stranglers' to emphasize how its members would mercilessly criticize each other's work. In the meantime, and perhaps in emulation (or in response to their exclusion, but this we cannot know!) a group of women writers set up a similar group called 'The Discussion'. Their intention was to emphasise positive aspects and to look for what was good in their colleagues' work, as well as to be encouraging and polite in their criticisms. Twenty years later, the university wanted to know what had happened to the two groups and commissioned a survey. It was discovered that, talent remaining equal, the two groups had achieved different levels of success determined by their differing behaviours. In fact, none of 'The Stranglers' had made a name as a writer, while half a dozen members of 'The Discussion' had become notably successful.

I often use this narrative with my students to illustrate the value of positive reinforcement, even if its gender sub-text makes me feel somewhat chauvinist. And it is this example that immediately came to my mind when I heard

Saija Katila calling this volume the 'positive book'. The strength of this metaphor resides in its communicating in simple terms an epistemic positioning that founds an identity as practitioners: in face of a 'strangler' mainstream other positionings, both identitarian and related to alternative practices, are possible. These two dimensions – of being and doing – are united in the critical-positive neologism, and they found an epistemology in which the production of knowledge is plural and pluralist, and based on experience.

PRODUCING KNOWLEDGE FROM EXPERIENCES

Thus far we have seen the meaning and theoretical importance of the shift from a universalist conception ('in the singular') of academic practice to a situated and pluralist vision of academic practices. The context and characteristics of the unequal relationship between university and society have thus become visible as the background from which emerges the will, possibility and epistemic positioning of practitioners who have experimented with alternative practices, and who testify through their personal biographies, as members of couples and groups, to epistemic positionings alternative to the mainstream. However, thus far diversity has been viewed in aggregate form and in relation to the mainstream. We must now consider diversity in the plural, the rich array of experiences which have recognized and tried to connect with a plurality of diversities in ethnicity, gender, religion, access to technological resources, and knowledge-producing epistemologies. These diversities have been declined in some cases in relation to different levels of teaching and in others in relation to research and methodologies to produce knowledges (in the plural) in relation to multiple subjects and plural methodologies.

I shall not go into detail on each of the relationships with diversity because each of them is, so to speak, unique. And also because the editors have examined them as a whole in their introduction, seeking to grasp elements that they may have in common and thereby determine what lessons can be learned to distil the secret of an actionable knowledge to render universities more inclusive and diversity-aware. I will instead consider the common elements, explicit or implicit, that constitute the epistemological and methodological premises of academic practices shared by this community of practitioners. These do not necessarily originate from the same matrix, but a family resemblance is evident in feminisms, post-colonialism, pedagogy of the oppressed and subordinate thought.

I shall now try to specify the epistemological principles that I believe can be identified in the various contributions to the book, apologizing to the authors for any unintentional over-interpretation of their thoughts. What in my opinion constitutes a shared epistemology derives from the following assumptions:

(a) *The value of experience as a source of knowledge.* Experience is a process and not a possession. Experience, according to Teresa de Lauretis (1984: 159), 'is produced not by external ideas, values or material causes, but by one's personal, subjective, engagement in the practices, discourses and institutions that lend significance (value, meaning and affect) to the events of the world'.
(b) *The practitioner's subjectivity as a means to produce knowledge-in-relationship.* Subjectivity (who I am) can be used both to enter into a relationship with diversity and to construct an engaged pedagogy. To educate (and to do research) is a practice of freedom, and in bell hooks's words (1994) it is a way of teaching where anyone can learn.
(c) *The practitioner's positioning* vis-à-vis *the object of knowledge.* The ideal of detachment is replaced by care, passion and engagement as necessary to produce a knowledge that counts as much for the subjects in the field as for those who relate with them. The ideals of compassion and emancipation found a positioning based on connection and care.
(d) *Respect for the other/others.* Respect for diversities helps 'nurture those places where worlds meet' (Bordo, 1992: 166; Billard, this volume).

I would like to conclude with Longino's words on epistemologies. She points to plurality as a feature of contemporary Western science and argues for local epistemologies rather than a single unifying model or methodology: 'If methodological rules and procedures are not claimed to be self-evident and context-independent, then their rationale [...] must lie in the aims and goals of the inquiring community (or in its traditions)' (Longino, 2002: 187).

A CONCLUSION IN THE FORM OF A METAPHOR

This book expresses the desire to compare and share experiences within a community of practitioners. It is therefore in a certain sense a book 'internal' to a community. But it also produces social effects that reverberate outside that community in the society at large. It offers a message of hope to those who fear that the university is becoming a self-referential world increasingly dependent on market logic. Moreover, it is a book which produces a sense of empowerment similar to that of the first feminist collectives when they broke the feeling of individualization and the sense of non-historicity of the female condition. Obviously, this similarity is only partial, and in a community of practitioners the sense of empowerment also derives from recognizing positionings other than the mainstream as possible and legitimate. For example, an epistemological positioning predicated on care and relationality can produce practices of teaching, research and administration which speak another language and legitimate courses of action other than those of control and pure efficiency. I shall not insist on this point because the entire book testifies to how practices of freedom are possible.

I shall conclude by recalling an image from a book emblematic of subordinate thought. The English-speaking Egyptian writer Ahdaf Soueif (1992), in her novel *In the Eye of the Sun*, describes the continuous movement between Egypt and England that becomes a metaphor for living in a state of translation. Soueif depicts the South of the world: that conception of the South explored by Antonio Gramsci and today rediscovered by subordinate thought. The South is a place of the mind and no longer a geographical entity because migratory movements have made it a state of continuous dissemination. The protagonist of Soueif's novel, a female Egyptian emigrant in London, says that she has not come to England empty-handed, but with knowledge that originates from the South of the world, from a positioning which claims autonomy of signification and legitimacy for the knowledge produced. It is not my intention to arbitrarily extend this metaphor to maintain that all the authors share a single epistemological positioning. But I would like to think that they, too, in accepting the editors' invitation have not come empty-handed, and that working for inclusion is to live in a state of translation.

REFERENCES

Barker, Ph. (1985), *Using Metaphors in Psychotherapy*, New York: Brunner-Mazel Publishers.

Barnett, R. (ed.) (2005), *Reshaping the University: New Relationships between Teaching, Scholarship and Research*, Maidenhead, UK: Open University Press and McGraw-Hill.

Bordo, S. (1992), 'Review Essay: Postmodern Subjects, Postmodern Bodies', *Feminist Studies*, **18** (1), 159–75.

Chandler, J., Barry, J. and Clark, H. (2002), 'Stressing Academe: the Wear and Tear of the New Public Management', *Human Relations*, 55, 1051–69.

Crane, D. (1972), *Invisible Colleges. Diffusion of Knowledge in Scientific Communities*, Chicago: The University of Chicago Press.

de Lauretis, T. (1984), *Alice Doesn't: Feminism, Semiotics, Cinema*, London: Macmillan.

Gherardi, S. (2009), 'Practice? It's a Matter of Taste!', *Management Learning*, **40** (5), 535–50.

hooks, b. (1994), *Teaching to Trangress: Education as the Practice of Freedom*, New York: Routledge.

Kerr, C. (1966), *The Uses of the University*, Cambridge: Harvard University Press.

Knorr-Cetina, K. (2001), 'Objectual Practice', in T.R. Schatzki, K. Knorr-Cetina and E.

von Savigny (eds), *The Practice Turn in Contemporary Theory*, London: Routledge.

Longino, H. (2002), *The Fate of Knowledge*, Princeton: Princeton University Press.

Parker, M. and Jary, D. (1995), 'The McUniversity: Organization, Management and Academic Subjectivity', *Organization*, **2**, 319–38.

Räsänen, K. (2008), 'Meaningful Academic Work as Praxis in Emergence', *Journal of Research Practice*, **4** (1), article P1, retrieved 3 June, 2009 from http://jrp.icaap.org/index.php/jrp/article/view/78/102.

Soueif, A. (1992), *In the Eye of the Sun*, New York: Anchor Books.

Index